#32-02 BKBUd 7/02

P9-DGV-542

BEYOND "e"

BEYOND "e"

12 Ways Technology is Transforming Sales and Marketing Strategy

Stephen G. Diorio

McGraw-Hill

New York   Chicago   San Francisco   Lisbon   London
Madrid   Mexico City   Milan   New Delhi   San Juan
Seoul   Singapore   Sydney   Toronto

McGraw-Hill

*A Division of The **McGraw-Hill** Companies*

1 2 3 4 5 6 7 8 9 0   AGM/AGM   0 9 8 7 6 5 4 3 2 1

ISBN 0-07-137649-6

This book was set in Janson by Matrix Publishing.

Printed and bound by Quebecor Martinsburg

How to Contact the Publisher

To order multiple copies of this book at a discount, please contact the McGraw-Hill Special Sales Department at 800-842-3075, or 212-904-5427 (2 Penn Plaza, New York, NY 10121-2298).

To ask a question about the book, contact the author, or report a mistake in the text, please write to Richard Narramore, Senior Editor, at richard_narramore@ mcgraw-hill.com.

Contents

Acknowledgments

Over the last 20 years, I have worked with hundreds of clients and sales and marketing experts, researchers, and academics. This book is a product of the research, experience, and ideas of many great people I have had the pleasure of working with over that time.

I am indebted to several people whose support was instrumental in writing this book. This book would not have been possible without the editing and coaching of Mia Amato and the guidance and support of Richard Narramore, my editor from McGraw-Hill. In particular, I am grateful to Dale Kutnick, the Chairman of the META Group, whose understanding of how technology will evolve is without peer and whose insights and ruthless editorial guidance shaped the thinking and logic of this book. In addition, I would like to thank Rick Bruner whose knowledge and insight into interactive marketing and Internet communications heavily influenced the first third of this book.

This book is informed by great research by several analysts and affiliates of IMT Strategies, the sales and marketing consulting company I founded in 1998. These include Marc Feldman, for research support and insight into viral marketing, event triggered marketing, and outsourcing; Laurie Heiss, whose practical selling experience was instrumental in developing the chapter on field sales; Greg Amrofell, for developing research on customer care and CRM; Rob Madonna and Greg Katz, for their data tabulation and primary research, which contributed much of the substance to this book; Audrey Manring, whose analysis of permission e-mail marketing and brilliant writing was an inspiration; Bill McKinney, who tested and molded much of this research to make sure it all made sense, and Eric Wilson for his diligent survey work.

Several top analysts from the META Group, a leading international information technology advisory firm, heavily influenced the book's analysis of the core technologies that are impacting sales and marketing strategy. In particular, I would like to thank Mike Gotta, Liz Shahnam, and Val Sribar for their help navigating the byzantine CRM technology landscape, and for their practical ideas on how organizations can make these solutions work; Peter Burris, who refined so many of the better ideas in this book and happily challenged the rest; Dave Yockelson, for his insights on online marketplaces and sourcing trends; Chuck Johnston, whose experience working with the leaders in the financial services and insurance industry gave me a glimpse of the future; and Maria Shaefer, for the exhaustive research into the human resources aspects of technology strategy crucial to understanding how technology would change the organization.

In addition, I would like to thank some of the leading experts in this field who have made direct contributions to chapters: Maria Barringhaus, who willingly shared her experience of leading the transformation of call centers; Professor Charles Jacobina, whose sage counsel and years of experience teaching online marketing and branding is reflected across the book; Fred Fassman and Rob Stagno of IBM, for their contributions to the chapters on interactive marketing and call center strategy; Jean Nives of Nielson/NetRatings who provided much insight on global e-marketing trends; and Stan Lepeak of Ajunto for contributing his vast knowledge on sourcing trends and making products ready for technology-enabled channels.

I am grateful to my agent Ron Goldfarb, Watts Wacker, Don Peppers, and the late Charles Trepper for teaching me what it takes to write a book.

There are so many other clients, associates, and friends who contributed to my marketing education and influenced my thinking. I wish to acknowledge here some of the outstanding minds I have been lucky enough to work with: Michael Kaiser, for showing me what great strategy looks like; Tony Ruegger, Professor Jeanne Rossomme, and Bob Gannon, with whom I worked at GE Corporate Marketing and whose ideas could fill several books; Dr. Rowland Moriarty, whose work in sales and distribution strategy was 15 years ahead of his time; Ann Zeller of the Direct Marketing Association, whose research and collaboration was invaluable. My thanks also to Jack Bergen for teaching me the communications business and trying to get me to write more effectively; to Karen Quinn who patiently absorbed too many of my ideas and discreetly pointed out the few that were good; and to Paul Hogan of Sealed Air Corporation who helped balance this exploration into new—and often "overhyped"—selling technologies with decades of real-world selling experience and practical advice.

Finally, I would like to thank my wife Lyn for her patience over the long hours and late nights needed to write this book, and my parents Ron and Arlene for giving me the confidence to express my opinions.

Introduction

Using Technology to Grow Revenue

Business leaders today are looking beyond e-business hype to understand how selling technologies can actually help them grow revenues and make their customers happier. For years, technology held out the elusive promise of turning sales and marketing systems into high-performance engines of revenue growth. Most of us are still waiting for the results, generally because we failed to recognize how technology has changed the playing field and did not adjust our game plans enough to exploit its potential.

Meanwhile, the best companies are cleverly taking advantage of established advances in communications networks, databases, and new media to stretch their sales and marketing budgets farther and stay one step ahead of the needs of their customers. The success of companies like Dell Computer, IBM, Charles Schwab, Amazon, and e-Bay shows that marketers who experiment with technologies as they emerge, and figure out how to best use new tools to support their selling approach, can gain competitive advantages in their markets.

The goal of this book is to show sales and marketing executives the 12 best ways to use technology to grow their businesses faster and get more mileage out of their sales and marketing dollars. This book spells out the most important actions leaders must take today and can help them rank the best opportunities that make sense for their organizations.

The winning strategies in this book are based on thousands of interviews with customers and sales and marketing managers in Global 2000 companies. They are also the culmination of more than 15 years of my personal experience advising some of the world's best marketers—companies that include IBM, General Electric, American Express, Citigroup, and Gillette.

Looking "Beyond e" to Your Marketing Technology Strategy

Despite the noise and confusion surrounding the e-business boom and its aftermath, most sales executives accept the fact that no matter what they sell, growing sales now require that they craft a technology strategy. Contrary to popular perception, the people who have been running sales and marketing in traditional businesses do "get it." Any seasoned sales and marketing professional can easily embrace the concepts of e-business and "customer relationship management." They also know the difficult part is learning how to "engineer" technology innovations into the sales and marketing process of a real company.

Businesses have successfully applied technology to their business for decades by automating factories and "reengineering" their supply chains. As a result, the cost of "making things" has dropped dramatically and the productivity of the average employee is vastly improved.

"Selling things" at lower cost has proven to be more challenging. Most executives are still struggling to understand how and where to use technology to improve sales and marketing performance. Mixing technology into the selling process is different from the factory because customers won't sit still long enough for engineers to "measure" them and design systems to suit them. Marketing creativity is hard for software programmers to code. And very few people really understand how technology is impacting customer relationships.

As a result, promising technologies like CRM, e-commerce, online markets, and sales force automation have failed to produce the results that sales executives are looking for. For example, most large sales forces have invested in (at least) one version of sales force automation software in the last 10 years, but less than one-third feel they realized significant results (according to Insight Technology, which conducts an annual survey of 122 sales force automation projects). When IMT Strategies studied 50 of the biggest CRM projects in 2000, they found that less than 10 percent could demonstrate positive results despite an average investment that exceeded $10 million per company. In fact, over three-quarters of these companies were still thinking about how to measure the return on these investments.

The recent raft of "dot-com" innovators promised to show us how to build electronic selling channels that cost less than our current ones. Most of these failed to displace their traditional competitors (eToys failed to knock off Toys "R" Us) and left a sour taste in the mouths of investors. Over 1000 online marketplaces were launched in the year 2000 hoping to assemble buyers and sellers into efficient electronic markets to make selling and buying easier. To date only a few have any significant transactions. Certainly none resemble the trading pit of the New York Stock Exchange.

This book shows how the best companies are using technology to build high-performance revenue growth engines. These marketing leaders will use these "engines" to grow market share the same way that Japanese automobile manufacturers were able to gain a large share of the U.S. car market in the 1970s.

Building High-Performance Growth Engines with Technology

In 1973, the average car built in the United States got 13 miles per gallon. That was the year of the first international oil embargo and the dawn of the "energy crisis." When the price of gasoline suddenly doubled, most drivers in the United States were under severe pressure to go farther on a tank of gas if they wanted to get to and from work and stay within their family budget.

At the time, Japanese car companies offered cars that were more fuel efficient. These cars got more miles per gallon than American models, which were sold on other features, like power, size, and leg room. One Japanese model—the Datsun 210—was rated as the most efficient car offered in America by the Department of Transportation, getting 33 miles per gallon. The car was two-and-a-half times more efficient than the average American car at the time. Over time this performance "gap" translated into rapid sales growth and increased market share. American car manufacturers worked furiously to close this gap in performance, but they could not do it fast enough to protect their market. By 1980, Japanese automakers owned 30 percent of the U.S. car market.

This message is important to all sales, marketing, and service executives because without it, they stand to miss out on a great opportunity. Organizations that can force themselves to think about combining technology with other sales and marketing resources to build powerful "engines of growth" will make more rational economic decisions about where to apply technology to boost their performance. The analogy is pretty simple. A sales and marketing team that is able to use technology to build a "growth engine" that is faster and gets more miles per gallon than the other guy's engine will win. For example, Dell Computer built a revenue growth engine that got far better mileage out of their sales and marketing dollars than the competition and enjoyed considerable success for over a decade. From 1990 to 2000 Dell used a combination of two "technology-enabled" selling channels—call centers and Internet storefronts—to sell PCs directly to consumers. It supported these channels with "product configuration" software to make it easier for people to understand and buy PCs online or over the phone. At the time the rest of the industry (including HP, Compaq, Apple, and IBM) were selling personal computers by using traditional selling approaches, made up of more expensive field salespeople and tens of thousands of business partners. These competitors were spending, on average, close to

20 cents of every sales dollar to pay for their sales and marketing expenses.

By comparison, Dell was able to sell PCs using its "direct" approach at closer to 12 cents on the dollar. This meant that for every dollar of sales and marketing budget they spent, Dell got back about eight dollars in sales. The rest of the industry was getting more like five dollars in sales for every dollar they spent on sales and marketing. To put it another way, Dell was getting eight miles per gallon while the other guys were getting five miles per gallon.

Dell took this highly efficient revenue-generating machine and challenged the industry to a race to see who could grow the fastest on a tank of gas. By the end of the decade, Dell had surpassed Compaq as the number-one PC seller in the U.S. market and was growing more than twice as fast as the rest of the competitors in the industry.

In the average company, there is plenty of room for technology to improve the sales and marketing engine that propels revenue growth. In most companies the revenue growth engine generally gets pretty bad gas mileage, only about four to five miles per gallon (i.e., four to five dollars for every dollar spent on sales and marketing). The average sales engine also accelerates too slowly—although double-digit growth is typically very hard to achieve.

Just like a new fuel injector and better-firing spark plugs can improve the performance of an engine, there are certain technological "parts" that can "turbocharge" your sales engine and help it run faster and better. Unfortunately, shopping for technology to improve your selling process is a lot like sending a teenager to an auto parts store to learn how to tune your car and get some driving lessons. He may walk out the door with a new carburetor and some spark plugs for his dad's old Chevrolet, but he won't necessarily be qualified to fix it properly and know how to manage the stick shift.

The solution is that sales and marketing executives have to spend time "re-engineering" the revenue generation engine to find the best parts to invest in. Analyzing the thousands of customer transactions and conversations needed to reach and sell to customers will reveal many places where technology can help. For example, IBM discovered that a technology-equipped call center representative can do many of the same tasks as well as a field sales representative, except 40 percent cheaper.

Many others have found that the Internet can help do a lot of the heavy lifting involved in customer service at fractions of what it costs to do it using retailer staffs, tele-reps, and salespeople. For example, e-Bay handles 200 customer queries every 20 minutes without the help of humans by using online "self-help" tools. A small greeting card company named Blue Mountain Arts used an Internet technique called viral marketing to build a national brand known to tens of millions of people on a shoestring budget. They were able to get customers to pass electronic marketing messages to their peers using online networks and digital greeting cards. Building a similar level of brand awareness using traditional media could have cost millions of dollars.

A recent Boston Consulting Group study found that sales and marketing organizations that "blended" Internet channels with other parts of the sales and marketing engine (like retail stores, paper catalogs, and call centers) were getting much better gas mileage. The average "clicks and mortar" company that employed the Internet as part of the system was spending about 13 cents of every revenue dollar on marketing costs. This is close to eight "miles per gallon," about twice as efficient as the best dot.com (Amazon.com got four miles per gallon according to the same study), and twice as efficient as the average company (often a competitor).

The Challenge of Fitting Technology into the Sales and Marketing Mix

So why aren't more companies getting more "miles per gallon" by using technology? It is not because the technologies don't work. The technologies available today are mature enough to dramatically improve your sales and marketing machine. The problem lies in several obvious and not-so-obvious areas.

The obvious problem is that the executives that run sales, marketing, and service organizations have limited time, money, and political capital to fully capitalize on the explosion of new technology happening around them. They are being asked to assess thousands of new technologies with the potential to grow sales and develop relationships.

The less obvious—and bigger—problem is that most sales and marketing leaders are failing to see how these technologies are changing the game. They are not changing how they package, market, and sell their products (and services) fast enough to exploit the opportunities new technology is giving them.

Twelve Opportunities for Sales and Marketing Executives

This book outlines 12 specific ways that sales and marketing executives can take better advantage of new technologies to grow their businesses, not just their Web sites. The original research cited here was conducted by IMT Strategies from 1999-2001, and it covered a cross section of technology trends changing the practice of sales and marketing, including e-business, interactive direct marketing, and customer relationship management (CRM) and online marketplaces. The analysis of the core technologies behind these trends was developed with analysts from the META Group, a leading international information technology advisory firm.

However, this book is not so much about the gear and the software but what they can do for you. It was written with the busy executive in mind and contains everything you need to discover opportunities that can deliver the biggest "bang for the buck" today while keeping the long-term growth picture in view.

Each chapter outlines how technology will impact a particular aspect of sales and marketing operations. The heart of each chapter lays out specific actions to take advantage of these opportunities. These recommendations are outlined in the form of short- and long-term management strategies.

For example, for many organizations the "pain" starts when they begin using new online channels and media to reach customers. The first section of this book discusses strategies for adapting the four Ps of marketing (product, price, placement, and promotion) to the way technology is changing customer behavior and markets. Chapter One shows how to repackage and redesign products so they can more easily be sold through the Internet channel or a mix of several technology-enabled channels. Chapter Two shows how online marketplaces are shifting the balance of power from seller to buyer, and how to survive and thrive under the golden rule (those with the gold still make the rules). Chapter Three discusses branding strategies to become relevant to the changing needs of online buyers, and how to take advantage of new media and networks to gain a competitive edge. Chapter Four shows how marketing managers can successfully integrate interactive direct marketing tools into their marketing mix, using disciplined experimentation to gain lower marketing costs.

Some of the worst problems are not technical. They involve conflicts that arise internally and affect relationships with existing selling partners. All organizations will have to wrestle with this problem as they add Internet channels and apply technology to other channels; the second section of this book shows you how to deal with this. Chapter Five thoroughly explains the bottom-line benefits for those who master the discipline of blending and managing many sales and marketing channels, including the numbers you need to show upper management why these disciplines can improve performance and grow revenues faster. Chapter Six describes methods that sales executives can use to add more value to their field sales forces, relative to other less-expensive tele-web and partner channels. Chapter Seven reveals how new, technology-enabled, peer-to-peer networking systems will affect your existing business-to-business relationships; it gives advice on how companies should deal with shifts in the balance of power among third-party selling partners and new media. Chapter Eight demonstrates how companies that are able to transform their call centers into a strategic "traffic cop" for a variety of online media and telephone communications can achieve great advantages, significant cost savings, and better sales performance.

The third section offers concrete advice about how technology will change the way managers run their sales and marketing operations. Chapter Nine shows how companies that organize around customers and processes (instead of products and business units) can get more out of their investments in CRM technology, customer data, and existing customer relationships. Chapter Ten tells how companies that can master delivering customer service across many channels gain an edge. Chapter Eleven explains how marketing managers can help ensure that their expensive customer relationship management (CRM) systems actually work, by designing in nine proven "customer exit barrier" concepts that will give them a huge advantage in the marketplace. Chapter Twelve looks at ways sales and marketing executives can manage a new universe of outsource suppliers, and anticipates that those that know what they are buying and get good at buying it will have an advantage over those who make bad choices or hire unqualified agencies.

Where to Start

Continued change is inevitable as new advances in technology and changing customer behavior spawn the emergence of innovative business models. The experience of leading organizations suggests that these changes will ultimately touch all aspects of sales and marketing, from operations to channels and markets.

One thing that sales and marketing executives already understand is that they will ultimately be held accountable for making sure that these technologies actually help grow sales and deliver returns to investors. After all, sales and marketing managers—not the information technology department—are the ones that control the revenue plan, selling resources, marketing budgets, and customer relationships. They cannot afford to let a dizzying barrage of new technology stand in the way of effective business management and timely decision making.

How will sales and marketing executives survive the next technology cycle? How can we turn technology chaos into advantage? What are the best opportunities to take right now? What is mission critical to you? This book helps you answer those questions for your organization, using strategies based on the innovations and forward direction of some of America's top companies. It provides a framework for ongoing success by breaking down how technology will impact the fundamentals of sales and marketing strategy. Looking closely at the 12 ways technology is most affecting sales and marketing, you will find insights for dealing with future technology innovations as they evolve and will be able to take competitive advantage of new opportunities that emerge in the landscape.

Sales and marketing managers need to separate what is important from what is not so they can make decisions fast. This book provides a framework for understanding the fundamental and most important trends that will distinguish the sales and marketing leaders of tomorrow.

BEYOND "e"

Designing the Product to Fit the Channel:

Making Products Ready for E-Business and Beyond

Y OU CANNOT PUSH A SQUARE PEG THROUGH A ROUND HOLE. To sales and marketing managers, the "hole" means channels to market. Channels, simply put, are the different ways companies reach customers. Human salespeople, distributors, newspapers, the Internet, or even an ATM cash machine are all channels. When the peg (read product) fits the shape of the hole (read channel), this usually means lower selling costs and fewer customer problems. Today, technology is changing the shape of the hole by enhancing existing channels and creating new ones. Making products ready to be easily sold, marketed, and serviced though these "technology-enabled" channels is becoming critical.

Product marketers need to factor in how technology—particularly the Internet—is changing the nature and mix of channels they sell through when packaging and designing their offerings. With proper design, all products can take advantage of the unique benefits offered by "technology-enabled" channels like the Internet—not just simple products that easily fit, such as digital music, news, financial services, and computer software. The makers of all products (from cars to detergents to raw goods for industry) can take advantage of technology-enabled selling channels if they take a different look at the traditional four Ps of marketing (packaging, promotion, placement, and pricing).

To take advantage of the opportunities created by new or enhanced channels, leading marketers are starting to redesign their "pegs" to fit a new or changing set of "holes." This chapter lays out six new design criteria that will be useful to marketing executives who seek to redesign their offerings for technology-enabled sales and marketing channels. Dell Computer, one of the earliest to recognize the discipline of making products ready for specific channels, shows how this strategy can work.

Dell Computer: Making Products Ready for a New Channel

In the early 1980s, a few innovators changed the personal computer industry. Stephen Jobs of Apple Computer and Michael Dell of Dell, Inc. had the same great idea: PCs needed to be simpler. Both set about the task in different ways. Jobs simplified the computer itself by inventing the Apple MacIntosh with its easy point-and-click instructions. Dell did something equally interesting. He simplified how PCs were sold. Jobs revolutionized the product and influenced how PCs would be made in the future. Dell revolutionized the distribution channel and influenced how PCs would be sold in the future.

Jobs and his friends built computers from scratch. On the other hand, Dell did not build computers; rather he assembled them from parts in his college dorm room. This perspective allowed him to embrace a powerful concept—*customized product configuration*. He concluded that since all the parts were basically the same, there would be value in buying a bunch of parts and then building a product configured to suit the needs of an individual consumer.

Over time, this focus on "configuring" products rather than building them let Dell as a company get very good at helping customers navigate thousands of possible PC system combinations available for sale. By applying this concept to the selling process, Dell learned how to translate what the customer wanted—in plain, not technical language—into a product recommendation or a customized computer built just for them. Dell made it easier for the average person without a technical degree to select and buy personal computers. The transaction could be accomplished without a physical product sitting in a store, and without the help of an expensive sales rep.

In practice, this meant that Dell could sell PCs over the phone at a time when other computers were still being sold through expensive field salespeople and retail stores. To make this happen, they laid out options in a print catalog so customers could see the choices they had; they used software to help call-center agents calculate the costs of options and add-ons on the fly while talking to prospects. And Dell used a new technology—the "fax back"—to immediately send proposals back to the prospects at the push of a button. Soon, Dell's selling costs were a third less than the competition, a significant gap in a business where margins were shrinking, as the price of personal computers continued to drop in the wake of the low-cost Apple product line.

In the mid 1990s, when the Internet came along, Dell found that the discipline of making the personal computer "ready" for the phone channel also helped them make it ready for online channels.

To adapt the PC for sale in online channels, they used new software called "product configuration software" that automated this process of product selection. This new "class" of software (pioneered by companies like Trilogy and Calico) does the complicated math needed to consider millions of possible alternatives and come up with the best set of options for a client. At Dell, this tool helped online customers navigate and understand very large and complicated product lines—the universe of PC products and features—and reduced the burden on the call center reps who coached these customers through the buying process over the phone. In addition, Dell's focus on configuration allowed them to become leaders in product customization and personalization because of the amount of information that could be processed quickly, then translated as customer orders sent directly to the factory.

Armed with these tools, Dell began to sell computers over the Internet in 1996 and was soon averaging over a million dollars in online sales a day. By the turn of the century they were doing over $13 billion in sales online a year—half of their total sales.

This focus on making products ready for technology-enabled channels helped Dell to grow faster for less money. By simplifying their products so they could be sold through low-cost tele and Web channels, Dell was able to get more mileage out of every sales and marketing dollar than their competitors, Compaq, IBM, HP, and even Apple. By the end of the decade they were growing at twice the rate as the rest of the industry and became the number-one seller of PCs in the United States. Their competitors are still scrambling to restructure and change their selling approach to close the cost-to-sell gap.

Exploiting the Unique Benefits of Technology-Enabled Channels

Dell is just one example of why, if you cannot fit a square peg through a round hole, then one thing you can do is redesign the peg to fit better. Technology is enhancing existing selling channels and creating new ones in every industry. These changes will ultimately change the way offerings are packaged and designed. In other words, the "peg" (product) remains the same, but the shape of the hole (the channel) is changing.

For example, most large companies are automating their sales forces and call centers with Customer Relationship Management (CRM) solutions (covered in Chapter 11). This is forcing product marketers to "digitize" product catalogs so they fit into salespeoples' laptops, and some are beginning to re-architect product specifications so they can be "custom configured" right in front of the customer on their computer screen.

Electronic channels place different demands on products. New Internet storefronts and online marketplaces that sell products directly online are forcing product marketers to digitize the way their products are represented or delivered so they fit better on

Top Reasons Retailers Cite for Not Going Online

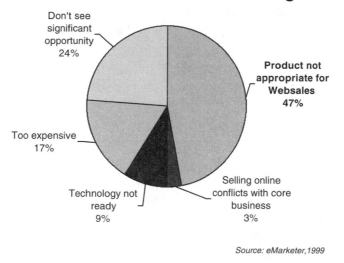

Source: eMarketer,1999

Figure 1.1 Top Reasons Retailers Cite For Not Going Online.

electronic "shelves," or change pricing on the fly to keep up with the rapid-fire bidding in online auctions.

Making products ready for technology-enabled channels represents an opportunity to marketers because most organizations are so focused on building technology-enabled selling channels that they have little time or money to focus on developing specialized offerings that fit those channels. More significantly, the concept of making products ready for channels is not yet on the radar screen of most senior executives. For example, almost half of retailers don't sell online because they don't feel their products are appropriate for the channel, according to e-Marketer.

Ultimately, things will have to change. The prevailing assumption that only certain products (e.g., CDs, books, travel) are Web-ready will be proven wrong.

For instance General Electric puts a lot of energy into boasting how they use online channels to support the sale of their "real world products"—plastics, steam turbines, and medical equipment. Car manufacturers like Chrysler and General Motors have aggressively looked deeper into dealer inventories and ultimately assemble custom cars. Professional services are another industry that can take advantage of the Internet. Executive search marketplaces, such as MonsterBoard, are among the most successful online marketplaces because of the Internet's ability to aggregate job hunters in one place and transport resumes and job postings with no paper or manpower. In the late 1990s an accounting firm, Ernst and Young, even started delivering tax consulting online through a Web site tool called "Ernie," inspiring a raft of imitators in all parts of consulting.

In the short term, marketers can begin simply by sorting out which products "fit" better in online channels, and which ones do not. For example, when Herman Miller, the office furniture producer, started building their electronic channels, they offered only a few simple home office products that were easy to buy online. Once they had gained some familiarity with online selling, Herman Miller added more products for home office users and offered an Internet configuring tool. It wasn't fancy: just a downloadable "Room Planner" that helped buyers to figure out if the desks and chairs they wanted to buy would actually fit in their cramped home offices. But it was important because the tool made it easier for remote customers to visualize and confidently select furniture for their home-based businesses. As a result, online sales at Herman Miller started growing at 38 percent each month.

Over the long haul to gain a competitive edge, product-marketing professionals will have to embrace two priorities:

1. Enabling product configuration and assembly that is fast and invisible to the customer;
2. Designing products and services that can be sold through any channel or mix of channels.

Here is how to begin.

Short-Term Strategy: Assess How Technology Is Changing the Channel

To begin to make their products ready for technology-enhanced selling channels, product marketers must first "measure the hole" they are trying to fit their products through. This means looking outside their organizations to find the new information that can be used by product design teams. Bob Villa, the popular host of the home improvement television show "This Old House," gives this same simple advice to home improvement novices—"measure twice, cut once."

Factoring distribution requirements into product design is nothing new in the world of business. In the automotive industry, the size, shape, and weight of cars and trucks is dictated, in part, by how these products will fit into railroad cars or maritime shipping containers. The standardized box and Tyvek pack sizes offered by Federal Express have little to do with how customers asked for packaging: They relate to how they will be stacked in airplane cargo holds. Designing in response to external factors creates a competitive advantage when it can result in efficiencies in product delivery.

In some cases it will mean altering the "container" to exploit an electronic distribution channel. A good example is American Greetings, one of only two companies consistently in the NetRatings Top 20 Web Sites listings that existed *prior* to the World Wide Web. Borrowing from online innovator Blue Mountain Arts, American Greetings repackaged its paper greeting cards so they could be purchased and customized electronically through its Web site and then sent electronically through e-mail. Adding capabilities unique to the channel, the "Web-ready" greeting cards include visual animations, music, and opportunities for the buyer to customize or personalize the greeting card with the recipient in mind.

To create products that are better suited for technology-enabled sales and marketing channels, marketers will have to learn more about:

1. How customer buying behavior is changing in all channels;
2. How competitors are selling or "bundling" offerings in your industry;
3. The specific ways technology is changing the channels you plant to sell through.

1. Watch for Changes in Customer Buying Behavior

Once customers get used to the benefits of buying through the Internet, they become a new kind of customer. This new customer expects, if not demands, highly personalized products, personalized services, and immediate delivery. Adapting existing products to meet such high expectations will involve changes in how organizations package, distribute, and configure products.

For example, customers will shop at online marketplaces that allow them to compare prices and products of many different suppliers, then select a vendor at a single mouse-click. As a result, manufacturers of commodity products such as steel, paper, chemicals, and plastics, and purveyors of indirect materials, such as packaging equipment and maintenance supplies, must tailor their products for online transactions. In simplistic terms, this involves providing digital product specifications and even visual screen demonstrations on Web sites to encourage virtual "tire kicking" and provide "extra information" that may influence a buyer. Eventually, "live," competitive bidding in these online markets will force marketers to become better at adjusting product pricing on the fly while still managing profit margins.

Online customers expect an increasingly wider selection of products and services through self-service electronic channels. But customers differ when it comes to the level of self-service they desire. Some customers will be "Hold-My-Hand-Harrys"—they require a great deal of assistance when they buy anything from a fishing hat to a mainframe. Other customers prefer minimal assistance: these are the Leave-Me-Alone-Larrys who are gruff to store clerks and find no joy interacting with human telephone reps. The Larrys of the world adore the Internet; to serve them well, organizations will have to become experts in managing a bigger collection of offerings for self-service.

2. Look at How the Competition is Selling

The example of Dell shows that marketers who look closely at how a product is sold have a good chance of gaining a competitive edge that lasts. Competitors are trying to set themselves apart by using technology in the sales and marketing process.

For example, in consumer financial services, new players like e-Trade and Ameritrade were able to enter the market by breaking apart the traditional financial services product "bundles" to take advantage of the unique benefits of the Internet channel. These innovators divided and conquered by separating stock transactions from financial advice and research. They offered lower transaction costs, more self-service, more options online to customers who wanted cheap trades but no advice. They were able to steal brokerage business from established players like Merrill Lynch and American Express Financial, who relied on high-priced stock trades to pay for the expert advice doled out by expensive human financial advisors.

New business models will create value in different ways by building services into structured pricing. Competitors typically accessorize mature products with desirable services—anything from automatic replenishment ordering, free returns and free delivery, to 24-hour technical support. Experiments in this zone also include leasing arrangements for products traditionally purchased, automatic free product upgrades, trade-ins, or creative financing for the buyer.

One extreme example in the auto industry was ModelE, now known as Build-To-Order, Inc. (btoauto.com). Initially created to serve custom car buyers among the ranks of the dot-com millionaires, ModelE planned a factory, with a Web site, that would allow high-end car buyers to literally design their own vehicles. This went much further than simply picking a custom color or shade of interior leather. If you wanted to put the engine of a Jaguar into the body of a Volvo, or build a hybrid of a Mustang and a Miata, the site's product configurators could show if it was possible and how much it might cost.

Now that the ranks of dot-com millionaires have thinned out, the company has turned its focus to the possibilities of selling normal cars with customized and highly specialized *service options*, to include some novel forms of purchase financing. Build-to-Order is still looking for a way to create new value from a bunch of spare parts and may one day realize its goal. Ford Motor Company was scared enough to try to knock off the upstart by claiming trademark infringement of its venerated Model T. Both Ford and General Motors have since outlined plans that will allow buyers more design input, through configurators on their own Web sites. Chrysler is already using data from configurators for market research.

3. Understand the Technical Requirements of New Channels

To design products that fit well in new technology-enabled channels they plan to use, marketers will need to better understand the technical "specifications" of these channels. The four Ps of marketing (packaging, price, placement, and promotion) still apply to product development. Technology just changes things a bit. For example, when looking at a potential distributor, marketers still need to ask how much capacity they have (read Internet bandwidth), what type of packing they require to ship safely (read digital containers), how much insurance is needed to guarantee delivery (read encryption), *and* what levels of support and installation they offer (read embedded service and self-help).

New product design teams should keep abreast of new methods to digitally represent and distribute products that were previously available only in a more physical form. For example, online channels are transforming the packaging of all written, audio, graphic, and video products. New media like HTML, writable CDs, multimedia, and wireless are merely alternate formats to paper books, plastic records, drawn decorative artwork, and videocassettes. Both publishing and the music industry are rushing to modify their offerings for digital distribution in a variety of electronic "containers"—for example, program formats such as digital MP3 audio and printable PDF files.

Publishers are also exploring new ways of pricing by factoring in time, medium, and context, which may have relevance to many other products and services. For example, *New Yorker* magazine allows their online customers to buy just a part of the magazine. For many that part of the magazine is their famous cartoons. This takes advantage of the Web's unique ability to sell content "by the drink" or in very small quantities. Accomplishing this same strategy at the newsstand would require a lot of scissors and thousands of cut-up magazines that nobody wanted.

Plenty of details need to be worked out. Novelist Stephen King, for example, experimented with online self-publishing by distributing a new work, *The Plant*, in text installments through his own Web site. Customers "paid by the chapter" and were on the honor system to pay by mail or credit card for each downloaded chapter. While many readers paid for the first few chapters, most apparently did not enjoy reading (or paying) this way. Payments began to fall off. True to his own cliff-hanger tradition, the author suspended future installments right in the middle of the story—until kinks in the value-capture mechanism (i.e., how to get readers to pay) could be worked out.

Making Vegetables "Channel Ready"

Companies that can successfully modify their products to take advantage of new channels can open up new markets. One of the earliest success stories out of what is now called Silicon Valley concerns two Sicilian brothers, Andrew and Stephen D'Arrigo, owners of a 28-acre vegetable farm in San Jose. In 1924, these innovators took advantage of a significant new breakthrough in product delivery—the refrigerated railroad car. They became the first California farmers to sell fresh vegetables, shipped on ice, to markets in Boston, and later, New York.

Getting fresh vegetables "ready" to be shipped across country required some attention to technical requirements of the new distribution channel. For example, they could only ship vegetables that could be safely stored at temperatures just above freezing and were least likely to wilt or rot during cross-country transport. Broccoli met this requirement and was therefore "ready for the channel." After more experimentation the brothers found their vegetables survived their bruising cross-country trip better when packed in straw, which also absorbed the water from melting ice.

In addition, to communicate the benefits of their product across 3000 miles without the benefit of a vegetable stand, the brothers used new forms of media (radio in 1927 and television in the 1950s). They ran ads to raise awareness of broccoli in East Coast markets and to promote their Andy Boy brand. (For more on modern branding initiatives, see Chapter 3.) The ads promoted broccoli specifically because while "channel ready," it was an old-world vegetable not yet common to American cuisine and therefore needed some introduction.

The D'Arrigos' approach was high-tech for its time and illustrates why modifying products to take advantage of new "roads to market"—whether they be dirt roads, railroads, or virtual highways—remains worthwhile. The brothers not only took their local business national, they helped develop a new business model for vegetable selling that left a lasting and dramatic effect on the nation's produce marketplace. Prior to 1925, vegetables supplied to major cities came from local farms no more than a day's drive away; today, nearly 100 percent of all the broccoli and lettuce found in U.S. supermarkets nationwide is shipped from California (to a lesser extent, Arizona, Florida, or Mexico). The Andy Boy brand still claims a significant market share.

Long-Term Imperative: Repackage Products to Fit Technology-Enabled Channels

Once you have measured how technology is changing the shape of the hole (the channel) it is time to redesign the peg (the product). To do this product managers will need to rethink the criteria they use to design products.

The best marketers are starting to sort and modify their offerings based on the type of channel they are being sold through. For example, even though books were among the first products to move online in large numbers, several material changes to the product were necessary. In the retail channel the binder art on the side of the book is important because it sits on a bookstore shelf. This is often the only part the customer sees while browsing. In online channels some new things are important. The theme and content of the book must be "architected" better to program good search engine "keywords" and other interactive links that make sure readers with interest find the book easily. Killer graphics and charts bring the content to life and make it look better online. And a large number of impartial, open-source reviews and referrals from actual customers are keys to making the sales.

In the short term this means resegmenting and repackaging products based on where they sell best. In the long run, this means redesigning products based on a new set of "channel readiness" criteria. This section will outline six new design criteria that will be useful to product marketers who seek to repackage and design their offerings to make them ready for "technology-enabled" sales and marketing channels.

Six Product Channel Readiness Design Criteria

There are six factors that will be important to making your offerings ready to take advantage of the unique benefits of online channels and a variety of channels working together:

1. Simplification: Making products easier to sell and buy online
2. Mass Customization: Letting customers have it their way
3. Dynamic Pricing: Surviving online bidding wars
4. Value Packaging: Redefining how value is created and paid for
5. Hybrid Distribution: Packaging for more than one distribution channel
6. Service and Support: Building customer service into products

These factors can provide a disciplined "scorecard" for setting priorities and sorting out which products are best suited for which channels. Marketers should think of these as a design template to direct the repackaging and redesign of products to ensure they have a better chance of working in technology-enabled channels. Each takes into consideration the external technical, consumer, or competitive information outlined earlier in this chapter and recommends design criteria and technologies that can help you adapt your products.

1. Simplification: making products easier to sell and buy online *This involves improving the ease with which customers are able to select, configure, and buy complex products, especially in online channels.*

Because of the practical limits of online distribution, only very simple and digital products or services can be delivered entirely through Internet channels. However, a wide universe of Web capabilities makes it possible for every marketer to use the Internet channel to streamline the purchase process. Marketers who take the extra step of making it easier for customers to select, configure, and buy their more complicated products, (not just simple ones) can gain competitive advantage. Something as basic as simplifying the way products are listed and categorized can make it easier for customers to find, understand, select, and buy your product using the Internet.

One enlightened example: RS Components (UK), which offers catalogs of business supplies and industrial products, made it easier for customers to quickly identify the products they needed by using personalized online catalogs. RS Components personalized these online custom catalogs to make specific product recommendations and used customer input to select only the parts that were relevant to each customer, from an inventory of over 100,000 components. This means customers don't have to thumb through massive paper catalogs and parts lists to find what they need.

Some of the technologies currently available that can help marketers simplify their products include:

One-click buying: Pioneered by Amazon, this patented technology provides a customer interface that simplifies the online buying process. Variants include "shopping cart" programs that automatically calculate tax and shipping charges as the customers selects products online.

Product configurators: This class of technology enables the personalized selection and configuration of individual products by permitting customers to browse and prioritize a large number of product features, options or part numbers based on personal buying criteria. Configurators can also automate price quotes, proposals, purchase-order forms and bills of manufacturing materials.

Natural language search: This technology, a notable example of which is Ask Jeeves, allows customers to formulate questions about what they want in plain English.

Artificial intelligence: This technology enables computers to guide and assist customers as well as anticipate customer questions, based on their past buying history or the flow of the buy decision itself. This technology can be highly useful in upsell and cross-sell. The process of purchasing a videocassette recorder, for example, may trigger a screen prompt for a sale on blank videocassettes.

2. Mass customization: letting customers have it their way

This involves "architecting" products to be readily configured and assembled to customer or channel specifications.

Nearly all products have to be assembled anyway—either in the factory, by a field service technician, or by frustrated parents staying up late on Christmas Eve. Winning organizations will design products that can be more easily "configured" to meet the needs of customers.

For example, General Mills permitted customers to customize their own breakfast cereal through the Web site of myCereal.com. This gave cereal-eaters the choice of millions of possible varieties. By comparison, a large supermarket might carry a few hundred different types of cereal. Along with a high degree of customization, General Mills could offer swift delivery of an individualized product, thanks to the use of product configuration tools.

Buyers can request the ingredients, textures, packaging, and even give the product package its own name. The company is able to factor in large amounts of customer information into the design of the product, including health, diet, portion size, allergies, and demographics. General Mills does charge a premium for customization, about two to three times market prices (about $8 per small box). But the cereal can be assembled and shipped the same day.

Other experiments in the packaged-goods area include personalized cosmetics from Procter & Gamble (Reflect.com) and customized coffee blends (Millstone.com). Two companies are selling customized sneakers online: Customatix and Nike. Chrysler's Web site, meanwhile, tracks 220 specific car options, features, and other attributes across its customer and prospect base. While it does not make personalized cars yet, it currently uses this information to model and forecast demand and reduce the cost of "mass customizing" its most popular cars in the factory. Mattel enables Barbie fans to custom-configure their doll with hundreds of possible permutations (e.g., hair and eye color, outfits, accessories) on its Barbie.com site. But it recently dropped the buying feature because too few visitors to the Web site actually ordered the custom dolls. (Mattel execs reported two stumbling blocks: adult buyers considered the delivery window for custom dolls weeks too long, and most little girls do not have credit cards.)

If online buyers want it "their way," they will generally reward a seller that can provide a highly personalized, individually customized, product or service. Certain technologies can help marketers develop customized or personalized products. They include:

> *Personalization/recommendation engines:* These systems build and recommend products or features based on customer's stated preferences, buying history, or behavior. Key vendors include Macromedia, Personify, and Net Perceptions.
>
> *Campaign automation and analysis:* These tools help marketers customize campaigns and promotions based on customer needs, channel preferences, and responsiveness. Some of the companies that provide these tools include Annuncio, E.piphany, and BroadBase.
>
> *Dynamic content management tools:* These Web content platforms enable marketers to deliver customized content and targeted marketing offerings. These are offered by companies like Vignette, ATG, and Broadvision.
>
> *Usage analysis/profiling:* These services give product marketers information to develop customized products and promotional offerings based on demonstrated customer behavior and interests. This capability can be provided by advertising and profiling networks such as Engage Technologies and DoubleClick.
>
> *Enterprise Resource Planning (ERP):* Several software companies such as SAP and Peoplesoft have spent years helping large corporations try to get a better handle on their pro-

duction processes for building products. After 10 years of trying, many of these systems are beginning to work. These Enterprise Resource Planning systems will play a big role in creating opportunities for marketers to produce and assemble more customized products. (They are also relevant to dynamic pricing: See below.)

3. Dynamic pricing: surviving online bidding wars *This means using fluid pricing models to deliver fast and accurate market pricing and to calculate product profitability "on the fly."*

Anyone with a Web browser can comparison-shop for anything from health insurance to cans of peas to tons of pig iron. And many online auctions require minute-to-minute price adjustments. In response, many marketers are being forced to monitor other Web sites and actively update their pricing to remain competitive. The best marketers are finding ways to deliver fast and accurate market pricing and to calculate product profitability in 24-hour cycles *or less.* This is an opportunity because a study by Pittiglio, Rabin, Todd & McGrath showed that most companies still change prices on a monthly or quarterly calendar.

For example, some electronics distributors use Web "spiders" (software programs that search the Web for a specific topic) to continuously benchmark their prices against those offered on competitive sites. Auction Universe, an online marketplace for a variety of goods, dynamically priced surplus inventory based on market conditions so they would be able to move product on the competitive Web channel.

As flexible pricing rapidly becomes a competitive necessity, marketers will have to take advantage of technologies such as:

> *Micropayments/digital rights management:* These technologies allow customers to pay for increasingly smaller increments of usage ("by the drink"), such as by individual page views. Vendors include iPin, Qpass, Cha!, and Reciprocal.
>
> *Auctioning software:* This software helps organizations participate in dynamic trading communities by enabling hundreds of different, market-based pricing structures (e.g.,

sealed bid, dutch, reverse auction). These are offered by vendors like Moai Technologies, OpenSite Technologies, (now part of Siebel Systems), and Fairmarket.

Data mining/segmentation: These data analysis tools allow marketers to better understand customer price sensitivity and value perceptions to enable individualized or discriminatory pricing tiers. These are offered by vendors like SAS Institute, DataSage, and Microstrategies.

Shopping bots/price spiders: This software enables marketers to set prices off of changing market price by continually searching the Web for competitive, comparable, or substitute pricing. A notable example is My Simon, which can be used by a retailer on her lunch hour to determine the "street price" of a trendy or hard-to-get item.

Enterprise Resource Planning (ERP): This software simplifies and speeds the costing, specification, and manufacture of products by automating back-office operations. Leading providers of ERP solutions include SAP, Peoplesoft, and Oracle.

4. Value packaging: redefining how value is created and paid for   *Marketers will have to rethink the "boundaries" they draw around their product to take advantage of the ways technology is enhancing their sales channels and exploit new forms of distribution.*

For example, is a car just a car, or is it really a "bundle" of machine, financing, undercoating, customized options, and a lifetime service contract? The answer depends on who you are. When the manufacturer sells the car to the dealer at a good profit, they prefer to consider a car as just a car to keep things simple. But auto dealers prefer to "package" the offering as a "bundle" when they can because they can make more money selling options and services to the end consumer.

Online sellers often gain an advantage when they bundle products traditionally sold by their competitors as separate items. Organizations must redefine the boundaries of their products; the goal is to optimally align the source of value to the customer ("value creation") with the basis for payment to the seller ("value capture"), with respect to specific channels.

This can often be a daunting task. For example, auto manufacturers like Ford are being forced to unbundle, or separate, their used and new car sales from Ford's in-house financing, and will forego the option of giving customers a "branded" service and local presence in order to participate in independent car-shopping portal Web sites and online trading communities such as Autobytel and Cars.com.

Innovators will find ways to redefine value boundaries in many ways, including repackaging traditional product bundles into smaller units for more customer flexibility, assembling new and innovative bundles of services and products into solutions, and experimenting with new compensation and payment models.

New online trading companies like E-trade, for example, also helped force the repackaging of the traditional relationship between stock brokers and customers by separating trading transaction functions (priced per trade) from advice and financial management (retainer or monthly/yearly management fee). While the discount brokerage model had been pioneered by Schwab and others, E-Trade concentrated its customer recruitment on the Web in the mid-1990s, when this was still a relatively new sales channel, and enjoyed a first-mover advantage there.

Redefining the Value of Service Products

New technology often gives our competitors the opportunity to blow our products to bits and "reassemble" them in ways that give them an edge. The impact that the Internet has had on the stock brokerage industry illustrates well the importance of value packaging and the benefits of rethinking normal product boundaries. Traditionally, stock brokers "created value" for their clients in the form of expert advice, which they gave freely to wealthy clients because they "captured value" (i.e., made their money) by conducting the technically simple transactions for fat fees (up to 5% of the principle amount invested). That meant that an individual who decided to invest $10,000 in a particular stock, during the course of an informative phone call with a broker, would pay perhaps $500 to the broker simply for implementing the requested transaction.

The Internet allowed a variety of new players to correct an obvious misalignment of "value creation" and "value capture." Ameritrade, E-Trade, and other online brokers broke apart this value bundle by letting investors conduct the transaction themselves for a flat fee of as little as $8. As for investment advice, self-service investors could soon find vast quantities of stock analysis available for free on the Web sites from Motley Fool, Raging Bull, and others. These sites could afford to give away advice and research for free because they got paid for ad placements on their Web sites (many for traditional financial services companies such as Merrill Lynch, Fidelity, and Paine Webber). Others like Financialengines.com, developed by a Nobel Prize-winning Stanford economics professor offered more personalized financial advice. For a fee ranging from between $50-200 per year, customers could input their personal and financial situation and the system would return individualized best-case, worst-case, and most likely future investment scenarios, much as a human financial planner would but at a fraction of the cost.

Full-service brokerage houses and thousands of well-trained financial advisors have reacted by adding Web-based self-service, or counteracting with advertisements that reinforce the benefits of "personal broker" relationships. Increasingly, "live" brokers are migrating to the top of the financial services food chain, selling only the most profitable financial products (like annuities) to richer clients who expect a higher level of customer care.

5. Hybrid distribution: packaging for more than one distribution channel *This means adapting and designing products for easy distribution through a variety of channels, including electronic channels and online business partners.*

Many products—including travel, stock brokerage, personal computers, and books—are currently sold through a variety of channels at the same time. Product marketing managers in these businesses are struggling to coordinate all the elements of product design across more than one channel. This can get complicated when you factor in pricing (multitiered pricing), packaging (both digital and paper catalogs), promotions (paper and email coupons), and placement (on the shelf and in the search engine). When multiple channel selling is involved, things start getting confusing pretty quickly.

Take the challenge of pricing across channels, for instance. For the first few years after introducing an online channel, Charles Schwab struggled with two-tiered pricing for telephone ($60) and Internet service ($30). This was because their costs and service levels were different in each channel. To keep customers from getting unhappy, and as a response to the lower prices and simpler offerings of other online brokerage competitors, they ultimately went with one low price for both channels. On the surface this cost them hundreds of millions of dollars in lost revenues as millions of customers got a $30 discount. However, the executives at Schwab were committed to "multichannel selling" and believed that the product needed to be consistently sold through more than one channel.

Schwab anticipates that over time, customers will buy higher-margin services over the phone and perhaps even get rich enough to warrant lucrative financial planning advice in person.

Making products and services easily available through many different channels is an opportunity because customers are becoming "schizophrenic" about which channels they prefer. For example, a customer might buy on the Web, complain on the phone, return to the store, and ultimately write a "snail mail" letter to the president looking for a rebate. The risk of not making products ready and consistent for all channels means customers will scream when the change of address they input on your Web site is not reflected in their conversation with your telemarketer four hours later. A recent IMT Strategies survey of 300 buyers showed that most of them check two or more sources (read channels) when buying. This means that there is a good chance that if the story is not consistent, customers will be confused or unhappy.

Marketers must design products for easy distribution through an increasing variety of electronic channels and third-party business partners, including online business-to-business trading communities and business-to-consumer Web selling. This may require product simplification, better product information, or new delivery and payment mechanisms.

For example, list brokers like Dun & Bradstreet and Axciom sell customized lists of prospects directly to salespeople through portal Web sites like Sales.com. They are able to do this by configuring their list products to align easily with the sales territories, industries, and software packages used by salespeople.

Marketers should investigate technologies like "electronic containers" that can fit through many different channels and media. Today's electronic containers are really a variety of software programs designed to package products for the technical parameters of online delivery. Adobe PDF, MP3, and Real Networks, for example, are digital formats for artwork and music that were quickly accepted as standards. In 2000, the U.S. Postal Service announced it would create a standardized method to certify the delivery of electronic documents; this is sure to have implications for private companies, such as Federal Express and DHL, which at best can only offer overnight document delivery between distant cities.

Marketers that plan to migrate products from physical channels of distribution to electronic channels must also consider computerized systems for billing online, accepting electronic checks, as well as warehousing and logistics (perhaps outsourced) to manage rapid delivery and returns.

6. Service and support: building customer service into products *This involves matching the level of product service and support to the requirements of the customer and to the technical needs of a selling channel.*

Customers usually show a preference for a certain level of support. The spectrum is broad from "Leave-Me-Alone-Larrys" (technically adept people who want to do it themselves online) to "Hold-My-Hand-Harrys" (people who value human interaction and have still not programmed the clock on their VCRs). But unlike direct sales channels, electronic channels may not offer human interaction to help customers understand, select, and purchase products. Therefore, when marketers design products for technology-enabled channels they should try to match the level of product service and support built into the product with the level of service offered in the selling channel and the needs of the customer.

For example, product managers can embed service and support within their Web sites or automatically link them to their telephone operations to deliver varying levels, depending on whether "Leave-Me-Alone-Larrys" or "Hold-My-Hand-Harrys" are shopping the Web.

Software developers Microsoft and Intuit have overcome the lack of retail sales support offered in computer superstores, for example, by embedding self-help knowledge bases and easy online customer support into their popular Office and Quicken products. Naturally, this support was biased towards their own products.

Businesses must invest in technologies to provide some level of automated buying support for less sophisticated or impatient customers. These technologies include:

> *Collaborative CRM.* These technologies facilitate online collaboration between customers and live agents during the product sale. Specific technologies include voice-over IP, co-browsing, automated call back, page push, and customer service chat.

> *Embedded service/service knowledge bases:* Best-in-class marketers will work to embed service into products using network, memory, and database technology to build instructions, help-desk support, and service into products themselves. Self-service products will require substantial investments in self-serve technical support, customer service, and frequently asked questions (FAQ) databases accessed over the Internet or embedded within the product.

> *Mail response management:* This class of technology uses artificial intelligence and business rules to read, sort, and respond to electronic inquiries, so marketers can respond more quickly to online customers and online prospects. Vendors include Kana Communications, eGain, and E.piphany.

More information on using these technologies for customer care is provided in Chapter 8.

Bottom Line

Mastering the discipline of Product Channel Readiness will become critical to success when new selling avenues appear. Product marketers need to factor in how technology—particularly the Internet—is changing the nature and mix of channels they sell through when packaging and designing their offerings.

Product Channel Readiness Assessment Scorecard

Simplified Overview

Product Channel Readiness Dimension	Scorecare Assessment Criteria
Simplification: Improving customers' ability to select, configure, and buy complex products, especially in online channels.	• Inherent product simplicity/complexity • Market complexity • Solution packaging • Level of assembly • Configurability & componentization • Level of engineering • Bundling with other offerings • Benefits explanation • Level of customer awareness
Mass Customization: Architecting products to be readily configured and assembled to meet customer or channel specifications.	• Level of Personalization • Customer segments • Ease of inputting requirements • Number of models • Build to order v. stock • Number of options • Lead time
Dynamic Pricing: Enabling fluid pricing models to deliver fast and accurate market pricing and to calculate product profitability on the fly.	• Market Price/"Street Price" vs. Factory Price • Dynamic/instant costing • Speed of commitment • "Cost plus" pricing • External pricing factors (service/support, risk, demand) • Value pricing • Price sensitivity • Market segmentation • Knowledge of the customer (lifetime value assessment) • Price complexity/terms and conditions
Value Packaging: Redefining product boundaries to optimally align value creation and value capture.	• Bundling • Level of packaging • Representation • Value-to-weight ratio • Differentiation • Customer awareness • Standards & certification of quality • Ease of use • Cost to customers • Benefits explanation • Value capture mechanism
Hybrid Distribution: Designing products for easy distribution through an increasing variety of electronic channels and business partners.	• Selling sophistication • Selling requirements (push v. pull) • Cycle time expectations • Transaction complexity • Ease of doing business • Fulfillment mechanism • Levels of communication • Virtual logistics
Service and Support: Matching the level of product service and support with the requirements of a particular selling channel.	• Service requirements • Customer sophistication • Self-service • Installation requirements • Installation agent • Relative availability of support • Quality, timeliness, and cost of service • Returns and repairs

Figure 1.2 The Product Channel Readiness Scorecard.

The Role of Online Marketplaces:

Maximizing Revenue Growth and Margins in Online Auctions and Exchanges

SELLING INTO ONLINE MARKETPLACES—Internet auctions, business-to-business exchanges, and other forms of electronic trading—will be inevitable for millions of businesses worldwide as more and more buyers start using them. General Electric, for example, will buy about $45 billion worth of goods and services in 2001. The company plans to make almost one-third of these purchases—$14 billion dollars worth—through online marketplaces.

No matter what your company sells, you can expect, and should project, that a significant percentage of your day-to-day customer interactions will occur through online marketplaces over the next two to three years.

This is both good and bad news for selling organizations. It's bad news because these online marketplaces will shift the balance of power from the seller to the buyer. If General Electric wants to buy in online markets, a seller must react, even if it means paying a fee for the luxury of posting your price list in a digital catalog and exposing yourself to more competition than ever before.

The good news is that online marketplaces offer sellers the opportunity to access global markets and define new markets. Smart selling executives will learn how to blend online marketplaces with traditional selling channels (e.g., field sales, telechannels, distributors, and Internet storefronts) to reach more markets and match the way customers want to buy. Ultimately, the real winners will find ways to use the information generated in these marketplaces to their own advantage, or add to their business by offering new, profitable services to buyers in these markets.

This chapter outlines how sales and marketing executives will have to change their approaches to pricing, channel management, and marketing in order to sell though online marketplaces. Eastman Chemical is one example of a company that moved quickly into online marketplaces to stay ahead of changing customer demands and the competition.

Eastman Chemical: Finding a Role for Online Marketplaces in the Selling Mix

In the $1.7 trillion chemical industry, old-world selling is coming face to face with new ways of buying. About 12 percent of corporate buyers currently purchase chemicals online. A growing number of online marketplaces, including early players such as e-Chemicals.com, ChemConnect, and ChemMatch, were set up to make it easier to buy and sell chemicals on a global scale. Because the chemical market is very fragmented—very few producers must sell to a large number of international buyers, ranging from producers of plastic soda bottles to producers of car parts—these online marketplaces offered chemical manufacturers the opportunity to reach this diverse group of buyers economically.

Eastman Chemical, a $5-billion manufacturer of specialty chemicals, saw online marketplaces as a new sales channel to complement its field sales force, its network of global distributors, and its new electronic commerce channel. Already noted for its strong field sales force, Eastman had recently added e-commerce as a new direct sales channel. Within nine months the new online storefront had registered some 500 customers and produced $10 million in sales.

Other buyers wanted to buy chemicals in online auctions. To learn how to reach them, Eastman took an equity stake in Chem-Connect, whose World Chemical Exchange hosts millions of dollars worth of transactions involving more than 5000 members from over 4000 companies in more than 100 countries. Eastman also has participated in other online marketplaces like Chemicals.com, which had built an online catalog of many chemical products.

Eastman Chemical recognizes that online markets are an "immature" channel and continues to re-evaluate all of the online marketplaces it sells in for their usefulness and longevity. For example, one promising chemical exchange, Chemdex, folded after three years because its members did not buy enough plastics to keep it afloat long enough to become established. And for now, sellers like Eastman and Dow Chemical are still "priming the pump" for ChemConnect's World Chemical Exchange until it catches on with other members. The two account for almost half the exchange's revenues.

Eastman currently projects that online marketplaces will account for 20 percent of its international sales by 2003. Longer term, as these marketplaces add value-added services (ChemConnect, for example, has introduced ChemConnect Logistics, a logistics information management service), Eastman should be poised to maximize margins and gain revenue through participation as well as through its equity stake.

Why Your Customers Will Use Online Marketplaces

The chemical industry is not an isolated example. In the year 2000, billions of dollars of online sales transactions, involving thousands of companies, were conducted through over 750 online marketplaces. More and more offerings—from headhunting services to agricultural products to secondhand factory equipment—are being marketed or sold through these online marketplaces every day. Online marketplaces may be slow out of the gate and still have some growing up to do, but it is likely that many of your customers are starting to buy through them.

The impact of online marketplaces on business-to-business (B2B) sales will be particularly great. *Purchasing Magazine*'s annual reader survey showed that 16 percent of buyers participated in third-party online marketplaces in the year 2000. A recent IMT Strategies survey of 260 businesses showed that 80 percent intended to either participate in an online marketplace or build one themselves.

This is because there are several good reasons to buy through online marketplaces. The Internet makes shopping and buying things much simpler and more cost-effective. For example, matching buyers and sellers, comparing offerings, and exchanging information are all much easier to do. Early consumer marketplaces such as Priceline.com or eBay illustrate clearly how online marketplaces do a good job getting many buyers and sellers into one place. The online auction site eBay conducted over $20 billion in transactions in 1999, among its one million registered participants—mostly individual folks interested in purchasing hard-to-find collectibles or bargains in secondhand merchandise.

The Internet also supports more flexible and efficient pricing. It used to be that auctions and "real-time" pricing were restricted to "elbow-to-elbow" bidding at stock exchange trading floors and elite auction houses. Today, networks like the Internet allow most businesses to take advantage of these efficient "market-based" pricing tools. For example, Priceline.com popularized the "reverse auction" pricing mechanism (cleverly marketed as "naming your own price") and as a result sold over 3 percent of all airline tickets in the United States in 2000 (according to self-reported figures). This represents an average of four seats per flight—significant in light of the slim margins that characterize the travel business. And 25 percent of corporate buyers already use or plan to use auctions and real-time bidding when they negotiate prices with their suppliers, according to the 2000 *Purchasing Magazine* reader survey.

For these buyers, the efficiency of Internet markets can translate into fairer prices, reduced transaction costs, shortened cycle times, and improved information flow. Industrial buyers are already seeing significant benefits from buying through marketplaces, reporting an average savings of 14–20 percent on their indirect purchases (like cleaning supplies) and semifinished goods (like circuit boards). Raytheon, for example, reported last year that it bought $100 million worth of goods in just three auctions on FreeMarkets, and had saved 25 percent over what it would have spent buying the same materials through traditional channels.

Understanding the Many Different Flavors of Online Marketplaces

Because of these benefits over 1000 online marketplaces have been announced in a variety of industries, most notably in commodities (e.g., specialty chemicals, steel, paper) secondary markets (e.g., parts, capital equipment, telephone bandwidth) and functional specialties (e.g., indirect procurement, energy management). They come in a bewildering array of different flavors—both large and small, private and public. And we can expect more marketplaces to be announced. Arguably, the U.S. economy could support thousands of specialized marketplaces if one considers having a unique marketplace dedicated to each SIC code. (The SIC code is a government designation for a unique industry—the U.S. economy is made up of over 3000 major industry classifications.)

This variety is a problem because it distracts sales management from the real issue—finding the best ways of using online markets to sell more. Whether you choose to call them auctions, exchanges, or fancier terms like "integrated captive supply chain," the simplest way to think about online marketplaces is that they make it easier for people to buy and sell things. Using this perspective to simplify matters, online marketplaces can be grouped into five primary flavors of online marketplaces, serving both the business-to-business and business-to-consumer markets.

1. *Online Buying Services*: These services offer support during the awareness and demand generation phases of the selling process.
2. *Auctions*: Auctions are online markets that are good at aggregating demand and matching buyers and sellers for a wide range of B2B and B2C products.

3. *B2B Exchanges*: B2B exchanges (also known as Vertical Exchanges) are independent trusted intermediaries that support most aspects of business-to-business commerce with vertical market and product-specific expertise.
4. *Industry-sponsored Exchanges*: This is when all of the major buyers in industries where buying power is concentrated, such as all the major car manufacturers, team up to build an online marketplace where all of their suppliers (which can number in the thousands) must go.
5. *Private Exchanges*: This is where individual companies like Wal-Mart and Hewlett Packard, who deal with a large number of suppliers and command a lot of buying power, create their own "private" or "captive" online marketplaces to reduce costs and improve information flow in their supply chains.

A deeper examination of the different types of online marketplaces and how they support the buying and selling can be found in the Special Section at the end of this chapter.

Online Marketplaces Will Give Your Customers More Power

Online auctions and exchanges tend to shift power away from the seller to the buyer. In many industries, buyers are banding together to "pool" their collective buying power and build exchanges that will exert greater control over their suppliers and squeeze costs out of the supply chain.

For example, in industries where buying power is concentrated but suppliers are numerous (as in the automotive industry, where three major producers are served by thousands of parts suppliers), buyer-managed exchanges such as Covisint (a partnership of Ford, GM, Renault, and Daimler-Chrysler) will become a battleground where all sellers, big and small, compete for market share. Eight such "industry sponsored" online exchanges were announced in the first six months of 2000 alone (including automotive, aerospace, travel, consumer packaged goods, retail, agriculture, energy verticals) and are now poised to harness more than $700 billion in purchasing power. By doing so they will force-march the participation of 250,000 American businesses onto the electronic selling floor.

Alternately, where both buyers and sellers are fragmented (such as in the small business market or a variety of aftermarkets), independent intermediaries ("middlemen") may step in to create and manage exchanges that are theoretically neutral trading ground. These exchanges are often called "butterfly," or "vortex" markets. For example, e-dentist.com sells dental supplies and connects 120,000 private-practice dentists with the opportunity to buy wares from 1000 manufacturers and 200 distributors. Parts-Driver.com, an exchange that serves the fragmented auto parts aftermarket, currently connects 210,000 independent repair shops to 80,000 jobbers and 600 manufacturers of replacement auto parts. Since independent trading sites make their income from transaction fees, their focus is also biased to buyers, in order to keep them coming back.

Only in industries where a few sellers have a high degree of control over market supply (such as specialty chemicals, personal computers, some types of insurance and airline travel) can sellers take the advantage by banding together to build "seller-biased" or "supplier-managed" exchanges. One that bears watching is Orbitz, a consortium of five airlines (Delta, United, Northwest, Continental, and American Airlines) that account for an estimated 85 percent of all U.S. air travel. The Orbitz Web site sells airline ticket reservations online, and it remains to be seen if it can compete successfully against the "buyer-driven" Web ticket marketplaces created by Priceline, Travelocity, and Expedia.

In general, online marketplaces increase the number of competitors, expose price differences, and often allow buyers to pool their buying power against sellers. In both business and consumer arenas, price information on online exchanges is routinely available and can be updated in minutes. Competing prices become "transparent," while buyers have the option to remain anonymous as they quickly amass data, pro and con, to compare offerings among sellers.

Short-Term Strategy: Tactics for Survival and Risk Mitigation

Sales and marketing executives need to be careful when choosing whether to participate in one or more existing online buying services, auctions, and exchanges; build their own online marketplace, or attempt both. Waiting it out, even in the near term, is not an option for most businesses. The danger of being left behind—and the long-term benefit of experimentation now—are too great. Businesses whose core customers decide to form an online exchange (as has happened in the automotive, packaged goods and chemicals markets) simply cannot afford to be shut out. Similarly, small businesses and growth-oriented companies should not miss a potential opportunity to redefine their industry or expand into new regional and global markets.

The Risks and Rewards of Online Marketplaces

A recent IMT Strategies study found that very small selling organizations were eager to enter online marketplaces; these firms anticipated getting new customers, increased visibility, and access to buyers. These small players felt they had nothing to lose competing with rivals in a new arena. On the other hand, larger companies were more reluctant to participate in online marketplaces: they feared price exposure, erosion of margin, and cutthroat competition from faster-moving, upstart rivals. They had everything to lose. The things these large organizations feared most were conflict between channels, changing existing selling processes, and losing control over product margins. Sellers should understand the risks and rewards of online marketplaces before diving in.

Online marketplaces pose several risks to selling organizations:

Exclusion from new markets;
Loss of margins due to product and price transparency;
Greater potential for customer attrition, resulting from greater ease of supplier and product discovery;

Channel conflict as online marketplaces overlap with and edge out traditional channels and distributors;
Volatility with respect to product demand and pricing.

The benefits of online marketplaces include the following:

Extended reach to regional, national, and global buyers;
Higher transaction volume;
Potentially lower customer acquisition costs;
Opportunity to redefine markets;
Opportunity to extract value from product and process expertise.

While it is important to move fast, organizations must also move strategically and develop ways to mitigate the risks involved. In particular, sellers must make a considered choice: Should they build an online marketplace and become facilitators, participate in one or more existing exchanges, or attempt both? To answer these questions, executives need to do some thinking—and some homework, and then some experimentation. Here are four key steps that sales and marketing executives should go through before making a choice:

1. Acknowledge the golden rule;
2. Find online marketplaces that fit your business strategy;
3. Know the nine essential ingredients for success;
4. Exploit short-term tactics to protect margins and boost share.

I. Acknowledge the golden rule Sellers must recognize that online marketplaces are being driven chiefly by buyers. They would be wise to remember the golden rule: Those with the gold make the rules. The more buying power a company can exert by forcing its suppliers to compete online, the more aggressively it will insist that its suppliers participate. For example, GE Aircraft Engines recently bought $50 million in indirect materials from 12 different auctions. Owens Corning, maker of glass fiber and composite materials, plans to migrate half of its $3.5 billion annual spending to online channels, including exchanges. Thus, before deciding how to participate, selling organizations must first understand how, and how fast, customer-buying behavior is changing in their particular market or set of markets.

Make no mistake; purchasing dollars are moving online. One annual *Purchasing Magazine* reader survey shows that the percentage of purchasers with access to the Internet has risen from 20 percent to 95 percent from 1995 to 2000. In the 2000 survey, 68% of respondents said they would use the Web to conduct purchasing transactions (up from 48 percent in 1999). And e-Marketer estimates that as many as 14 million consumers will use auctions to buy things by 2003.

The trick for sellers is to accurately anticipate and monitor how and how quickly their buyers are adopting online marketplaces. This is the only way to avoid being left out, and the best way to gain first mover advantage in certain online marketplaces.

2. Find online marketplaces that fit your business strategy

Eastman Chemical is an example of a company whose participation in online marketplaces was guided by a strong set of business objectives. It took an equity stake in an online chemical exchange, ChemConnect, to augment its sales force and Web sales with the goals of expanding market coverage and unearthing new opportunities. Executives at Eastman predict that by 2003, 50 percent of the company's business will be transacted online—and 20 percent of that will be sales created through online marketplaces.

Every selling organization wants to increase its customer base and make more sales more efficiently. Leaders will be recognized by their ability to pick the right online marketplaces for their organizations.

Here are some strategic trade-offs to consider before moving into an online marketplace:

Margins Versus Volume: Many sellers will have to decide if they are willing to trade lower profit margins for the greater customer access offered in online marketplaces. Many suppliers who sell in reverse auction Web sites willingly swap lower product margins for the benefits of acquiring large numbers of new customers to whom they can resell over time. "Predatory pricing"(the practice of price slashing to get customers in the door) is a familiar marketing tactic in the offline world and can be extremely effective in online marketplaces as long as the discounts are justified by (1) greatly reduced customer acquisition costs and (2) a very high lifetime value of the customer.

For example, two early (and now defunct) online marketplaces, Mercata and Mobshop, pioneered the concept of "aggregating demand" by getting hundreds of buyers to "pool" their buying power to drive down the price of consumer electronics—like DVD players. This concept of "pooling" buying power is now an important element of many online marketplaces. Mercata was successful in getting hundreds of buyers to participate in these "reverse auctions" and buy things as a group.

Some high-end electronics manufacturers (say Harman-Kardon) might view selling DVD players this way as a risk. A thousand avid stereo buffs could form a buying group and drive the price of its offered product down so low they would never be able to recoup the research and manufacturing costs for the high-end machine. Others see this as an opportunity to acquire hundreds or thousands of customers at one time at a low cost. Mass marketers (like Matsushita or any of its distributors) pursuing "Generation Y" consumers would happily slash the price of a comparable DVD player in order to gain the names, addresses, and e-mail addresses of 1000 youthful customers who buy this one product and then happily accept pitches for other home electronics. Given that the average cost for acquiring an online customer has ranged from $40 to $120 in recent years, a sales executive might consider a discount of up to $120 a reasonable price to pay for access to certain new customers.

Ease of Doing Business Versus Efficiency: Not every product warrants real-time trading. Paper clips and most consumer package goods are too inexpensive and commoditized to justify the effort. Priceline.com discontinued its food shopping operation, Web-House Club, for this reason: The time it took for members to find the best prices on a can of beans didn't justify the savings even to the most dedicated penny-pinchers.

Some items in a product line may not be eligible for online marketplaces because they are part of "preconfigured" purchases via EDI (e.g., direct materials replenished daily at the factory). Other products are too highly engineered or customized (such as engineered subassemblies for aircraft and automotive products) and so can't attract large buyer groups. In these cases, ease of doing business the old way will tend to outweigh pure price competitiveness in the eyes of buyers, diminishing the value of an auction.

Exclusion Versus Inclusion: Businesses must wrestle with the question of whether online marketplaces will consolidate industry buying power to the extent that nonparticipants will be left out, or whether new markets and opportunities will result from "playing the field." For example, the introduction of vertical exchanges in the aerospace, automotive, and home appliance industries may give a small supplier access to buyers in all three industries, whereas previously a firm with limited resources and geographic reach had difficulty serving "many masters" of large size.

Where sellers combine to create an exchange, traditional rivalries will remain a factor. Dell Marketplace, which sold office supplies and was hosted by Dell, 3M, Motorola, and Pitney Bowes, was never able to attract other major suppliers to the venture. Buyers were not enticed by such limited product offerings, and Dell Marketplace folded after four months.

Market Coverage Versus Control: If an online marketplace provides the opportunity to cover more of the market, it may also result in less corporate control over the sales process. In auctions where prices are "dynamic," the seller will have less control over price changes. Sellers also have little control over product information (for example, in product reviews that are published online).

Attempts by sellers to defy the "democratic" nature of the Internet (where participants vote on what is best) have usually been ham-handed and not successful. An early effort known as Brandwise.com was an online buying service that claimed to provide objective product recommendations and consumer audience reviews of appliances such as washing machines and dryers. As the Web site was funded by Whirlpool, a major appliance manufacturer, the project's credibility was dubious at best, and the site has since been taken down.

Cost of Arbitrage Versus Pricing Gaps: Selling organizations need to anticipate the possibility that online marketplaces will create "gray markets" (loopholes for resellers, that allow middlemen to take advantage of price differences across global markets). For example, a global marketplace may expose the fact that your product sells for 50 percent less in Prague, Czechoslovakia than it does in Columbus, Ohio. A business that has grown used to selling products at very high margins must weigh the risk that prices will become "transparent" (where everyone sees your pricing), margins will shrink, and that arbitrageurs will be avidly monitoring the electronic trading floor, poised to strike.

3. Understand the nine critical ingredients of success Should your company build or sponsor its own online marketplace? Executives considering building or sponsoring an online marketplace must make sure they have the critical ingredients needed for success. Nine ingredients (below) are essential to success in an online marketplace, and none of them—surprise—are about the technology. The necessary hardware and software can be bought or rented from solutions providers such as Moai, Ariba, and Ajunto relatively easily. Online auctions can be up and running in less than 30 days using off-the-shelf software. It is much more important to bring to the table certain strategic assets if you want to create your own online marketplace. The high "mortality" rate of online marketplaces in the last year indicates that companies ignore these nine ingredients when they rush in to announce an online marketplace.

A company that takes on the role of marketplace intermediary should ideally be a master of its field. Marketplaces involve more than just conducting transactions on the Internet. Relationships, information, and power come into play. In order for commerce to happen, buyers and sellers need to know things like "Who is selling?" "Which products are the best?" "How limited is supply?" and "How much are buyers willing to spend?" The good marketplace host should be recognized broadly for its expertise and ability to provide this "value-added information." Organizations that already publish reports or provide inspection, licensing, or quality certification services may be ahead of the game here.

Nine Critical Ingredients
for Building an Online Marketplace

INGREDIENT	SELF-EVALUATION QUESTION
1. VALUE-ADDED CONTENT	Do I have access to value-added information relevant to my market and industry (e.g., demand forecasting, product assessment)?
2. EXPERTISE	Do I have market-leading expertise in either specific markets (e.g., timber machinery) or functional processes (e.g., energy management, logistics)?
3. TRUST RELATIONSHIPS	Am I a trusted intermediary with credibility and strong industry relationships who can help reduce risk and monitor product and participant quality through regulation, appraisals, inspections or certification?
4. LIQUIDITY	Do I have the ability to deliver or attract a critical mass of volume, buying power, buyers, usage and transactions?
5. FINANCING	Can I deliver material financing and/or manage credit risk in the marketplace?
6. SOURCING	Do I have the ability to attract and connect many buyers and sellers (e.g., possess either a strong customer/supplier base or marketing expertise to acquire the same)?
7. SELL-SIDE LEVERAGE	Do I operate in seller-managed markets (i.e., with a high concentration or sellers) or do I have the dominant share of a unique niche market?
8. FIRST MOVER ADVANTAGE	Am I the first to the market in my specific niche or can I successfully redefine the market?
9. RESOURCES	Do I have the financial and technological infrastructure, resources or partnerships to scale the marketplace to reach critical mass?

SOURCE: IMT STRATEGIES 2000

Figure 2.1 Nine critical ingredients for success.

Trust relationships are also important. A company needs credibility with all parties to be a "trusted intermediary" in trades. If your list of friends or "client Rolodex" is not very deep in the offline world, it is not likely that going online will make you any more popular.

Liquidity—the volume of sales transactions that happen in the market—is vital. Without it markets will not survive. Organizations that already gather and attract large numbers of buyers or sellers will find it easier to build the high volume of transactions required for a successful exchange. Businesses that already do a lot of buying from smaller companies may find sufficient players to justify building their own "private" online marketplace for goods and services; selling organizations that dominate their markets or hold unique market positions also have an edge. Organizations that currently provide financing or help their buyers or suppliers manage credit may have the "power" to move these functions online as well.

Organizations that cannot identify strong assets like these should experiment with online marketplaces as a participant at first. If building an exchange makes sense over the longer term, sales executives should begin cultivating these nine "success" assets internally to lay the groundwork for a future online marketplace opportunity.

FreeMarkets: Assembling the Right Ingredients into a Marketplace

FreeMarkets, a business-to-business online marketplace, was an early success story because it brought many (but not all) of these nine essential ingredients to the table. The company was a first mover. It started in 1995 by helping to facilitate a variety of online exchange transactions between industrial buyers and their suppliers, focusing on MRO, semifinished and custom goods. FreeMarkets is one of the few companies that demonstrated (and not just advertised) that it could bring real buyers and sellers together. In 2000, FreeMarkets generated revenues of $91.3 million helping businesses conduct $9.9 billion in online transactions. It claims to save buyers an average of 15 percent savings.

Early customers included a "who's-who of industry," including Emerson Electric (which does 25 percent of its procurement online), General Motors, United Technologies, Navistar, Raytheon, and buyers from over 100 industries. Its transactions to date have involved more than 130 supply verticals, including injection molded plastic parts, metal fabrications, chemicals, printed circuit boards, cardboard packaging, and coal.

FreeMarkets established more credibility providing value-added information to its members in the form of an extensive supplier knowledge base. This online database provided members with critical, current information about the delivery capacities of thousands of suppliers worldwide, as well as details about suppliers' manufacturing processes, quality assurance, and market focus. This data helped ensure that suppliers that bid had capacity on hand, so FreeMarkets could offer quick turnaround on trades. It enabled price and product "transparency" by not allowing sealed bid contracts.

FreeMarkets has accumulated a high level of expertise in important areas of purchasing job function like managing online RFQs (requests for quotations) and the supplier selection process. It provides these to its members in the form of proprietary "Web-based sourcing" software as part of the service. It also staffs a multilingual call center to facilitate international sales in 30 languages.

Even a leader like FreeMarkets does not have all nine ingredients in its marketplace. Because buyers are fickle and move from market to market, the primary challenge for FreeMarkets will be to add more buyers to build enough liquidity to be profitable. Even though transaction volumes tripled in 2000 (from $2.7 billion to $9.9 billion), the management team does not predict profits until 2003. FreeMarkets may not achieve the "sell side" leverage or dominant share of any one vertical market to keep its biggest buyers around. As a case in point, General Motors, one of FreeMarkets' first customers, was one of the first defectors to start its own exchange, Covisint, with the other large car manufacturers. And where buyers go, suppliers will follow.

4. Seven short-term tactics to protect margins and boost market share Organizations selling into online marketplaces face myriad risks (described previously) in the short term. Clever marketers are actively starting to experiment with short-term tactics to find ways to participate in online marketplaces without turning their products into commodities and shrinking their profit margins. For example, many sellers are "counterattacking" by redefining value boundaries or retiering pricing. Others are using "predatory pricing" tactics by selling certain products into an exchange at no-margin pricing in order to acquire customers and attempt to upsell them (at generous margins) offline.

Here are seven tactics to try:

1. Redefine Value Boundaries. Profit margins erode and pricing becomes "transparent" when online markets allow customers to easily make apples-to-apples comparisons between products by supplying ratings, reviews, or other kinds of product comparison information. Marketers can transcend competition on price by cleverly bundling solutions, increasing minimum order sizes, or establishing pricing tiers to make things "apples to oranges" again.

2. Discriminatory Pricing Practices. Marketers can develop proprietary or complex pricing schemes that discourage comparison shopping. Building customer-specific products, redrawing market segments, or negotiating exclusive volume purchase agreements (VPAs) can all be used to justify different prices. For instance, the airline industry has created pricing schedules that "discriminate" against business travelers by scaling prices against specific rates, short cycle times, and length of stay. Pricing practices can usually be justified by geography (delivery issues), unit volume (frequent-buyer or volume-buyer discounts), or acknowledged supply-and-demand peaks (seasonal or weekday/weekend, etc.).

3. Elevate Service to Add Value. Marketers should strap on, bolt on, or weld on value-added service to every product they offer through an online marketplace. Online customers routinely pay higher prices for "free" delivery, liberal returns, product guarantees, service warranties, online user support, and other perceived value-adds. Retail and distributors can justify service premiums on commodity products since most online marketplaces today offer few services beyond matching buyers with sellers and providing some product and price information. For example, because few online marketplaces today offer customer support or on-site service, there is a potential advantage for distributors in bundling service into pricing and creating a local service company that customers can drive to.

4. Speed. Differentiate your wares by offering speedier delivery. A component delivered in eight hours is worth more to some buyers than the same component delivered eight days from now. In both consumer and business markets, faster fulfillment has proven to be a plus factor in pricing. Faster pricing can provide an edge. Marketers who become good at developing costs in "real time" can react more quickly to changes in demand and high-speed bidding. For instance, superior pricing models and capabilities will allow sellers to quickly decide where to participate (or rationally decide not to) and better understand and optimize margins in fast-paced bidding.

5. Loss Leader Approaches. Make the goal of online marketplaces acquiring new customers and leads, and choose a product that is likely to appeal to first-time customers. Use a loss leader (e.g., extremely low-priced) product as a way of acquiring customers and leads at low cost, with the expectation of upselling them offline. Depending on customer lifetime value, a lower cost of customer acquisition may offset low or even negative product margins.

6. Arbitrage/Gray Market Leverage. Arbitrage means taking advantage of short-term differences in market prices. Marketers should explore the possibilities of "arbitraging" price differences between or across Web sites, supply chains, or countries. Anonymous exchanges and global auctions provide an opportunity to exploit disorganized pricing and take advantage of "gray markets." For example, the price difference between olive oil in two different countries may be large enough to justify buying from one and selling to another.

7. Positioning. Exploit ways to gain favorable positioning in an online marketplace. This is always a viable strategy when dealing with online buying services such as product review sites. Paying for prime position or public relations exposure is one option, but don't rule out gaming the software. For instance, American Airlines garnered 35 percent of transactions on its captive Sabre exchange, where, coincidentally, all airlines were listed alphabetically (see case study).

American Airlines: Managing to Be First Among Equals

American Airlines was an early innovator in online marketplaces when it introduced Sabre, the first electronic reservations network to serve the travel industry. Ostensibly an open system, it eventually included all of American's major airline competitors and linked thousands of travel agents. It reaped quick benefits as an online marketplace facilitator; the airline garnered 35 percent of its reservation transactions over the network. Of course, Sabre listings were alphabetized on computer screens—so American Airlines flight listings usually came up first.

Antitrust pressure eventually forced American Airlines to spin off Sabre as an independent organization (which was later sold to EDS). Undaunted, they turned to other strategies to regain competitive advantage. By segmenting its product and customers, American Airlines is able to deploy tiered pricing through its online selling channels. Consider, for example, that 70 percent of executive platinum members have logged onto the AA.com Web site, where average ticket revenue is noticeably higher than the low-margin sales generated by low-cost online auctions that attract budget travelers. The lack of comparative pricing information within online auctions protects this differential pricing. In public markets the complexity of American Airlines posted prices makes comparison-shopping difficult.

The company also recently joined four competitors (United, Northwest Continental, and Delta) to create Orbitz, an online reservation service. It allows a consumer to browse comparative fares in an "unbiased" database that shows all available flights, but it also includes "exclusive" online fare deals to compete on price points with online ticket discounters such as Travelocity and Expedia.

Long-Term Imperative: Three Strategies for Creating Value and Maximizing Margins

Short-term tactics such as discriminatory pricing and arbitrage that rely on confusion and imperfect information may protect margins and revenue today when online marketplaces are immature and inefficient. Over time, these tactics will become less tenable because markets will evolve towards greater efficiency—and value will be rewarded more than cunning.

In the longer term, online marketplaces offer selling organizations another viable selling channel to cover existing markets and access global markets. The real winners will find ways to use the information generated in these marketplaces to their advantage (for example with better forecasts of what customers will actually want to buy in the future) or provide new and profitable services to these markets to help them run better (for example, helping move products to market or inspecting goods bought online to ensure quality and standards).

Perhaps the best illustration of how to take advantage of the potential of online marketplaces in the long term is the New York Stock Exchange (NYSE). Two hundred years ago, the NYSE was only one of twenty-four competing stock exchanges in New York City. It has survived to outlast all of them, growing to manage $8.9 trillion dollar's worth of transactions in 1999. Yet for all this transaction volume, the income generated from transaction fees was a mere $75 million during 1999.

What is significant about this story is that the profits from the all the services that provide support to the traders and investment bankers who use that exchange—ranging from take-out Chinese food, pizzas, coffee, limousine services, haircuts, shoe shines—far exceed the money being made on the transactions within the exchange itself.

Even more significantly, the information generated by the exchange, in the form of stock updates, trend and performance analysis, generates *even more money*. Media companies turn this information into profitable news programming (e.g., CNBC, Moneyline, CNN Financial). Financial analysts repackage and sell this information to investors in the form of stock newsletters, financial Web sites, and securities analysis. And investment bankers use this information to build new and highly profitable products like sophisticated derivative securities, futures contracts, and other financial instruments.

The lesson to sales and marketing executives is that providing services to an exchange and using the information generated by the exchange may prove a more profitable growth path than the transactions that happen within them. Within the next several years, organizations that facilitate online exchanges will get less revenues from shrinking transaction fees but will gain higher revenues on services and the sale of timely, market-related information products. Value-added services and information will become the primary source of revenue and profit.

To win in this environment, sales and marketing leaders will devise strategies that focus on three keys to success

1. Add online marketplaces to the selling channel mix;
2. Provide value-added services to online marketplaces;
3. Leverage the information generated by these markets.

I. Integrate online marketplaces into the selling channel mix

To become an effective part of the selling equation, online marketplaces need to be viewed as a potentially powerful new selling channel that augments existing sales resources such as direct field sales, third-party distributors, and Internet e-commerce. To be complementary, not a source of conflict, online marketplaces must be managed in concert with these other methods of selling. One reason American Airlines is so successful online is that it has developed a disciplined "market coverage" model (more on this in Chapter 5) that matches specific products with channels with customers. For example, America uses online auctions such as Priceline.com to sell off its excess inventory—that is, its share of the industry's estimated 500,000 empty seats that go unsold each day. At the same time, it continues to use travel agents, its telephone call center, and its Web site, AA.com, to sell higher-margin travel packages and business fares.

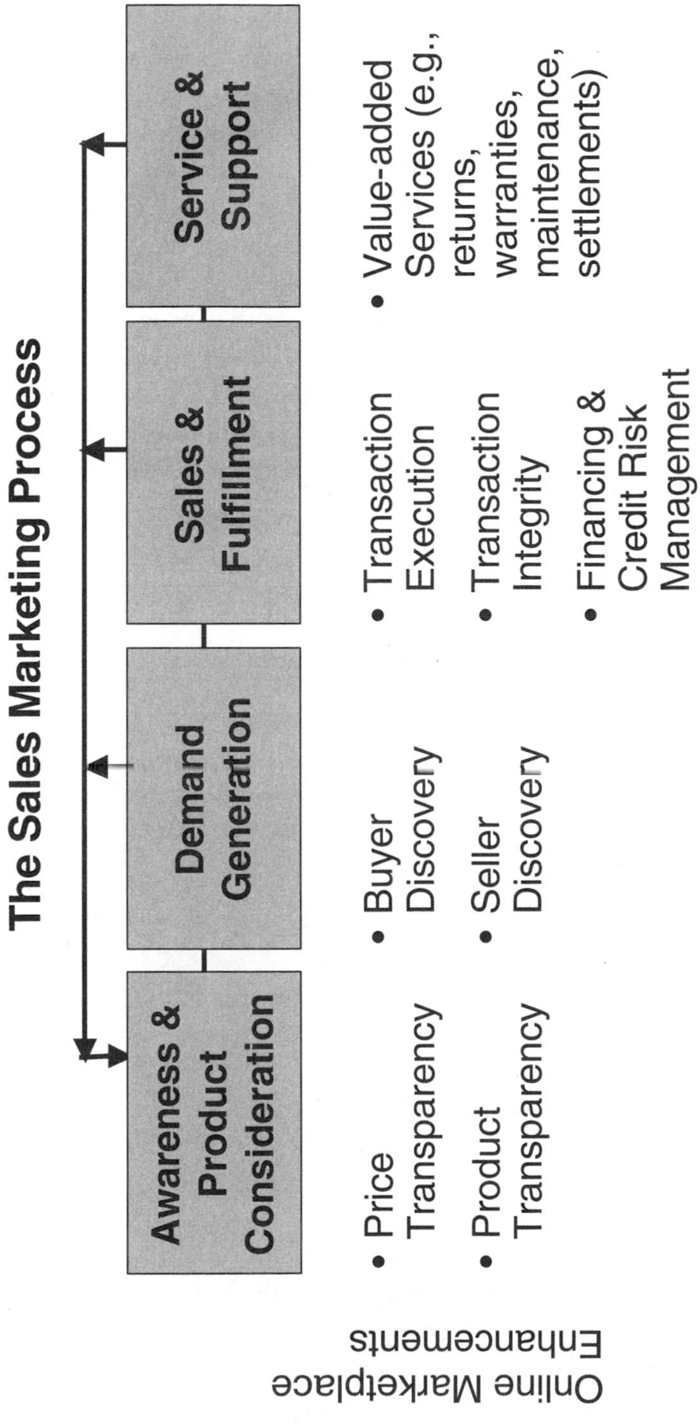

The Sales Marketing Process

Awareness & Product Consideration	Demand Generation	Sales & Fulfillment	Service & Support

Online Marketplace Enhancements

- Price Transparency
- Product Transparency

- Buyer Discovery
- Seller Discovery

- Transaction Execution
- Transaction Integrity
- Financing & Credit Risk Management

- Value-added Services (e.g., returns, warranties, maintenance, settlements)

Figure 2.2 How online marketplaces help the selling process.

2. Provide value-added services to online marketplaces The most successful players in online marketplaces will create additional value, perceived by buyers who use the exchange site. An organization that hosts or manages such an exchange creates such value merely by eliminating transaction inefficiencies between buyers and sellers; this is why members usually agree to pay the host organization a transaction fee.

For example, FreeMarkets (see Case Study, this chapter) offers global customers a multilingual call center that provides support and service in more than 30 languages. One of its other main attractions is a supplier database that includes detailed information on 9000 suppliers in 50 countries and is updated every day.

Other examples of services that can be sold within an online marketplace include:

- Settlement of disputes
- Inspection and appraisal
- Quality assurance
- Escrow
- Customs clearance service
- Shipping validation
- Logistics support

Even selling organizations that merely participate in online marketplaces will be wise to offer some of these third-party value-added services to other participants. While helping to streamline and perfect the transaction process for the whole population, offering services to other members enlarges the organization's assets within the exchange. It can enhance the perception that the company is an expert or "trusted intermediary," which may improve its positioning—and it then becomes more noticeable among larger rivals. Fees charged to other members would be a viable source of revenue, as well.

3. Leverage or sell value-added information generated by these markets Internet marketplaces assemble and generate a lot of valuable information. Clever marketers will find ways to profit by using this information, for example, to develop forecasts of supply and demand. Established exchanges such as the Chicago Mercantile Exchange generate tons of information about current "supply and demand" conditions for meat, wheat, and other commodities. This information is turned into valuable "products" like options and forward contracts that help buyers of grain, milk, and pork manage business risk and lock in supplies at a given price. As online exchanges mature, they will reveal predictors of demand.

Any company participating in an online marketplace should be alert for opportunities to capture, process, and resell transaction data. Information generated as a "by-product" of online marketplaces can create value by improving predictability and mitigating risk. This may encompass:

Industry performance benchmarks

Forecasts of consumer demand

Futures and forward contracts

Aggregated industry catalogs

For example, the auto industry exchange Covisint says it plans to offer suppliers an information portal where they can retrieve real-time plant production schedules from various manufacturers, as well as consumer demand forecasts indicating what makes and models of automobiles will be popular. Market research is another opportunity. For example, a sporting goods manufacturer might monitor consumer activity on online buying services to bolster other trend data on the relative popularity of scooters, skateboards, and inline skates in order to better predict the future sales of helmets, knee pads, and wrist guards.

The organization that can supply an instant-by-instant snapshot of sale and supply curves, or provide accurate long-term planning forecasts, has an information product that may be worth far more in the global arena than the manufactured product it started with.

Keeping some of the information for yourself is also good strategy. American Airlines recognizes that online marketplaces such as Priceline.com and Orbitz are a low-cost means of acquiring new customers, plus a rich source of behavioral information to facilitate upselling. It is leveraging this information to personalize its products (through personalized email and tailored frequent-flyer offers) so it can sell higher-margin projects to these bargain hunters.

Bottom Line

Sales and marketing executives will have to change their approaches to pricing, channel management, and marketing in order to sell through online marketplaces like Internet auctions and business-to-business exchanges.

Special Section: The Five Flavors of Online Marketplaces

The simplest way to think about online marketplaces is that they make it easier for businesses and consumers to buy and sell things. The pieces of this puzzle will emerge more clearly when you look at these marketplaces in the context of how buying and selling actually occur in most businesses (see Figure 2.3).

In order for business to be conducted, all buyers and sellers must walk through several basic steps. The process generally starts with a prospective buyer thinking about buying something (product consideration). They then move to contacting a seller to investigate the specifics of the offering (demand generation). If the product or service meets a particular need, a sales transaction occurs (sales and fulfillment) and a relationship begins (service and support). In reality a whole bunch of research, promoting, haggling, contracting, delivery, and servicing goes on in between the cracks.

What online marketplaces do is help buyers and sellers perform one or two steps of the buying process. In select cases more mature marketplaces can offer help with many

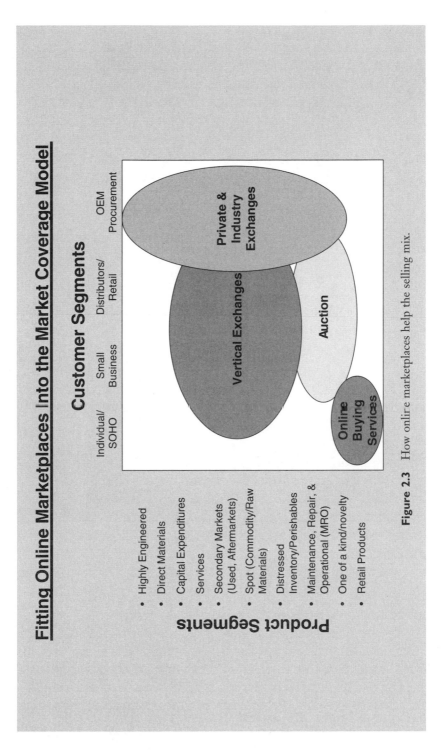

Fitting Online Marketplaces Into the Market Coverage Model

Customer Segments

| Individual/ SOHO | Small Business | Distributors/ Retail | OEM Procurement |

Product Segments

- Highly Engineered
- Direct Materials
- Capital Expenditures
- Services
- Secondary Markets (Used, Aftermarkets)
- Spot (Commodity/Raw Materials)
- Distressed Inventory/Perishables
- Maintenance, Repair, & Operational (MRO)
- One of a kind/novelty
- Retail Products

Private & Industry Exchanges

Vertical Exchanges

Auction

Online Buying Services

Figure 2.3 How online marketplaces help the selling mix.

steps of the buying process and be quite useful. The more parts of the process a marketplace can make happen easily, the more useful and valuable the marketplace will be. When assessing the potential of an online marketplace as part of their strategy, managers can simplify the process with this checklist of seller and buyer benefits.

- *Price and product transparency:* the ability to easily locate and compare products and prices;
- *Supplier and seller discovery:* or the ability to get many buyers and sellers in the same place—often called "aggregating demand and supply";
- *Convenient and reliable transactions,* by matching buyer and seller orders and accommodating a wide range of pricing alternatives such as different types of auction formats or real-time bidding. These are often called "market-making mechanisms";
- Ultimately, *a range of value-added services* associated with the selling process, including logistics, inventorying, financing, forecasting, advertising, catalog management, and more.

The hundreds of online marketplaces currently in existence differ in some important ways. They provide different levels of information to the buyer and seller such as price, availability, or range of substitutes. Some will provide more services than others such as quality assurance, financing credit risk, and customer support. They offer a wide variety of pricing formats such as Dutch auctions, reverse auctions, real-time transactions, and collaborative negotiations. In some cases the technology needed to run them (e.g., Web shopping agents, content management, levels of database and transaction infrastructure) will be different.

Individual online marketplaces will also differ by products sold and markets served, as well as by size and scope. Moreover, online marketplaces in different vertical markets will offer different levels of control to the buyer, seller, and market facilitator, as well as defining the role of each player in a slightly different manner.

Smart executives will sort through this mess by asking how an online marketplace can actually help make buying and selling happen in their markets. Here is a way to think about the five forms of online marketplaces and how they might apply to your business:

1. Online buying information services These services offer comparative price and product information to prospective buyers: They can create product awareness and product demand. For example, Gomez.com offers analyst reviews of sites and services, while Epinions.com solicits customer opinions through open source reviews (or reviews of reviews). Their Web sites help introduce buyers to new vendors and usually include product reviews, product recommendations, or other selection aids.

Early examples include *shopping agents*, such as mySimon, evenbetter.com, R U Sure, Buy.com, and Best Buy. Variants are *price aggregators* such as Carprices.com and Quote-smith.com, which cut to the chase and help consumers find a bargain price for a certain product that is sold over many different Web sites.

Online buying services primarily target to consumers, as well as to small business/home office (i.e., SOHO) markets. Most do not have transaction capabilities but will provide (usually for a fee) a link to a seller's commerce sites or a different site where transactions can be done. They can be a useful way to introduce a product to a geographically dispersed audience.

2. Internet auctions Auctions are online markets that match buyers and sellers for a wide range of business-to-business and business-to-consumer products. They are popular and employ a variety of market-making mechanisms (e.g., reverse, Dutch, English, and sealed-bid auction types) to meet buyer needs. Auctions offer minimal information; as in real-world auctions, buyers must come equipped with their own notions of product value if they hope to find a bargain or even a "good" price. Other examples of auctions include Amazon.com, Yahoo!, NexTag.com, QXL.com, Priceline.com, Perfect.com, and Fairmarket.com (auctions).

Online auctions are viable for sellers in retail; novelty; maintenance, repair, and operations (MRO); distressed inventory/perishables; spot purchases of commodities and raw materials; and secondhand capital equipment. eBay started as a one-on-one, individual auction offering an array of used, one-of-a-kind, collectible products. Today it is also used by wholesalers offering small lots.

3. B2B exchanges   B2B ("business to business") exchanges are independent, trusted intermediaries that support business commerce with vertical market and product-specific expertise. *Vertical exchanges* deal with specific vertical market and product categories. They offer real-time, dynamic pricing and considerable product information in their realm of specialty.

For instance, eSteel helps 1700 members buy and sell steel products such as hot-rolled, cold-rolled, coated, and plated steel. Like many successful vertical exchanges, eSteel is a neutral organization not affiliated with any industry player. It has created a niche as a trusted intermediary, serving all members of the steel supply chain including producers, distributors, fabricators, converters, trading companies, and large end-users.

Other early examples of vertical exchanges include Paper-Exchange.com (pulp and paper), e-Chemicals, CheMatch (industrial chemicals), DoveBid.com (capital assets), InterX-ion (bandwidth), and FreeMarkets (industrial materials). These online marketplaces are used for MRO procurement, spot purchases of commodities and raw materials, capital equipment, secondary markets, distressed inventory, perishables, and some direct materials such as semifinished and engineered products.

Functional exchanges do not market products, but market services or solutions that automate or support specific business functions or processes (such as human resources benefits management or energy management).

Employease is one example of a functional exchange that helps companies that manage employee benefits and administrative services to sell their services to human resource executives who are looking for efficient ways to outsource these tasks. A Web site that aggregates jobseekers and corporate search firms, such as hotjobs.com or Monster.com would also be an example of a functional exchange that pulls in individuals as well as businesses.

Other early examples in a variety of service industries include tradehub (import/export), Imark.com (capital equipment and raw materials purchasing), Celarix (global logistics), YOUtilities (energy management), MRO.com (MRO purchasing), and Citadon.com (building/real estate project management).

4. Industry-sponsored exchanges These online marketplaces are usually launched by major industry buyers. In industries where buying power is concentrated, they give a small group of buyers even more power to command a view of vendor options. For example, in early 2000, the big three automotive manufacturers—GM, Ford, and Daimler Chrysler (and subsequently joined by Renault and Nissan)—announced shared sponsorship of Covisint to create a parts buyer's paradise for the participating automakers. Cargill and Dupont teamed up to develop Rooster.com to serve agricultural markets.

Small industrial suppliers can join industry exchanges to find a level playing field, or at least a different avenue to the big-time buyer. Other examples include GlobalnetXchange (uniting retailers such as Sears and Carrefour) and Exostar (aerospace). It should be expected that corporations that set up industry exchanges will keep the exchange close to its parent company in order to increase market valuations, generate favorable press, and use corporate buying power to directly control industry supply chains.

5. Private exchanges   This is a trading community built by one buyer that deals with many suppliers, or a Web community that links a group of companies that already have established strong, interconnected relationships. Many large companies like Hewlett-Packard and Wal-Mart cannot wait for "public" online marketplaces to grow up. They have set about building private exchanges that seek to achieve the benefits of online marketplaces within their own supplier base that "public" exchanges run by a third party have yet to achieve. According to an annual *Purchasing Magazine* reader survey in 2000, most purchasing managers showed a preference for automating existing supplier relationships through private marketplaces, over participating in third-party managed exchanges. For example, Hewlett-Packard buys so much plastic for its computers and printers that it has set up an exchange that buys plastic cheaply in bulk quantities and sells it back to its hundreds of subcontracted molders and sub-assembly suppliers at huge savings to all. Companies like Wal-Mart are so large they can gain large benefits just from getting thousands of their own suppliers communicating to share information to reduce purchasing costs and inventories.

CHAPTER

How Technology Changes Branding:

The Changing Rules of Awareness, Identity, and Loyalty in the Twenty-First Century

T HE IMPACT OF THE INTERNET ON BRAND STRATEGIES IS ENORMOUS. It has changed the competitive playing field and created a land rush to establish brands in online channels. Never before in the history of business have so many companies launched so quickly—or competed so hard to achieve brand awareness—as in the first three years of mainstream e-commerce. This has forced established companies to struggle with either dragging their existing brand assets online, or abandoning these million-dollar assets to build a new brand through a complementary "dot-com" initiative.

This choice is only the beginning. To become relevant to online buyers and take full advantage of new media, marketers must rethink their brand investments. They must intelligently balance their brand strategies between the physical and online worlds. They must cleverly blend traditional media with online approaches to provide customers with a rich, interactive experience.

The well-publicized battles between Barnes & Noble and Amazon.com are more than entertaining to executives who are not in the bookselling business: they exemplify the importance of continually adapting online branding strategies to gain or regain a competitive edge.

Battle of the Brands: Barnes & Noble Versus Amazon.com

Barnes & Noble came to the online book business late—in 1997, two years after Amazon.com had established a strong online brand and a huge customer base. This initial disadvantage was compounded by the fact that Barnes & Noble lacked certain strengths necessary to bring a brand online.

Barnes & Noble had a little problem with what's called "customer segment affinity." In other words, people who visited Barnes & Noble's retail bookstores enjoyed the cozy ambiance of soft lighting and sofas that combined the feel of a library with an upscale coffee bar, and rarely bought stuff online. Amazon's customers were "Web heads," at ease with their computers. And having ceded "first mover advantage" among online book buyers to Amazon, Barnes & Noble didn't bother to innovate. Its initial Web site was difficult even for its existing customers to find. Internet search programs cannot digest an ampersand, and the first Web address, barnesandnoble.com, proved unwieldy.

Eventually, they stopped banging their heads against this wall and started using the assets they had. Barnes & Noble created a new, separate brand: bn.com, that was separate yet complementary to the retail channel. Instead of trying to lure its current bookstore customer online, the new goal was to offer the best of both worlds to all of the folks who preferred to buy books online and offline as well.

When it became clear that customers that bought books from both companies were the most profitable customers of all, bn.com took the brand fight with Amazon literally to the streets: in major cities, such as New York, it promised same-day delivery of books purchased online. It also pursued a "hybrid" customer—one who shopped online but would go to a bookstore to pick up an order or return one.

It was still losing the battle. As late as holiday 1999, a Nielson/NetRatings survey showed that while 47 percent of bn.com's customers shopped at Amazon.com, only 17 percent of Amazon's customers also shopped at bn.com. Six months later, Amazon.com declined to renew a three-year contract with America Online, and Barnes & Noble leaped quickly to secure its expensive keyword slot. AOL subscribers typing in the keyword "books" would now find a link to bn.com, not Amazon. And six months after that, Barnes & Noble reported a 25 percent increase in online book sales.

Amazon, experiencing a slowdown in its own sales, had already switched to more cost-effective branding tactics. As the effectiveness of banner ads and keyword placements waned, it had concentrated on securing exclusive linking arrangements with thousands of Web sites to be the preferred online bookstore. By the time it jettisoned the six-figure annual fee for the AOL "books" keyword, it had amassed 450,000 exclusive affiliate network partners. Unlike the keyword sponsorship, it does not have to pay for the referrals unless a customer actually buys.

Amazon.com continues to innovate and enlarge its brand with experiments in viral marketing, personalized product offerings, and strategies to woo "Generation Y"—consumers 12 to 19 years old, who buy music products, not books, on Amazon.com.

Barnes & Noble continues to retool bn.com as a support system to the brand experience of its retail settings. Freestanding bn.com kiosks now appear among the leather armchairs, for example, to help re-introduce the newer online brand to its demographically older customers.

Extending Brands into Electronic Channels

Barnes & Noble is not alone in their struggle to bring an existing brand online. To most established organizations, brands are valuable assets on the balance sheet. In consumer product marketing they can be a considerable expense. Coke spent $4 billion, IBM spent $1 billion, and Microsoft spent $3.7 billion last year to create and maintain awareness of these household brand names. Brands are assets because a strong brand helps create product demand and solidify customer loyalty. The power of a brand name justifies higher margins and builds influence over distribution channels.

Historically, marketers built brands slowly, over time by investing in mass-media advertising (TV, print, radio, and transit ads such as billboards and bus shelter posters). But the Internet is changing the meaning of a brand, the nature of brand loyalty, and the effectiveness of traditional branding investments made by marketers.

If nothing else, early Internet innovators such as Blue Mountain Arts, Pets.com, and eBay demonstrated the Internet's ability to build brands fast and cheap. A look at the Nielson/NetRatings "Top 20" on any day can be revealing. The brands listed are all known to over ten million potential customers (the lowest-ranked Web site gets over 10 million visitors per month), and yet most of the NetRatings "Top 20" Web companies didn't even exist before 1995.

Economically, online branding approaches allow marketers to cut through past constraints of geography, timeliness, and cost of creating a branding message that may be seen by millions of people in a single day. This new level playing field is often bad news for older brands. Access to online knowledge, especially through the online marketplaces discussed in Chapter 2, for example, provides a buyer with an overwhelming barrage of product choice. In a global business market, a potential customer who encounters your brand or product name first on the Internet may have no previous information to rely on—they haven't seen the TV ad or the glowing trade journal product review. Because of these factors, brands on the Web must be equipped to stand naked as independent entities, stripped of past attributes, but ready to acquire a new reputation.

e-Branding: An Accident Waiting to Happen?

Why are well-established brand names such as Procter & Gamble, Disney, Tiffany, and NBC still struggling to transfer their brand assets online? One clear reason is that most marketers have not been paying attention to what works and what does not. Amazingly, there remains a severe disconnect between how customers

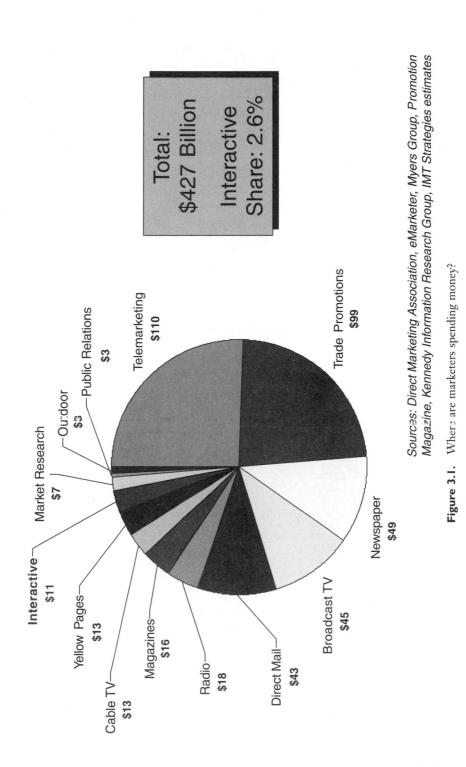

Total:
$427 Billion

Interactive
Share: 2.6%

Market Research
$7

Outdoor
$3

Public Relations
$3

Telemarketing
$110

Interactive
$11

Yellow Pages
$13

Cable TV
$13

Magazines
$16

Radio
$18

Direct Mail
$43

Broadcast TV
$45

Newspaper
$49

Trade Promotions
$99

Sources: Direct Marketing Association, eMarketer, Myers Group, Promotion Magazine, Kennedy Information Research Group, IMT Strategies estimates

Figure 3.1. Where are marketers spending money?

Top Methods of Discovering New Web Sites

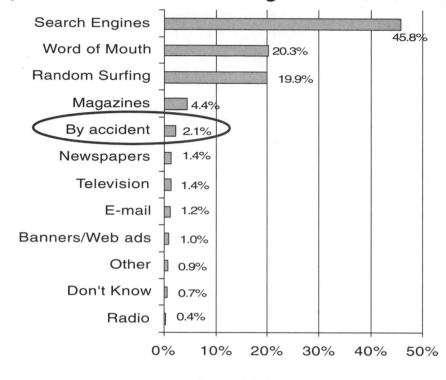

Source: IMT Strategies, 2000

Figure 3.2. Meanwhile, where are visitors coming from?

find new Web sites and where companies are focusing their branding investments. The evidence is obvious and easy to discover. In one IMT Strategies phone survey of 360 typical Web users, for example, customers were asked to identify the primary way they discovered new Web sites. Without any prompted choices, fully 45.8 percent cited *search engines* as their top choice. Another 20.3 percent cited *recommendations from friends*, and 19.9 percent credited *random surfing*.

In fifth place were the 2.1 percent who cited "by accident" as their primary means of finding new sites. And after that? "By accident" outranked virtually everything on which marketers were actually spending money—television, banner ads, newspaper and radio—each of which was the top pick of less than 1.5 percent of respondents.

Good branding on the Web shouldn't be an "accident." Nor should it be a marketing money pit or a leap of faith. To avoid this, marketers need to review their own brand strengths and weaknesses, and be courageous enough to totally reconsider their current branding strategies and past investments.

Short-Term Strategy: Figuring out How and Where to Extend Your Brand Online

Marketers who have spent millions of dollars to establish brand familiarity are now trying to figure out the best ways to transfer that existing brand to the Web. Before getting started, there are two things all marketing executives should do to evolve a successful brand strategy:

1. Assess how easily your existing brand can be transferred online.
2. Align brand investments with the way that customers actually behave online.

This may sound simple, but most marketers are not asking the question of how and where their brand makes sense online. Some marketers may find, after thoughtful analysis, that their current or well-established brand name does not translate well to a Web environment. To reflect this reality, marketing goals for existing Web selling channels may need to be redefined, if not completely overhauled. One option is to create a new brand for online use that complements the existing brand in the real world. A lesson should be taken from Barnes & Noble, which floundered online for several years before relaunching its Web business as a separate company with a new brand name, bn.com.

I. Assess How Easily Your Existing Brand Can Be Transferred Online

The first step is a thoughtful assessment of how easy it will be to transfer your existing brand online. To make this more than just a guess, it is useful to have a scorecard to guide the process. The following scorecard is based on the experience of market leaders and factors in several dimensions that make a real difference when moving a brand online. Six factors that are very important to consider are:

1. *First mover advantage: do you have the advantage of being first?*
2. *Customer segment affinity: do your customers rely on the Web?*
3. *Innovation and creativity: does your company enjoy a reputation for marketing innovation and creativity?*
4. *Information richness: does the product offer high information value?*
5. *Brand experience portability: is your customer's usual brand experience adaptable to an online channel?*
6. *Domain readiness: is the brand name "domain ready?"*

Sales and marketing executives should consider this as a screening tool: before wasting millions of dollars to move a brand online, it is better to consider issues that may indicate that the better strategy would be to create a new brand for online sales. The Scorecard can help identify where your competitive advantage lies; help determine where to focus Web investments for maximum return. If an organization has an existing but poorly performing Web initiative, the Scorecard analysis may help to pinpoint areas of weakness, inherent in the brand, that are holding a venture back.

Figure 3.3 maps the transferability for nine well-known brands.

Six dimensions of brand transferability

1. *First mover advantage: do you have the advantage of being first?* Many winners invested early in online initiatives: Federal Express, for example, introduced its online package tracking feature in 1994, long before many of its customers had even heard of the Internet. Dell and Land's End were early adapters of e-commerce. First mover status counts for a lot. Only a few offline retailers have been able to establish themselves online, and only three are regularly listed in the NetRatings "Top 100." In particular, JC Penney has leapfrogged its traditional competitors in this new arena.

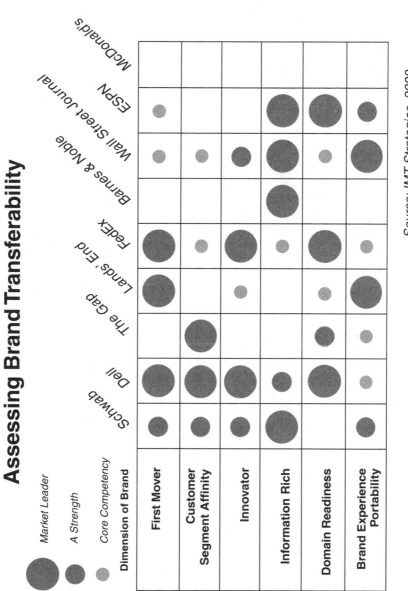

Source: IMT Strategies, 2000

Figure 3.3. Transferring brands online.

2. *Customer segment affinity: do your customers rely on the Web?*
   Some customers have no problem being drawn to online
   channels. Buyers who deal with computer manufacturers
   such as Apple, Dell, and IBM tend to be more familiar with
   computer-enabled transactions. Others, say, customers of
   Dunkin' Donuts or K-Mart, may be less adventurous technically or have fewer opportunities to use online media.
   K-Mart's response to this challenge was to create a new
   brand to cater to a small but affluent "Generation Y" segment of its customers with obvious affinities: bluelight.com
   sells CDs, cell phones, fashion clothing, and trendy youth
   products to this segment.

3. *Innovation and creativity: does your company enjoy a reputation
   for marketing innovation and creativity?* The online branding of Scope mouthwash illustrates how even a simple product can engage customers with fun, interactive experiences.
   Procter & Gamble developed a Scope "kiss"—a customized
   multimedia e-mail message "sealed" with puckered lips,
   which customers could download and send to others via
   e-mail.

4. *Information richness: does the product offer high information
   value?* The Web's search and interactive possibilities are
   ideal for selling data-heavy purchase decisions, such as financial services and travel planning, and for digitally rich products, such as software, music, books, and timely news. For
   example, ESPN's brand extension online into was a no-
   brainer, because its primary product—up-to-the-minute
   sports results—could be translated online into multiple levels for stat-crazy consumers. Challenged with selling mere
   clothing, The Gap invents context and content out of whole
   cloth: its Web site uses interactive games and stories to
   involve the customer in a richer brand experience.

5. *Brand experience portability: is your customer's usual brand experience adaptable to an online channel?* Direct sellers, such as
   catalog retailers, which encourage a high degree of self-
   service in product selection and purchase options, enjoy
   some built-in advantages when moving their brand to the
   Web. Companies like Lands' End have already accrued
   brand equity through arm's-length customer relationships,

so they don't have to recondition customers to a buying experience that differs from their expectations. The brand experience of shopping a paper catalog is easily transformed, and enhanced online. For example, Land's End has experimented with "digital avatars"—computer-generated customer surrogates that help a buyer visualize how clothes will fit on a model with exactly their measurements.

Until more intimately sensory experiences can be transmitted by the Internet, portability for some brands remains elusive. Barnes & Noble failed to follow Amazon.com's success online in part, in its first online incarnation, because the brand equity for the Barnes & Noble experience rested on the "high touch" (comfy chairs, soft music, coffee bar, friendly sales help) of its brick-and-mortar stores.

6. *Domain readiness: is the brand name "domain ready?"* On the most basic level, organizations need to consider domain readiness issues, such as registering all variations of trademarked names into typeable Web site addresses, known as "Internet domains." This has been a problem faced by Wal-Mart, Procter & Gamble, and others. Chrysler, for example, neglected to register common misspellings of its brand name, leaving its customers to contend with a crop of porno sites with domains such as "Chrystler.com."

Tricky spellings and names with symbols in them can still be a hurdle to the 45 percent of customers using search engines to find suppliers. More commonly, likely domain names may have already been registered to someone else in an unrelated industry. MacNeal & Schwendler, a decades-old maker of transportation simulators, faced both these problems and eventually changed its corporate name to MSC.Software, rather than lose customers among the Internet jet set.

Online is not for all brands

Fundamentally, some organizations will realize that their essential business does not port to cyberspace, no matter how big their brand may be. The fast-food giant McDonald's, one of the world's most popular brands, scores pretty low on the Brand Transfer Readiness Scorecard for a number of good reasons.

McDonald's never had first mover advantage. While very few restaurants have established themselves on the Web, in many cities delicatessens and cafes that deliver to office workers were quicker to add Web ordering to their fax and phone ordering.

And unlike delis that sell sandwiches to office workers, McDonald's customers don't spend their days staring at a computer screen. Its main audience remains small children and parents who take their kids out for a treat. Romping through plastic tables and playground equipment, crayoning Ronald-McDonald coloring books, and wrapping little fingers around the prize in the Happy Meal are customer experiences that simply don't transfer to the Web.

While a laggard online, McDonald's has been an innovator in other forms of marketing, notably cross-promotions with movie companies such as Disney—opportunities where it could borrow content, to provide some data or entertainment value that might go on a Web site. Unlike Disney, McDonald's products are not information-rich on their own—no one really wants to see a nutritional analysis of a bacon double cheeseburger.

The final nail in the coffin was McDonald's failure in domain name readiness on several counts. The name is not easy to spell; this has opened the doors to a fuzziness in domain control. "Mac-Donalds.com" and similar variations continue to exist on the Web under the ownership of others, largely because the company was slow to register the names it would need to successfully protect its franchise in cyberspace.

Organizations whose brand equity does not translate well to the Internet have many paths to follow. One path is not to go online at all, to stay out of the game. That's probably a better option for some companies than the second path: wasting money online.

A third path is to create a new, separate brand—a new online venture that can be complementary to marketing and sales efforts in the real world. Barnes & Noble's later launch of bn.com and K-Mart's efforts to attract a younger, hipper audience with its bluelight.com. are two successful examples of this strategy. A third example is Fingerhut, a well-branded catalog company that did business online for five years under the name andysgaragesale.com.

A fourth path is to rely on a partner to get online. Toys "R" Us was able to re-establish its brand online, after a disastrous customer service season, within a year by partnering with Amazon.com, which had an untarnished reputation for customer service. (See Case Study, this chapter.)

Marketers should not forget the fifth path: innovate like crazy. For every twenty widget-makers convinced that widgets do not sell online, there's probably one widget entrepreneur still dreaming of a way to make it work.

Most marketers, however, don't have the time or resources to dream up new branding strategies. For these executives, the smartest move is to put money into online branding strategies that take into account how people really discover companies and products on the Web.

2. Align Your Online Brand Investment with Changing Customer Behavior

Good branding on the Web should not be an accident, nor should it be a sinkhole for marketing budgets. The days are long gone when an Internet startup would be handed millions of dollars for outdoor billboards and posters, saturation TV commercials, and the purchase of banner ads that result in a miserable response rate. Not even the big guns could get this right. NBCi.com wound up spending $5 million a month on a TV ad blitz (all of it in trade from its parent company NBC television) and aggressively cross-promoted the Web site on its TV programs, only to find that the number of new Web site visitors actually dropped by more than a million at the peak of this campaign.

A big part of the problem has been that marketers assumed customers would behave the same way in online channels as they do in the physical world. They assumed that tried-and-true media would work just as well to get the message across to online customers. Neither of these assumptions was true.

The simple analysis of how customers find Web sites (see Figs. 3.1 and 3.2) illustrates an important point. Traditional marketing investments—television advertising, print ads, bus shelter, and billboard blitzes—are often less effective in building long-term visibility and brand equity over the Web. In the study illustrated above, Web users say they have a better chance of finding a Web site "by accident" than by TV, print, and radio. Web banner ads on the most heavily visited Web pages of Yahoo and AOL, while still credited for boosting initial brand awareness, continue to fall in popularity (and ratecard pricing). So what does make a difference?

The clues can be found by looking at how customers actually behave online. For instance, online buyers overwhelmingly prefer search engines, word of mouth, and random surfing to other marketing vehicles. And if the online audience finds businesses primarily through search engines, random Web surfing, and friendly referrals, then online brand investments should concentrate first on the three techniques that capitalize on these preferences:

1. Search engine optimization
2. Affiliate networks
3. "Viral" marketing promotions

While no organization is going to shift its entire TV ad budget (which exceeds $100 million for some) into these new areas, these cost-effective techniques are well worth understanding. They work better simply because they are consistent with the way people actually navigate the Internet and search the Web. These techniques have a better chance of succeeding because they create more opportunities for a customer to interact with your brand online. Marketers *must* better align their branding investments with customer shopping and buying behavior, and start to concentrate on the three most logical online branding strategies.

Search engine optimization: getting 20/20 vision

Nearly half of all Web users use search engines (searchable information Web sites such as Excite! InfoSeek, Google, and Yahoo!) to discover new sites: more than 50 percent of all online activities include use of a search engine. Known user behavior includes a reluctance to scroll down more than a few pages of search results.

Marketers must therefore strive to improve their position (also known as ranking) in search results, so the brand will appear among the first few pages (and ideally in the top ten rankings) of a search engine listing. This is not a trivial concern: according to Compaq's analysis of 500,000 Alta Vista inquiries, 85 percent of the search engine's users never looked past the first page of results presented in response to a question. The goal to shoot for is 20/20 vision: be in the top 20 listings of the top 20 search engines. To achieve this goal, some companies assign work teams to make the ongoing adjustments to maintain a high position on search engines. Other companies will find a variety of outsourcers who will do this work.

While the emergence of new top-level domains (beyond .com, .net, and .org) will give many existing Web ventures a second chance to gain rank, there's no excuse for not at least trying to improve current positioning. The disciplines required can be described as "white magic," "black magic," and "green magic."

White magic is the accepted practice of building a Web page's hidden source code with certain keywords and phrases, for the benefit of search engine spiders (automated search programs) that file and rank Web sites by the relevant content. This is basic procedure for any new Web site. Tactics include analyzing the source code of a successful competitor's Web pages to help identify the most effective keywords. Old pages can be recharged by the creation of "pointer pages" at a later date; these use new code to redirect searchers to old sites.

Black magic is a borderline discipline. The proprietary algorithms used by search engines to automate ranking can be rigged, or at least reverse-engineered to artificially raise position. In defense, reputable search engines will change their relevance criteria without notice, and penalize the more blatant attempts to game the software. (This discipline is likely to have a limited life as search engines continue to adopt pay-for-placement ranking models.)

That's what green magic is all about: businesses that pay the largest fee to certain search engines will be given the number-one positions. Green magic is good news for marketers; there are always going to be opportunities to buy your way to the top of a listing page. Portals are providing more and more opportunities for marketers to gain access in the form of paid sponsorships or purchase of a keyword. All search engines are under intense pressure to improve revenues, and as prices for ad placements fall, paying for positioning will become the dominant discipline for raising a search engine ranking.

Affiliate networks: being everywhere customers go online

As 20 percent of Web users cite "random surfing" as their top means of finding new sites, marketers must have extensive Web links to other, audience-appropriate sites to maximize their visibility and reach to possible new customers. Online affiliate networks are contractual arrangements between Web sites; typically, there is a monetary reward for referring customers. This can be a commission or bounty based on click-throughs, sales leads, or completed transactions. Because they are performance-based, they are generally much more cost effective than online banner ad campaigns, which use a standard cost-per-thousand (CPM) pricing.

Online marketers should carefully plan and manage partner programs that give them a broad reach of links on affiliate sites across the Internet. Goals should include affiliations with highly trafficked sites, as well as with less trafficked sites with likely affinities to the customer base. In the business-to-business sphere, Web site affiliations with well-branded industry leaders can lend cachet and respectability to lesser-known companies, and can do a good job generating qualified sales leads among specialized audiences. Affiliate networks can be managed in house, using off-the-shelf software, or may be outsourced by an "affiliate network solutions provider"—a service company that finds the partners, sets up the links, monitors traffic, and supervises the payments.

Viral marketing: harnessing electronic word of mouth

Often the most powerful recommendation for a company is that of a satisfied customer to a friend. The 20 percent of Web surfers citing word-of-mouth by friends as their top means of finding new sites suggests that companies need to continue to experiment with new variations on old incentives (e.g., electronic coupons, online loyalty currencies) and simple mechanisms (e.g., Web-based e-mail forms, pass-along e-mail newsletters) to enlist their customers as online marketing advocates to others.

This strategy is often referred to (regrettably) as "viral marketing." Highly cost effective, it achieved notoriety through a handful of instances where marketers found they could motivate millions on shoestring budgets.

A recent IMT Strategies study found that companies with incomes under $100 million were more likely to experiment with viral marketing, whereas companies over $100 million were more likely to have never tried it. Only 23 percent of companies showing revenues over $500 million described viral marketing as "very important"—an indication of how poorly this powerful tool is understood by upper management.

Viral marketing works because customers look to one another to seek out independent and trustworthy evaluations of a business and its offerings. It is worthwhile to target points of interaction where customers are most likely to function as advocates, and where in the purchase cycle a potential customer is likely to turn to an existing customer for his or her opinion.

Hotmail, a free e-mail service that is also an advertising network, is an early, classic example of viral marketing. In 1996, Hotmail included the tag "get your private, free e-mail at http://www.hotmail.com" at the close of every e-mail its subscribers sent. With each e-mail sent, a new potential customer was exposed to Hotmail's offer. Each new Hotmail registrant became, in effect, an implicit evangelist in the ranks of Hotmail's geometrically growing customer sales and marketing force. Consequently, Hotmail gathered 12 million subscribers in eighteen months at a cost-per-acquisition of just over four cents per subscriber ($500,000 investment in marketing). It later built this base to 40 million subscribers, demonstrating that the communication patterns of online users can continue to drive a viral marketing campaign.

Good viral marketing requires an online environment that encourages customer-to-customer communications. For consumer companies, viral marketing capabilities can be built into the online sales engine—for example, allowing users who have just completed a purchase to either post their opinions of the experience, or forward information about their experience to an e-mail network of family and friends. Other methods to encourage passing along information to others include online wedding, baby, or gift registries, making gift certificates available electronically, and hosting issue-oriented bulletin boards or chat rooms.

When creating a viral message, the right motivating trigger points might evolve out of research into the most frequently asked customer questions, e-mail responses, and customer complaints. This can also identify high-advocacy customers more likely to actively share information.

Other nontraditional brand investments that make sense

No one will make money online without repeat visits by customers. The previous focus on building brands fast and gaining new customers quickly often meant that important technology tools and interactive techniques for customer retention, such as personalized product offerings and automated customer care, were given less emphasis. Smart marketers have learned that service, relevance, and reliability are highly important to online brands.

The multi-million-dollar battle for dominance in the online retail toy business fought between eToys and Toys "R" Us, for example, ultimately turned on customer service issues, and wound up being won by neither company. Amazon.com emerged as the top Web toy seller strictly on the basis of its reputation for customer service. In plain terms, the best dollars spent online are those spent on customer care. (For more on E-Care, see Chapter 10.)

Battle of the Brands II: Toys "R" Us Versus eToys

Few people seem to remember that Toys "R" Us was the darling of the stock market crowd in the 1970s when it brought the "superstore" concept to retail children's toys. As retailing entered the Internet era, Toys "R" Us had at its peak 1500 stores and was recognized as the number-one toy retailer.

Toys "R" Us built a brand experience that brought customers into noisy, cavernous warehouses, where bikes and dolls and baby strollers were packed to the rafters and children were drag-racing around the aisles in shopping carts. Despite these unappealing features, adults packed the store, especially during the holiday season, because the Toys "R" Us brand was esteemed for its breadth and depth of inventory. Whatever the hot toy of the moment was, a parent could find it at Toys "R" Us.

Online, Toys "R" Us got a late start into electronic selling. First mover advantage went to eToys.com, which became the fifth-most-visited retail Web site over the 1998 Christmas season. Toys-rus.com came in a dismal 33rd in the same year's ranking (by NetRatings) and posted a $132 million net loss for the quarter.

Ratcheting up its brand advertising, both online and offline, Toys "R" Us was determined to out-brand its upstart rival during Christmas 1999. Its efforts to draw customers to its Web site were so successful that the retailer began to run out of toy stock. Unable to fill orders, it began notifying customers who had ordered well in advance that it couldn't deliver Christmas toys by December 25. On December 10, the Web site quit taking orders online entirely.

In the debacle that followed, lawsuits were filed, thousands of disgruntled customers were issued credits and $100 gift certificates, and the company paid a $350,000 fine to the U.S. Federal Trade Commission to settle claims that it had misled customers. Hundreds of news reports disparaged the company name. While eToys also reported some inventory problems, the brand damage was far worse at Toys "R" Us.

In mid-2000, Toys "R" Us announced an alliance with Amazon.com, which had begun selling toys on its book-related Web site. In the new alliance, Amazon would cover online sales and customer service, and Toys "R" Us would supply product expertise, inventory management, and regional warehousing. By "borrowing" some customer service cachet from Amazon, and refocusing on its own strengths, Toys "R" Us was able to rebuild its reputation to online buyers in time for Christmas 2000. By April 2001, eToys announced it had run out of operating capital, and went out of business.

The Toys "R" Us experience underscores the importance of customer care in branding. No online initiative is worthwhile if a customer's Web experience damages the reputation of the brand. In the end, Toys "R" Us found it was best to "cobrand" with an experienced partner. For many traditional companies, sacrificing corporate ego—partnering to brand online instead of going it alone—may be the better path to building an online reputation.

Long-Term Imperative: Three New Keys to Sustaining Brands over Time

Once you have mastered the basics, you have to buckle up for the long-haul drive. Over the next three years, branding by your competitors will also concentrate on creating the rich customer experiences that will promote long-term loyalty. This means that marketers should continually experiment with new approaches, measure their success or failure, and refine their branding activities based on results from important customer segments.

Marketers will have to do three difficult things extremely well:

1. **Learn to merge online and offline marketing media (e.g., telephony and TV with the Web) to create compelling multimedia brand experiences;**
2. **Create branding strategies that appeal to the critical emerging segment of Generation Y consumers;**
3. **Apply direct marketing measurement techniques to determine the response levels and usefulness of all branding investments.**

1. Be a Master of Media Convergence

The convergence of media represents a significant opportunity for marketers because it offers them the means to foster intense interactivity and brand "immersion." Best-in-class organizations will mix multiple media in innovative ways to create this immersion.

The convergence of the Internet and television experiences is no longer a prediction but is a burgeoning reality. According to research from NPD, 49 percent of all Web users watch television and surf the Web simultaneously, and new companies are working hard to close the gap between those two media experiences. America Online's acquisition of Time Warner portends an acceleration of this trend, combining AOL's dominance in the online world with Time Warner's extensive holdings in print, film, cable, and broadcast television.

Leading-edge marketers like Nike were early movers in combining these two media in integrated marketing campaigns. Most early experiments used television spots that encouraged viewers to log on to a special, temporary Web site to partake in an interactive experience. Nike, for example, launched a special series of ads during the Olympics that looked like harrowing action films: in one, a woman athlete on the U.S. team runs from a man with a chainsaw. To get to the end of the story, viewers had to log on to the special Web site, then push past product messages first.

Other marketers will follow and refine this hybrid approach as the technological interplay between TV and the Web (including hand-held Web devices) becomes a more seamless experience. Also of concern is the rapid convergence of telephony and the Internet, through various hand-held devices and wireless digital communications. Net access can only become more ubiquitous, through public kiosks, hotel-room terminals, exercise equipment, common appliances, and more.

2. Look Out for Generation Y

Generation Y embodies the demanding audience of the future. Marketers will have to develop new branding strategies that capture the loyalty of this potentially lucrative but supremely challenging youthful customer segment.

It is the perpetual role of youth to challenge society's status quo assumptions, in business as elsewhere. In the case of Generation Y, today's teens and preteens, no generation since their Baby Boom parents represents as large a demographic bulge or will have as great an impact on the conventions of marketing. This group (60 million strong, born from 1979 to 1994) has grown up in a post-vinyl LP age of 3D video games, 500 cable stations, and high-speed Internet access.

As a result of their "power-user" media savvy, Generation Y tends to be cynical of, if not immune to, traditional brand marketing tactics. By the time they come of buying power age, their finely honed media filters will screen out most commercial attempts for their attention. Many of today's leading marketers will be caught unprepared for the new challenges in establishing loyal brand relationships with this new breed of consumer.

Long-time youth-oriented brands, such as Coke, Levi Strauss, and Nike, are struggling to remain credibly hip and relevant with Generation Y. The Web alone won't be enough to enable marketers to form lasting relationships with this segment. Convergence—richly interactive brand experiences that combine Web promotions with print media, live event sponsorship, electronic music, and digital movie-making—may be the best way to keep their attention.

Raised with a joystick, remote or mouse in hand, Generation Y consumers are always one click away from taking a brand interaction one level deeper—or switching allegiance to a competitor's product. To navigate this razor's edge between customer retention and loss, companies must be able to quantify the success of their branding efforts quickly and make adjustments faster than ever before.

cKOne: Targeting Generation Y with a "Cyber Soap Opera"

The branding campaign for cKOne, a fragrance product of Calvin Klein Cosmetics, is a great example of intelligent online branding. It effectively targeted and reached Generation Y; it effectively integrated online and offline media, and it used the principles of viral marketing and audience collaboration to pull prospective customers back, again and again, to a Web site rich with interactive play.

The product itself is tailored to "Generation Y"—it is a cologne meant to be used by both men and women. The ads (print, TV, and transit advertising) simply showed different beautiful young models with their corresponding e-mail addresses. The only "message," for example, would be something like "tia@ckone. com," in very small print. Embodying the enigmatic "cool" of the Calvin Klein brand, there was no other copy.

Anyone curious enough to send a message to one of the addresses soon began receiving friendly messages back. While the replies were not truly personalized (one could declare one's love to Tia to no avail), they were written as if the recipient were a close confidant of the models, all employed as characters in a cyber-soap opera.

People who continued to respond could also exchange mail with the other characters, who often had a different point of view. While none of the e-mail messages explicitly referred to any Calvin Klein products, and no products were sold on the ckone.com site, the continuing storyline drew people into a brand experience around the cachet of cKOne.

Importantly, the success of the branding campaign could be measured directly by simply counting the numbers of people who stayed with the story. Although every e-mail update—two or three messages a week—contained instructions for unsubscribing at the bottom, only a small percentage dropped out, prompting the project to continue into a second year.

A campaign like this capitalizes on the strengths of Internet branding: it caters to a young audience, uses a combination of media to attract interest, employs viral marketing, and can be measured accurately in terms of brand response. Not surprisingly, copycat campaigns have cropped up since, include fcuk.com, from youth fashion retailer French Connection.

3. Apply Direct Marketing Measurements to Branding Investments

The classic joke among brand marketers—"I know half of my advertising is wasted; I just don't know which half"—is not funny to senior management any more. All marketers must demonstrate a return on investment (ROI) of their online marketing programs, in the same way they can, must, and do demonstrate the ROI of old-fashioned direct mail. They will be accountable to management to show more tangible returns. Under the pressure of retaining long-term customer loyalty, marketers are embracing the powerful brand response measurement techniques created for the Internet, and using them to monitor the success of all branding initiatives.

If e-branding is the natural child of branding and direct mail, this new trend is a logical next generation of brand building and direct response techniques. The online promotion for cKOne is a good example of an effective "direct brand response" campaign. Other companies such as Nike and Volkswagon have also used traditional brand advertising vehicles (e.g., television, radio, and print ads) featuring toll-free telephone numbers and/or Web addresses where consumers are encouraged to find out more details or place an order.

Online banner ads that encourage a viewer to "click through" to the company Web site can simultaneously count branding impressions (the number of times the ad is downloaded to a viewer screen) while enticing the consumer into ever-deepening levels of lead qualification that lead in the end to a direct response offer.

Given that banner advertisements are increasingly less successful in encouraging click-through (the average click-through rate, or CTR of a typical online ad is .01 percent, or one person in ten thousand), you can expect that consumer and business magazines with online divisions will be less timid to experiment with quantifiable brand response. Electronic variations on the old "reader reply card" may be just the tip of that iceberg, though advertisers themselves will lead the way with interactive campaigns, as they face increasing pressure to demonstrate the ROI of brand marketing programs.

Brand response will not only permit marketers to measure and modulate brand impact; it will enable them to capitalize on the emotive aspect of brand with unprecedented efficiency. Consider point-and-click television, which will make it possible to translate consumers' emotional reaction to an ad into an immediate purchase response through TV-commerce. The next generation of TV product placement, for example, is likely to allow viewers to freeze-frame during an episode of *Friends*, learn details about Jennifer Aniston's wardrobe, and then buy a copy of her blouse directly from Calvin Klein. This sort of "emotional interactivity" will epitomize future branding strategies, drive profits, and garner customer loyalty.

Bottom Line

Traditional marketers must totally rethink branding strategies and investments if they want to remain relevant to customers that attend to new media.

Interactive Direct Marketing:

New Tools to Improve Marketing Performance and Anticipate Customer Behavior

Direct marketers have a new arsenal of highly targeted, interactive direct marketing tools available to help them grow sales, reduce costs, and better understand their customers. Tools such as targeted Web marketing, e-mail direct marketing, and online market research are changing the way marketers reach their customers.

Marketing executives must pay close attention to these newer tools for two important reasons. First, these tools can significantly improve sales and marketing performance. Second, they provide marketers with a new ability to anticipate and influence the way customers will buy.

Executives who do not understand or at least experiment with these tools will miss out on major shifts in customer buying behavior. Learning how to integrate interactive direct marketing tools into the marketing mix is best done through disciplined experimentation. General Motors (GM) illustrates how an established business with an aging brand and entrenched physical distribution channel adapted to changing customer behavior by using this new set of tools.

General Motors: Gaining Customers with Interactive Direct Marketing

GM relied on mass media advertising and a single channel for distribution (its brick-and mortar dealers) to reach customers for nearly a century. Then General Motors realized that a lot of its customers were shopping the Web for new cars and used cars, as well as for offerings of car-related services, which represented a high-growth, high-margin category for the auto industry. In 1999 a J.D. Powers study showed that 16 percent of new car buyers shopped on the Web. By 2001 well over 65 percent of GM's potential customers were looking online for cars. And a new set of virtual middle-men—such as Autobytel, Microsoft Car Point, AutoSite, and Autoweb.com—were starting to steal customers and business from more traditional dealer channels. These electronic intermediaries were stepping in front of dealer networks to capture car sales, gain better customer information, and establish valuable online customer relationships.

In response, GM got serious about interactive direct marketing. The company spent aggressively on Internet advertising and promotions, outinvesting its industry and, in fact, the rest of corporate America, to become a leader in online advertising. Spending $24.4 million in 1999 and $47.9 million in 2000, GM invested more than any company in online media than any other company, according to Competitive Media Reporting.

They developed an online brand, GMBuyPower.com, and tested other online marketing programs that took advantage of GM's offline assets—such as local dealerships, deep inventories, and custom factory orders. For example, GM used online promotions to provide incentives (valued up to $50) for customers to give them more detailed information about themselves so GM could start an online relationship with them. They also used the Internet to distribute $500 e-coupons encouraging prospects to take test drives of GM cars at local dealerships. GM even partnered with several popular Web intermediaries, such as Auto-Trader Online and AutoSite, to get better access to online buyers, even though those sites offer competitive cars and price comparisons. Online ads were purchased to drive prospective customers to GMBuyPower.com, inviting them to search a database that at present represents the inventories of three-quarters of GM's U.S. dealers.

Rather than watch 65 percent of their customers go online without them, GM adapted to find ways to incorporate powerful interactive marketing tools into their mix, alongside television advertisements and its more traditional dealer promotions.

Interactive Direct Marketing is the Future of Direct Marketing

Direct Marketing is important to sales and marketing executives because it delivers against a top management imperative—improving customer relationships. For decades, direct marketing programs such as direct mail and telemarketing have offered better targeting, greater personalization, and more efficient use of marketing dollars. According to the Direct Marketing Association (DMA), spending on direct marketing has now overtaken spending on traditional mass-media brand advertising, and now represents nearly 60 percent of all total U.S. advertising expenditures.

Now, interactive tools such as e-mail and targeted Web advertising can take direct marketing to another level. Not only are these tools more interactive, they also are more measurable, and in many cases they perform better.

Electronic mail, for example, has established itself as a significant conduit of business and personal communication. Over one-third (37 percent) of the U.S. population currently uses e-mail, according to a recent study by eMarketer. Americans presently send more than three times as many e-mails per day as postal letters, according to research by the U.S. Postal Service. According to a Harris Poll, 66 percent of households earning more than $75,000 per year use e-mail.

Not surprisingly, in a recent IMT Strategies survey of 160 marketers, "permission e-mail" was ranked as their number-one marketing investment priority. By the year 2000, U.S. spending on the interactive marketing tools profiled later in this chapter had reached $11 billion. According to IMT research, U.S. marketers will invest on average 2.5 percent of their marketing budgets into interactive direct marketing tools in 2001. Expect that share of marketing dollars to triple in the next three years, as marketers gain experience incorporating these new tools with traditional marketing programs.

Improving Marketing Performance and Learning about Changing Customer Behavior

Interactive direct marketing (also known as IDM) can be inexpensive compared to telephone and direct mail. And compared to other forms of direct advertising, it can give businesses a better understanding of customer behavior and what drives people to buy.

When e-mail marketing programs are executed properly they are very cost-effective. E-mail marketing campaigns typically get conversion rates (the ratio of actual orders per message or envelope sent out) of over five percent. This means that 5 percent of the people contacted respond to the offer, at pennies per mailing. These performance levels are much higher than traditional direct mail, which gets lower response rates on average (1–3 percent) and can cost over a dollar per envelope if printed graphics or purchased mailing lists are involved.

Other interactive direct marketing tools have the potential to improve your marketing effectiveness as well. For example, Affiliate Networks (services that bring in new customers from third-party Web sites) give marketers a fast, easy, and inexpensive way to put up "storefronts" in thousands of highly targeted online realms. Services like BeFree can create networks of thousands of specific Web sites quickly (within days) and cheaply (usually with no setup costs and on a pay-for-results basis). And new "online customer behavior analysis tools" can help marketers make decisions based on facts, not assumptions.

2000 Corporate Interactive Direct Marketing Spending

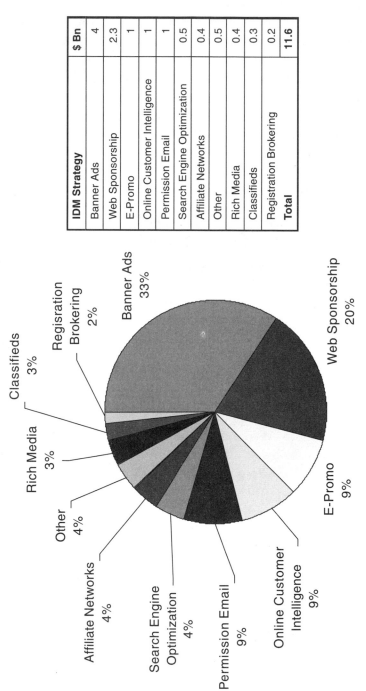

IDM Strategy	$ Bn
Banner Ads	4
Web Sponsorship	2.3
E-Promo	1
Online Customer Intelligence	1
Permission Email	1
Search Engine Optimization	0.5
Affiliate Networks	0.4
Other	0.5
Rich Media	0.4
Classifieds	0.3
Registration Brokering	0.2
Total	**11.6**

IMT Strategies estimates, Internet Advertising Bureau

Figure 4.1. Where are marketers spending online?

2004 Corporate Interactive Direct Marketing Spending

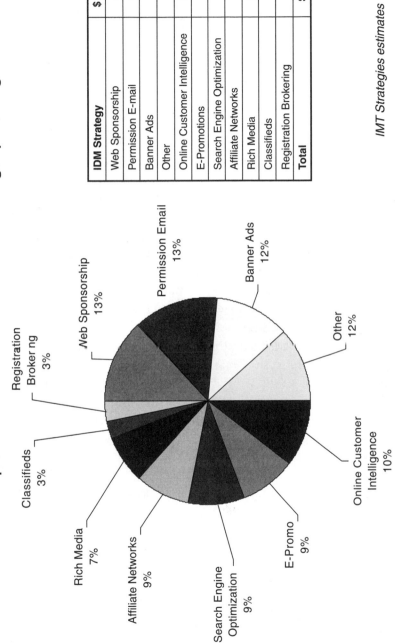

IDM Strategy	$ Bn
Web Sponsorship	4.5
Permission E-mail	4.5
Banner Ads	4
Other	4
Online Customer Intelligence	3.5
E-Promotions	3
Search Engine Optimization	3
Affiliate Networks	3
Rich Media	2.5
Classifieds	1
Registration Brokering	1
Total	**$34**

IMT Strategies estimates

Figure 4.2. A forecast of U.S. spending on IDM by 2004.

This alone is an opportunity to grasp. Most marketers are not following their customers online in a meaningful way because they don't know how to target them exactly. This is because targeting the online customer in the here and now is like shooting at a moving target. Savvy marketers taking aim at online customers must lead them by a few steps if they are going to hit the target. If they shoot too far behind, their marketing performance will suffer relative to the competition, like many established retailers who lost share to newcomers who were quicker to serve customers online. If they shoot too far ahead—as in the case of Webvan and other dot-coms set up for online grocery shopping—they will have to "chalk the investment up to experience" and adjust their aim anew.

Better understanding customer buying behavior lets marketers adapt to where and how customers are buying. For example, using audience segmentation technology from the vendor Personify, the online wine seller eVineyards.com was able to carefully analyze the buying patterns of its e-commerce customers according to segment clusters (e.g., "window shoppers," "information seekers," "wine experts," and "gift buyers"). The company soon realized its most profitable customers were not wine aficionados, as they had previously presumed, but rather wine neophytes. As a result, the company was able to shift marketing resources toward online ads that reached this more profitable customer base with higher conversion rates. In other industries, analyzing online buying patterns can save businesses money by directing programs, sales incentives, and promotions to help migrate some customer interactions to low-cost electronic channels, including self-service and automated replenishment.

Leading marketers like IBM and Procter & Gamble have traditionally been aggressive experimenters in new technologies. They know that if and when they "crack the code" of a new marketing formula, a single marketing success can make up for a lot of failures.

P&G and the tiny TVs

Procter & Gamble is an established company that has boldly experimented with new tools to get consumers to buy in old ways. Many years ago, in the pre-Internet age, P&G spent over a million dollars to test a customer messaging threshold: it put tiny TV sets in supermarket shopping carts. The concept involved a series of laser triggers, so that when a customer wheeled the cart down the cereal aisle, for example, the TV would display a commercial for Cap'n Crunch.

This highly original attempt at real-time interactive marketing nosedived miserably through technical difficulties. Kids would wheel the carts to a distant end of the parking lot and steal the TV sets, or the equipment would fail or break and store workers wouldn't know how to fix it. But what if it had succeeded? To Procter & Gamble, it was worth a million dollars to find out if customer buying behaviors would change in what was even then a mature product market.

Procter & Gamble continues to see value in experiments. In one single year, P&G conducted over 200 Internet ad campaigns, with dozens of online marketing and technology partners. To market approximately 30 of its brands on the Web, the company invested more than $4.4 million in Internet programs. Yet this represented less than 0.2 percent of its $3 billion advertising budget. While Procter & Gamble is wedded to traditional customer behavior, since most customers will likely continue to buy its packaged goods through supermarkets, any experience gained will be valuable if and when more consumers begin to automate their purchases of staples such as laundry detergent and toothpaste.

Currently, most of its competitors prefer to stay in their "zone of comfort," using proven tools such as printed coupons or television advertising to serve well-understood customer buying behavior. When customers migrate to online sales channels, any organization that has already done some testing with interactive direct marketing tools will enjoy a competitive advantage.

Short Term Strategy: Mastering The Interactive Direct Marketing Toolkit

The interactive direct marketing toolkit is made up of a variety of technology-enabled marketing tools. New and refined tools are constantly being introduced. Most marketers and their agencies are still struggling to understand the large number of interactive direct marketing tools and services at their disposal. On a certain level, senior executives cannot be expected to keep up with all of the latest interactive "solutions," nor can they be expected to deal intimately with the more technical aspects of data management. But to take advantage of the benefits of adding interactive direct marketing tools to the marketing mix, marketing executives must at least have a general understanding of the media involved. To get a better overall grasp of the possibilities, it helps to realize that most fall into the following three general categories.

Targeted Web marketing tools

These tools help marketers target and segment customers who use the Web to improve the level of effectiveness and reach of companywide Internet initiatives. Such tools include *online incentive programs*, *targeted Web advertising*, and the *affiliate marketing networks* discussed in Chapter 3, when these are used not only for branding but also for direct-response selling.

Incentive programs such as online coupons and sweepstakes cast a wide net to draw in potential buyers (20 of the top 100 busiest Web sites offer games or promotions). Web targeting tools and services can now serve up online ads to the computer screens of individual consumers, based on interests and geography, or in real time while customers are shopping with competitors. Affiliate marketing services help expand new markets through reseller networks of virtual business partners, or through Web sites that offer prequalified sales leads.

E-mail direct marketing tools

The average e-mail marketing message is on average five times more efficient than direct mail and 40 times more effective than Internet banner advertising, and it costs just pennies to deliver. "Permission-based" e-mail direct marketing has evolved the medium far beyond unsolicited "spam" to a targeted marketing tool that—when executed properly—can cost-effectively build customer relationships and reach out to many new prospects. Successful "permission-based" e-mail models maximize performance on the fly, use high levels of personalization, and are sensitive to privacy issues. Marketers commonly use eight separate models of e-mail marketing, depending on whether they are aiming for customer retention or looking to acquire new customers. (These eight are described in the "Technology Overview" Special Section at the end of this chapter.)

For example, in 1996 American Airlines online channel, AA.com, saw a new opportunity to integrate e-mail into their marketing plans and created NetSAAver, an opt-in e-mailing list that lets passengers know about last-minute discounts on flights to various cities. By the year 2000, more than two million people subscribed to this e-mail list, both within the United States and internationally. Through it, American created a new, cheap, and effective channel to liquidate otherwise unsold seats. Most other airlines have since developed similar e-mail programs.

As American gained experience with permission e-mail marketing, they started devising more sophisticated programs like Sale AAlert. This personalized e-mail program, a type of reminder service, allows travelers to register on their own personalized AA.com pages which city they live in and which cities they frequently visit (e.g., for work, family, friends). When flights between customers' home and "favored" cities go on sale (e.g., due to airline price competition or seasonal changes), AA.com sends off personalized e-mail alerts to relevant subscribers. Before Sales AAlert, if American Airlines wanted to promote sales on airfares to specific cities, they had to place national newspaper ads announcing the new prices and hope customers would respond. If customers called back on the phone they had to wait while an agent found the details for their particular city. With AAlert the deal goes immediately and directly to the consumers most interested in traveling to those cities. To respond, they only need to click once on a link embedded in the e-mail message, and they're immediately able to begin the reservation process.

Permission e-mail has proved to be an extremely cost-effective marketing vehicle for the airline, compared to traditional channels, notably direct mail. Typical conversion rates for up-sell offers were generally in the high single digits for both NetSAAver and Sale Alert. This was slightly higher than direct mail response rates. But with much cheaper execution costs, it was five or more times as cost-effective as direct mail. With results like these, American is looking for ways to build and maintain its permission lists to gain even greater benefits from interactive direct marketing. This represents a very large opportunity; as of 2000 only 6 percent of the AAdvantage program's 32 million members, all of whom get postal mail from American, had opted-in to their permission e-mail programs.

Online customer buying behavior analysis tools

Online customer behavior analysis is the who, how, what, when, where, and why of e-business. Tools include *profiling services* that provide detailed information about customer purchase behavior as well as the *personalization and segmentation software* to analyze this behavior in real time. Analysis tools can also be used to measure the effectiveness of campaigns, and provide raw data for campaign research and future product development.

The IMT Strategies survey estimated that over $ 1 billion was spent in 2000 on online buying behavior analysis and tools to understand how customers behave online and develop data that prove e-business works. Half (51 percent) of the e-business managers surveyed reported using third-party software and solutions to measure Web performance.

Today, over 1000 organizations use Web "panels" (groups of Internet users assembled by companies such as Nielson/Net Ratings, NetValue, and Jupiter/Media Metrix) to benchmark their online performance and understand where customers like to shop online and what they respond to. The smartest marketers will develop proprietary online panels dedicated to gathering accurate intelligence on the behavior of specific prospects and customers.

Online customer buying behavior analysis tools can generate behavioral profiles that go beyond purchase history and demographic data about customers. This data can help anticipate critical customer buying behavior trends that can be exploited to gain competitive advantage in the following areas:

Direct marketing cross-sell and up-sell programs

Determine customer preferences for electronic channels and interfaces like e-commerce, kiosks, ATM, and Web/ telephone integration

Decide the adoption of automated self-service to help speed and simplify the buying process

Decide participation with electronic intermediaries, such as affiliate networks or online trading marketplaces

Determine customer willingness to adopt fully automated replenishment (applicable to both business and consumer buyers)

Create appropriate levels of virtual self-service and low-cost online support to serve different kinds of customers

The Technology Overview section at the end of this report provides an overview of the interactive direct marketing tools discussed above.

Successful marketers must have a working knowledge of these tools to capitalize on their potential and manage the risks. There are several pitfalls to consider. Innovators must deal with rapid technical evolution, industry consolidation, privacy, and marketing infrastructure issues. Hundreds of companies provide interactive direct marketing products and services currently, and despite ongoing consolidation of the industry, hundreds more are launched each year.

Even best-of-breed "point solutions" solve only part of the overall online marketing equation—and these are by no means household-name companies touting industry standards. In practical terms, this can create problems when the organization wants to upgrade software, or integrate functions with marketing systems from different suppliers. As the industry inevitably consolidates, even some of the best suppliers will disappear. Many will be merged into larger software companies or marketing agencies, or will go out of business. (For more help on choosing technology partners, See Chapter 12.)

Long-Term Imperative: Mainstreaming interactive direct marketing tools into the marketing mix

A marketer's portfolio of interactive tools can be managed in the same way as a stock portfolio. Most professional investors will allocate a small portion of their funds to new or risky stocks. If these "speculative" investments don't perform as well as current investments they will get dumped. If they perform better, resources may be transferred out of older instruments to what is now viewed as a "better investment."

For many companies, interactive direct marketing is still an experiment. These experiments are funded out of a separate budget and not put in competition with traditional marketing programs. Many mature businesses have "dabbled" with interactive direct marketing while upper marketing management continued to focus on business as usual—that is, deploying older tools.

New tools that work should become fixtures in the marketing budget. For example, if permission e-mail programs can remain five times more effective in eliciting a prospect's response than traditional direct mail, they deserve to be a part of the mainstream marketing budget, accountable and visible.

The ongoing challenge is deciding how fast to move interactive direct marketing initiatives from the "experimental" stage to a mainstream activity of the sales and marketing team. And before successful experiments can become line-budget, mainstream marketing programs, some operational challenges—internal turf wars, conflicts with agencies and outside partners—should be expected. Smart managers will anticipate issues and have measures, processes, and operational rules in place to succeed.

The framework below illustrates the balancing act sales and marketing management must perform over the next two years.

Direct marketing leadership means finding the best possible combination of new and old marketing tools to meet the needs of current and future customer behavior in order to maximize sales growth. Trial and error will be involved. To remain competitive, organizations must move out of their "zone of comfort" and experiment to continually assess how fast customer behavior is chang-

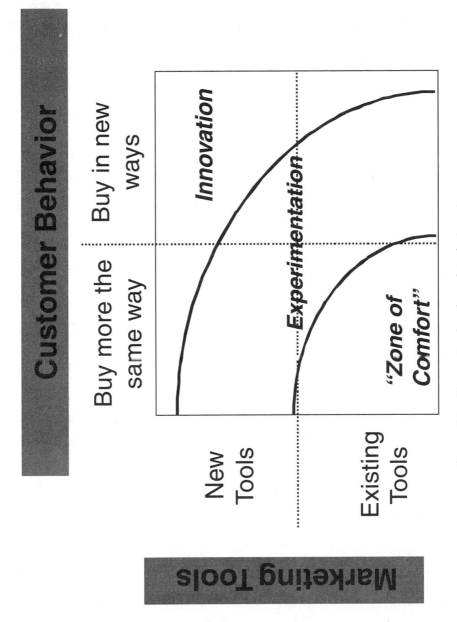

Figure 4.3. Fine-tuning the sales and marketing mix.

ing and how aggressively to adopt new marketing tools. For example, 50 percent of established mail catalogers are experimenting with Web commerce programs according to a recent DMA survey. Direct marketing innovation carries greater risks but holds a promise of greater rewards.

To make the right choices, organizations must do a better job of testing the performance of new tools and tactics. Three long-term strategies can help shape the best ways to integrate new tools into the evolving marketing mix:

1. **Build ROI models to test new tools and learn;**
2. **Start managing new customer data streams;**
3. **Negotiate control over customer data.**

I. Build ROI models to test new tools and learn

The key to getting results from new Web marketing tools is to think more like scientists and continually "test and learn." To figure out which tools work best, marketing managers must demand that each initiative build in a method to measure the project in terms of marketing performance, what value is created, and what the return on investment (ROI) is. ROI models will be necessary to justify the reallocation of marketing resources to increasingly targeted and sophisticated interactive direct marketing programs. Their effectiveness relative to traditional marketing programs will have to be demonstrated in real numbers to justify shifting budget dollars out of "entrenched" marketing budget items such as TV advertising.

Marketers are not applying the direct-marketing discipline of test and measurement to interactive marketing as aggressively as they should. As late as 2000, the majority (over 70 percent) of marketing organizations in the IMT survey did not measure response rates (neither "click-through" nor conversion) of their interactive direct-marketing campaigns, despite the availability of built-in measurement tools and software. And 94 percent of e-business managers surveyed agreed they were not capitalizing adequately on the potential of the Internet to measure campaign results.

But why not? Direct marketing managers run constant experiments to test which catalogs, telephone, and direct mail programs work best. One reason is marketers are having a difficult time measuring the performance of online marketing tools on an "apples-to-apples" basis with other marketing investments. A common and early mistake is to measure what is easy (like hits and clicks) rather than what is important (conversion rates). Smart executives will draw a line of "acceptable" marketing performance goals for interactive direct marketing experiments. They will keep what works—the programs and tools that fall above the line—and throw out any that fall below the line of acceptable performance.

The Importance of Measurement : From Counting Clicks to Customer Intelligence

The earliest direct response initiatives on the Web, 1997–2000, counted nothing more than "eyeball traffic," or the number of users who would perform a "click-through" to reach a home page if they were elicited by an online banner advertisement or e-mail communiqué promotion. As retrievable data from server logs became more available, e-marketers were able to further break down hits into useful data, such as the number of new (also called "unique") monthly visitors, the time spent viewing the organization's pages, how many pages were viewed, and number of repeat visits as a percentage of all traffic. While more sophisticated companies took the logical next step of comparing traffic patterns with "conversions" to actual sales, surprising numbers didn't even bother to measure the effectiveness of campaigns. A year 2000 study by IMT Strategies of 50 "best-in-class" Web companies revealed that 30 of the 50 companies had no metrics in place at all, and were spending their online dollars with no accountability, in some sort of "leap of faith" that profits might occur.

By 2001, after a long season of broken "business models" and busted budgets, savvy e-marketers stopped chasing traffic and began hunting "conversions." Businesses were switching wholesale to interactive programs that got results: either direct sales, or user registration, or at the very least a prospect's participation in a quiz, contest, or game that would garner a scrap or two of customer intelligence data.

Once metrics were installed, e-mail marketing proved to deliver superior performance compared to other Web marketing initiatives. Some marketers commonly achieved a 15 percent response rate for e-mail pitches that drove prospects to an organization's Web site. (To understand the relative impact, just imagine if 15 percent of all the people who viewed a bus-shelter ad poster actually walked into a retail store.) And this was at a time when "click-through" rates for Web banner ads had fallen from response rates nearing 5 percent, to a dismal .01 percent. As a result, the use of electronic mail for marketing increased dramatically, and banner advertising either declined or was upgraded to include a richer level of interactivity.

2. Start managing new customer data streams

Interactive direct marketing programs such as e-mail will grow the amount of information organizations collect about customers by an order of magnitude. Executives should anticipate a dramatically increased volume of inbound customer response and customer data. A successful online interactive direct marketing campaign, for example, launches thousands of outbound customer messages and will result in vastly higher levels of inbound customer response. Each inbound message increases the opportunity for a direct sale but arrives burdened with the need for speed, since online customers have far greater expectations for an immediate and satisfactory response. Processing inbound customer data quickly will be a critical management challenge.

Mainstreaming interactive direct marketing programs will require big investments in hardware, software, data processing, staff training, and data capacity. For example, businesses will need data warehouses—on their own premises or off-site—to organize and house this large volume of customer data. In the year 2000 over 30 percent of large companies had built very large customer databases that exceeded a terabyte in size according to the META Group. By comparison, in 1990 only a handful of companies had built databases about their customers that approached that size.

The variety of sources and types of data will expand as well. Companies must organize this information so it can be useful. This will be necessary to manage the expanding number of data streams from new media (the Internet, freestanding electronic kiosks, etc.), multiple selling channels (telemarketing, partners, direct sales, e-commerce), and online customer analysis programs (data mining, personalization, audience segmentation).

To ensure that this data is useful, marketers will need to define a common centralized "master customer profile" to effectively target interactive marketing campaigns and collect valuable market research and competitive information. This will also be necessary for clear governance over customer relationship and privacy programs. Sales and marketing executives, as the primary owners of the customer relationship, must recognize—early on—the need to define this profile. For example, the online music company CD now can personalize over 100 different elements on an e-mail based on customer information (past behavior, purchases, and profile forms). A customer database must be "architected" to make sure that all of these valuable pieces of data have a home and can be retrieved by marketers who need them.

Another important reason to get a handle on customer data is that customers will want to see it more and more. Forward-looking marketers need to realize that ultimately, customers want total control over electronic relationships. An IMT Strategies customer survey showed "communication control" and "content selection options" were the top two personalization features preferred by online customers. In the near future, customers will require higher levels of control and access over their customer profiles and opt-in message status so they can manage the relationship more. They will want to update their own profiles and dictate how they will be treated, and when and where they will accept a marketing message—even from a company they already buy from and trust.

The Privacy Issue: The Importance of "Asking Permission"

Privacy considerations are critical to designing online marketing program policies and management practices. Soon, an effective privacy policy will be the price of entry for doing business online. However, ensuring customer privacy costs money and resources.

Modern marketers must understand the full concept of "permission marketing." It means just that: asking permission in the form of opt-in (this means "positive consent" or "please check yes to confirm we have a relationship").

IMT Strategies research has shown that Internet users make a clear distinction between welcome messaging and unsolicited commercial e-mails, i.e., spam. Marketers developing permission e-mail strategies must recognize that crossing over to the wrong side of the permission e-mail marketing/spam divide, as even well-intentioned marketers will do, can result in long-term damage to customer relationships and brand equity. More than 80 percent of the respondents in the survey said they felt negatively towards unsolicited e-mails. Less than a third say they have ever responded to these more than once. And opinions sharpen over time. Customers with over two years of Internet experience were 30 percent more likely to be negative about unsolicited messages than newer online users. Similar studies from other research teams suggest this percentage may be closer to 40 percent.

Asking permission marketing can be good for your brand. In the IMT survey, 69 percent of customers felt "asking permission" to have an e-mail relationship was "good marketing" or "superior customer service." A phone survey of over 400 adult e-mail users found more than half felt positively about permission (while most of the remaining were "neutral"). Significantly, nearly three-quarters of those surveyed said they responded to permission e-mails with some frequency.

---

4. Negotiate control over customer data

Customer data is becoming like gold. It is the basic "stuff" that runs all targeted marketing and customer relationship management (CRM) programs. Like gold, everyone wants it. It is also a transferable asset and tends to get moved around in complex selling organizations from one department to another. Sometimes it is hoarded by business partners. Sometimes it is lost.

As a result, organizational issues and fights will occur over the data. For example, one department may establish an "opt-in" e-mail relationship with a customer based on a promise to not share the information. Once they put the e-mail address in the central data warehouse, other departments (or distributors) could access the information and send that customer a marketing promotion. This can cause conflicts between departments and with customers.

Smart managers will find ways to negotiate control or access to the customer data they need to make interactive marketing programs run. They must assure that their needs are met when master customer profiles are compiled, and they have a say in defining company protocols and structures to allow access to data when it is needed. They must also be alert to making sure that valuable customer data is not lost (or borrowed or stolen) when marketing campaigns are outsourced to third-party agencies.

Marketing executives will need to negotiate all these issues. This takes power, money, or some of other form of persuasion. Some solutions are not new. For example, manufacturers who sell through third-party distribution (like supermarkets) would like access to customer names. In some cases they are swapping trade promotional dollars (programs that benefit resellers or retail distributors, for example co-op print advertising or cash shelving allowances) for access to the customer data (like e-mail addresses) they need to make future interactive marketing promotions more successful.

Citicorp POS Information Systems: Wrestling Customer Data from Grocers

Back in the late 1980s, Citicorp got into the marketing information business. At the time, most supermarkets had added technology to their stores in the form of bar code scanners and sophisticated cash registers. These tools let them "capture" data about sales transactions at the cash registers. The problem was most grocers were just dumping this information into accounting records and not using it for marketing purposes.

Citibank had the clever idea of matching those transactions with the people who made them. They did this by using "frequent shopper programs" like GreenStamps where the customer had to scan a card to get points. This let them attach the customer name to those transactions.

They talked several supermarkets into handing over their customers' names and all the information about what they were buying from cash registers. In return they helped these supermarkets run targeted direct-marketing campaigns to drive customers into the stores. To make the deal sweeter they bought the data at one cent per transaction as well.

Supermarkets like Vons, Ukrops, and Dominicks handed over all their customer data. Citibank built a very large customer database. At one point they had over 6 million names and the database was one of the first to reach terabyte size. It was a direct marketer's dream.

The brains at Citibank did all sorts of customer analysis on this data and tested how effective ads, promotions, and coupons were at growing sales. This helped packaged goods manufacturers like Procter and Gamble and General Foods to test which ads worked best and helped them target customers more effectively. For example, because they knew what everybody bought, they could create a list of the top 1 percent of beer drinkers or families that bought diapers for the first time. Citibank thought all sorts of marketers would find this incredibly useful and would spend billions to buy this valuable customer information service. They were wrong.

This ambitious database marketing effort failed within a few years because marketers were not sophisticated enough to take advantage of all that targeted marketing. At that time, mass media advertising was still the mainstay of marketing budgets, and the World Wide Web was still years away. Retailers would just as soon distribute coupons the old-fashioned way in newspapers, instead of rifle-targeted direct-mail campaigns at one dollar per envelope.

Citibank also learned that customer data is expensive to collect and maintain. The database technology was new, and one penny per transaction fee did add up. To their surprise, the cost of acquiring and maintaining the stored information exceeded $50 per name per year. Considering that the going price for a targeted mailing list was $50 per 1000 names, Citibank would have had to sell each name to 1000 marketers just to break even.

Privacy considerations were the final blow. Eventually, supermarkets stopped giving the information away because of the pressure from privacy advocates and the desire to control their own customer data. Today, most of these supermarkets run and administer their own frequent shopper programs and have 100 percent control over their customer data.

This "bleeding edge" failure illustrates how much things have changed in the last decade and puts the opportunity that marketers face in perspective. Most marketers have embraced the concept of one-to-one marketing. Direct marketing spending is now on equal footing with mass media advertising. Interactive marketing programs like e-mail are far less costly than direct-mail campaigns and easier to customize. Customer data warehouses have gotten less expensive, larger, and more common. For instance, the META Group predicts that within a few years almost half of Global 2000 organizations will have customer databases of a terabyte or more.

The control of data and privacy remain as thorny as ever. This imperative is clear: negotiate control over customer data with distribution partners and offer customers much higher degrees of control over the use and access to their information as well as their e-mail boxes.

Bottom Line

Marketers need to apply direct-marketing disciplines to the broad arsenal of new, interactive direct-marketing tools in order to dramatically grow demand, reduce costs, and learn more about their customers.

Special Section: The Internet Direct Marketing Toolkit

Recent years have seen the advent of a wide array of promising new interactive direct marketing technologies. Here is a brief overview of some material developments to which marketers should pay careful attention.

Targeted Web Marketing

The Web is still a rapidly evolving medium. Leading marketers and solution vendors have demonstrated a range of powerful online customer targeting techniques—many unique to the Internet—that can dramatically improve sales and marketing performance. A variety of strategies, from behavior-based targeting to online incentive programs to affiliate networks, can substantially improve online response rates, delivering high penetration, acquisition, and retention of customers for relatively low costs.

Targeted Web advertising

As response rates for banners have dropped to below 1 percent on average (that is, the "click-through rate" of Web users who click to interact with a given banner ad), selling organizations have largely abandoned generic Web advertising for more targeted ad placements that encourage higher conversion rates. Among Web users who click-through on banners, only around 1 percent typically convert to online sales, according to many merchants and networks. Effective strategies to boost conversion levels include:

Segmented target advertising

Content Affiliation/Sponsorship: Simple as it sounds, one of the most effective audience-targeting techniques is to position an online ad near related editorial content: for example, car ads with automotive news, bank ads with investment tips, bridal gown ads with wedding advice. Leading online media buying agencies, such as Modem.Poppe, Lot21, Agency.com, and Anderson & Lembke, specialize in targeted ad placement.

Geographic: Regional products and services can use several methods to target ads geographically. Several services customize their content according to zip codes, such as *TV Guide*'s online listings, Weather.com, and MapQuest. Other quality sites serve exclusive local niches, such as entertainment listing services Sidewalk and CitySearch and the *New York Times*. In addition, some large sites and most ad networks, such as DoubleClick, AdForce, Flycast, and AdKnowledge, can target visitors geographically, using Internet Protocol address information.

Demographic: Many sites collect at least some demographic data on their visitors so they can target ads according to gender, age, income bracket, and other known characteristics. Leading ad serving systems, such as NetGravity and Accipiter, can easily facilitate this type of targeting where sites collect the data.

Behavioral: Customers' actions often better predict future behavior than their demographics or stated intentions. For this reason, several sites and networks use algorithm-based targeting techniques, such as click-stream analysis, psychographic profiling, neural networks, vector analysis, and collaborative filtering, to track and predict what ad message a given user is most likely to respond to. Leading technology vendors include Engage Technologies, Aptex, Andromedia, and Net Perceptions.

Keyword: Search the keyword "airfare" on any major portal like Yahoo!, Alta Vista, and Excite and you are guaranteed to get an ad for a travel service. Costs for keywords can range in the million-dollar zone for portals such as AOL, to pennies per search at sites such as GoTo.com, which displays to users the price paid by the advertiser. Marketers must experiment with different phrases on various search engines and carefully track which keywords produce the best results on which engines.

Cross Sell/Competitive: Imagine Macy's salespeople handing out 20 percent discounts to customers waiting in line at Nordstrom's cash registers, or Land's End being able to call a consumer just as he or she is browsing an LL Bean catalog. Impossible in traditional marketing, but it's happening online. Services such as Alexa Internet and NetZero have developed techniques for showing ads to consumers outside the standard Web browser frame that enable them to, for example, show an ad for Barnes & Noble while a surfer is on Amazon.com's site.

Retention/Remarketing: These tools direct multiple ad exposures to an individual online. For example, the Web ad network DoubleClick pioneered a way to target Web ads to surfers who have already visited a marketer's site. The service, called Boomerang, relied on "cookie" files (a basic feature of most browsers) to tag visitors as they arrived at the marketer's site. The service then "followed" the customers after they left for other sites and showed them ads that might bring them back to buy. Then the ad engine automatically served the same ad to the same individuals when they visited any of the hundreds of other sites in DoubleClick's network.

Shopping History: Online ad serving networks often have the capability to combine consumers' offline shopping histories with online banner targeting, though early attempts to exploit this information have drawn legal challenges from privacy advocates. The marketing potential of matching offline and online consumer behavior remains to be realized at this writing.

Online incentives and promotions

Green stamps, coupons, and airline miles are examples of incentive marketing programs or so-called "loyalty currencies" in traditional direct and retail marketing. Various vendors have spun incentive marketing in creative new ways to use the Web and e-mail to lift customer acquisition rates, improve brand loyalty, and aid the capture of data for market research.

Loyalty programs from companies such as Cool Savings, Cybergold, MyPoints, and Netcentives offer consumers redeemable prize points, instant discounts, and actual cash rewards for filling out demographic forms, reacting to promotional messages or making online purchases. Points from systems such as these are redeemable for airline miles, CDs, gifts, telephone credit, and other enticements. Retailers such as Long's Drugs have experimented with online coupons with the help of SmartSource.com's U-pons program. The shopping portal GiftCertificates.com will tailor incentive programs for a business-to-business clientele. Meanwhile, companies such as WebStakes, ePrize, and NewCanoe specialize in creating sweepstakes, contests, and special promotions to drive traffic for online marketers.

Affiliate networks

Affiliate networks enable marketers to cover thousands of niche market segments through networks of Internet business partners. Amazon.com pioneered the model of affiliate network channels on the Web. At this point, Amazon.com has more than 450,000 partner sites signed up to generate sales leads for a commission rate that averages 15 percent.

Hundreds of merchants have followed Amazon's lead and introduced affiliate networks of their own. Because reseller sites are compensated strictly on a performance basis, the affiliate model can be an extremely cost-effective marketing strategy for generating traffic and reasonably qualified leads, helping extend market coverage, and—more to the point—resulting in actual sales. Affiliate network services such as, Be-Free and LinkShare provide sales lead tracking, payment management, and even relationship brokering for merchants and resellers. (For more on the value of affliate networks in branding, see Chapter 3.)

E-mail direct marketing

Permission-based e-mail direct marketing has matured into a viable direct marketing program. After learning that customer tolerance for unsolicited commercial e-mail (a.k.a., spam) is extremely low relative to print direct mail, most large, well-branded companies are investing in building "double-opt-in" lists and permission-based e-mail marketing programs. This was after discovering that permission-based e-mail marketing performs significantly better than direct mail in driving customer responses and building customer relationships. It is important, however, to distinguish among the different types of e-mail marketing, not all of which produce equal results. There are eight primary models of e-mail marketing, which fall into two business objectives: customer retention and customer acquisition.

For customer retention/up-sell

Customer Relationship E-Mail: The most widely practiced model of permission e-mail marketing invites existing customers and new prospects to submit their e-mail addresses in order to receive occasional announcements and promotional offers. While this sounds straightforward, successful strategies take into consideration all known variables that affect response rates, including type and quality of offer, frequency, message formatting, subject lines, copyrighting, and (in the case of richer Web media) the size of electronic files.

Companies generally see the highest rate of response from in-house lists they've built with the active consent of their existing customers and prospects. This is permission marketing at its most effective. When highly personalized to individual customers' needs and desires, response rates that exceed 20 percent are not uncommon. Sending messages to an in-house e-mail list is also more cost-effective than using a third-party, purchased list. Maintaining high levels of response over time can be managed by controlling the frequency or volume of messages to avoid saturating consumers. Leading e-mail marketing software and service vendors include Digital Impact, Media Synergy, Exactis, Message-Media, and Post Communications.

Online Corporate Newsletters: Similar to customer relationship e-mail, corporate e-mail newsletters are sent to recipients who have opted to receive regularly scheduled editorial updates of niche news, advice, training, company announcements, and other information, punctuated with marketing offers. Pampers.com, for example, offers a weekly advice column for new parents; the advice changes as the customer's child presumably grows in maturity, from newborn diapers to toddler pull-ups. Online newsletters are also used for business-to-business communications: the caveat here is that business subscribers expect high levels of information value and unique content. Software and service vendors include the same as above for customer relationship e-mail, as well as L-Soft and Lyris.

Reminder Services/Scheduled Alerts: Reminder services are calendar triggers that consumers and business clients can sign up for. For example, e-commerce sites usually offer gift reminder services for anniversaries and birthdays. A variation, the replenishment service, sends an e-mail prompt to a printer customer, for example, giving notice that the printer cartridge purchased six months earlier is likely to need replacing soon. Vendors include high-end e-mail marketers mentioned above as well as Post Communications and Life-Minders.

For new customer acquisition/prospecting

Permission List E-Mail Marketing: Businesses seeking to target a large number of new prospects can pay to access the subscribers of permission list managers. Such third-party services take permission marketing to the next level by asking consumers to choose what kinds of offers they want to see. Consumers are typically lured by a contest to provide details of their shopping interests in exchange for highly screened offers, often featuring special discounts or loyalty currencies (like frequent flier points). A manufacturer of golf equipment, for example, could use this kind of e-mail list service to pitch discounted golf clubs to people who identified themselves as golfers.

List managers do not release e-mail addresses to the marketers; rather, the marketer supplies the message content to the list manager, who relays it to subscribers who have indicated an interest in golf, a percentage of whom may click through to the advertiser's site directly. On the downside, the quality of leads depends upon the reliability of the vendor, the strength of its permission policies, and the veracity of its customers: caveat emptor. Leading infomediary services include MyPoints and YesMail.

Sponsored Editorial Newsletters: These are independently published newsletters and discussion forums that help marketers target niche interest groups and communities. Though online, they have a similar feel to printed special-interest publications, and many accept advertising sponsorship. Thousands of specialized e-mail newsletters exist devoted to such wide-ranging topics as Internet marketing, dog grooming, car mechanics, and more. While most have small circulations, others have over a million subscribers. This low-tech, low-cost approach can be especially effective in business-to-business sellings. Media buying services that can place ads with e-mail newsletters include Lot21, Modem.Poppe, Penn Media, Flycast, and NewCanoe.

Sponsored Discussion Lists: E-mail remains a widely used medium for open discussion forums, where members of a shared list send messages that are duplicated to the entire subscriber base devoted to a common theme, such as Java programming, scuba diving, or photography. Over 90,000 such lists have been catalogued: one example worth exploring is the ClickZ Forum, an ad-supported discussion group made up of e-mail marketing executives. An increasing number of nonprofit e-mail communities accept advertising sponsorship. Enabling services include Topica (incorporating Liszt) eGroups, eCircles, and OneList.

Advocacy (Viral) Marketing: "Viral marketing" is a referral-based e-mail marketing technique where customers spread the marketing promotion of a company among themselves— that is, like a virus. More often known these days as advocacy marketing, it is generally seen as a positive and highly efficient grassroots marketing technique by both consumers and marketers. Much like the popular MCI "Friends and Family" campaign, a company enlists customers as implicit or explicit advocates, encouraging them to endorse its products and services to friends and associates.

The classic early example of the power of this model comes from Hotmail, which used viral marketing to build a foundation of more than 40 million registered users. Many other companies, such as Procter & Gamble, have found that offering a benefit, such as a personalized greeting, coupon, or contest entry, to both senders and receivers increases the pass-along rate. A Mother's Day campaign for Scope mouthwash, for example, allowed participants to send an animated "kiss" to loved ones. Advocacy marketing tends to be a grassroots effort; one specialist vendor is NewCanoe.

Partner Co-Marketing: In the world of traditional direct marketing, it is common for companies to rent or sell access to their customers' names and addresses to other businesses. In the world of e-marketing, however, a company merely acquiring a list of e-mail addresses from another runs a risk of permission problems and acquiring a reputation for spam. Permission-savvy marketers now use a compromise position in which one company sends a message to its own list on behalf of a partner.

For example, Land's End might send a message like this: "Dear Land's End Customer, to thank you for your loyalty we would like to let you know about a special offer from our corporate partner, Sharper Image." Again, the third party does not release the list to the marketer, but relays the message under its own brand. Digital Impact has offered a service, E-Mail Exchange, aimed at cross-promoting customer lists among its corporate clients, within a permission framework.

Online customer buying behavior analysis

Understanding online customer buying behavior provides organizations with valuable customer market research to build better e-business strategies. Various new online customer-buying-behavior analysis tools and services enable marketers to better understand how their customers buy currently and forecast how they will buy in the future. Enterprise marketing automation (EMA) tools enable marketers to analyze both online and offline marketing data in an effort to design and deliver better marketing campaigns. The key tools and strategies of online customer buying behavior analysis include the following.

Audience segmentation
Web site analysis tools enable marketers to analyze and segment their Web site visitors according to behavioral clusters, such as "tire kickers," "information seekers," "discount seekers," and "core constituents." This helps businesses identify

their most profitable online customer segments by finding the behavioral clues that differentiate a good prospect from a bad one. Marketers can then design products, marketing programs, and content for different segments and track segments against how visitors discovered the site to better target future ad campaigns. They can also correlate behaviors to identify cross-sell opportunities, such as demonstrating a high propensity among backpack buyers to also buy sweaters. The leading vendor in this category is Personify.

Personalization

These tools help marketers personalize services for individual customers by collecting information about them when they visit the company's Web site. "Personalization" includes a range of tools that help marketers create profiles of individual consumers, then deliver targeted marketing offers. Many such tools rely on sophisticated data algorithms such as collaborative filters, vector analysis, and neural networks to recognize patterns in observed behavior to predict future customer actions. These tools can also predict what ad message or promotional offer will lead to the best response. Leading personalization vendors include Art Technologies Group, BroadVision, Net Perceptions, and Vignette.

Profiling

Profiling services look beyond a single Web site to gives marketers a more complete picture of online customer behavior by analyzing the behavior of customers across many Web sites. A few large service providers, such as Engage Technologies, Cogit, and DoubleClick, collect and aggregate customer buying behavior data with large networks of sites. These services have tracked Web users with anonymous serial numbers across other sites in the network, noting the pages they visit and other actions. This way, members of the service can know that a new visitor, while anonymous, has demonstrated an interest in, for example, golf, home mortgages, and chemical engineering, and their individual sites can use this extra information to personalize content or target messages.

Enterprise marketing automation

For years, direct marketing solutions and service providers (service bureaus) have assisted marketers in the design, execution, and analysis of traditional direct-mail and telemarketing programs. These services enabled marketers to conduct targeted offline marketing campaigns (direct mail, telemarketing, print ads, and even public relations) with cycle times that often exceeded 90 days. The recent new generation of direct marketing software—known as enterprise marketing automation (EMA)—is designed to help marketers automate the process of designing, executing, and analyzing sophisticated direct marketing campaigns. The value of EMA is to speed the campaign cycles, so marketers can learn more about customers and react to changes in customer buying behavior faster. These solutions help marketing organizations deliver a combination of both online (Internet and e-mail) and offline direct marketing campaigns.

Leading marketing automation vendors include, but are not limited to, Annuncio, Market First, E.piphany, and Prime Response. Significant spending will go to marketing automation tools that are combined with Web personalization platforms (e.g., Net Perceptions, Vignette) that analyze, package, and report Web information.

Campaign management and reporting

Nielson/NetRatings and Jupiter/Media Metrix are the leaders in ranking top media sites and analyzing general Internet user behavior based upon large panels of Web users (upwards of 70,000 panel members each) who have agreed to install software that tracks everywhere they go on the Internet. One may consider them the Web equivalent of TV's Nielson families. NetValue, a European-based company, has taken a similar technological approach, although it lets businesses create their own panel of users to gain intelligence on preferences and online behavior for product and promotion research.

Site audience research/Web audience ratings

Simpler forms of data analysis are still useful when fine-tuning Web sites, such as usability studies to detect flaws in navigation or transaction functions, or competitive surveys of ranking, hits, repeat visitors, or length of page view or sessions. E-business customer intelligence runs the gamut from immediately deployable online audience satisfaction surveys available through E-Satisfy.com, to complex demand modeling and custom data mining research offered by firms such as Eucid. Other third-party software and solutions to measure Web performance include online survey service companies (e.g., Harris Black Interactive, Greenfield Online) and site audience analysis (e.g. Macromedia Aria, Accrue).

CHAPTER 5

Managing Multiple Sales and Marketing Channels:

Blending Channels for Growth and Profitability

MULTICHANNEL SELLING—selling through a combination of field sales, retail, business partners, direct marketing, call center, and electronic selling channels—is already common in the high-technology, retail, and financial services industries. It is fast becoming a fact of life in mainstream businesses.

Any business that expects to grow profitably and to effectively cover their markets will have to master the art of selling through a coordinated mix of multiple channels. This is because when sales and marketing resources work well together, the result is usually lower selling costs, happier customers, and more reliable results. When channels are not managed properly, sales opportunities tend to slip through the cracks, and sales and marketing costs get out of control.

To make many different online and offline selling channels work in a unified way, sales and marketing managers will need a new game plan for planning, measuring, and coordinating their sales and marketing resources. They must become like a "soccer coach" to place each player in the right position on the field, explain the rules, draw up the plays, and keep the score.

Covad Communications is one example of a company that reached out for greater control to improve its selling performance, as it coordinated the efforts of hundreds of selling partners with call centers and online marketing programs.

Covad Communications: Getting Selling Channels to Work Together

Covad Communications Group (Covad) sells high-speed Internet and data services over standard copper phone lines. Over 90 percent of Covad's business comes from the small and medium-sized business market.

Covad sells these services through a multichannel selling system that is made up of a combination of third-party business partners—Internet Service Providers (ISPs) and a smaller key account sales force. They also use the Internet and call center channels to generate demand and support business partners. Though in a difficult market, it has enjoyed 4-digit growth and the number-one market share. With more than 300,000 subscribers, it is one of the top ten broadband suppliers in America, competing head to head with "Baby Bell" spinoffs such as SBC Communications and Verizon. To grow market share quickly in the new and highly competitive Digital Subscriber Lines (DSL) market, Covad knew it had to get its combination of resellers, field salespeople, call centers, and Internet channels to work together.

At first things did not run very smoothly. For example, to acquire new customers Covad invested heavily in "pull" marketing and advertising programs to generate leads for its call centers to qualify and its business partners to close. These included print, online, and radio ads convincing homeowners to switch over to DSL from regular phone access to the Internet. While these campaigns were successful in pulling in between 200 and 500 leads per day to the call center, it was discovered that most of the ISP business partners were not following up these leads, because they felt the leads were of poor quality or "not ready to close."

Covad had to start getting these different sales and marketing resources playing like a team. To get online leads quickly into the hands of the regional partner best positioned to make a sale, it added an automated customer tool and an online reseller locator to the Web site. To improve the process of qualifying leads and following up on them quickly, it invested in a "lead flow management system" by Marketsoft. The software was linked to a centralized call center and an interactive Web site that gave potential customers a choice of interaction points—and streamlined the passing along of relevant information to business partners. These technology tools made it easier for the call center and Web channels to coordinate their efforts with the resellers (ISPs).

The software also allowed Covad to measure the performance of each ISP in following up leads. Though its partners were widespread geographically, Covad was able to regain control of the early part of the selling process. They established new rules and goals for the resellers regarding response time, location, vertical market specialization, and other key management criteria. An immediate result of this new scorecard was that Covad's ISP business partners were following up on three-quarters of the leads sent to them and converting a higher percentage of these leads into new sales than before.

And when many ISPs went bankrupt in the millennial dot-com bust, Covad's ability to monitor and measure the effectiveness its ISP business partners helped it survive as rival independents such as Northpoint Communications failed. And it was able to use its Web-enabled call center to sell DSL directly to consumers while revamping its business-partner strategy.

Why Managing Multiple Sales and Marketing Channels Is Important

The Covad example shows why the number of sales and marketing channels you have is less important than how well they all can work together. Managing channels is important because customers and cost pressures will force organizations to sell through more channels in the future.

Defining Channels

"Channels," simply put, are the different ways companies reach customers. Channels are the human salespeople, distributors, newspapers, the Internet, or even ATM cash machines—that allow organizations to reach, sell to, and service their customers. Broadly defined, channels can include anything that can interact with a customer and conduct business.

Channels come in many different types and roles. For instance, the role of a sales channel is to generate revenues while a marketing channel is responsible for generating leads and awareness. Service channels are meant to deliver technical support, field service, or customer service.

It is important to remember that channels are "resources" that cost money and must get results. A "sales channel" has a discreet revenue objective and set of costs associated with it. For example, a tele-sales channel might expect to get 20 dollars of sales for every 3 dollars of cost.

It is also useful to think of channels as "pipes" that carry products or handle phone calls because they have limited capacity and can reach only so far. This is particularly relevant to, say, a call center where an agent only has the capacity to complete 30 to 40 calls a day maximum or a sales rep who can only spend 240 days on the road a year.

Over the last several years sellers have found it increasingly difficult to achieve rapid growth cost-effectively using tried-and-true selling approaches. For example, it is not as profitable to sell personal computers in an "in-the-flesh" sales meeting as it once was. Having a cup of coffee with a field sales person can cost up to $400 when you factor in all the costs it takes to put that sales rep in the field. If the coffee talk yields the sale of a desktop personal computer, the cost of the cup of coffee can be many times more than the gross margins made on the computer itself.

Lower cost-selling channel alternatives—such as Internet and telephone—have proven to be a more profitable and (in most cases) more convenient for selling these products. For example, a similar conversation with a productive and automated call center rep could cost as little as $35 to the seller. This means if the selling organization can "migrate" that PC transaction to a tele-channel or Web channel, they have a better chance of showing a profit. If customer questions can be answered online instead of on the phone, more money is saved and the call center agent is free to answer another call. Further, if customer questions can be routed to a Web site and answered by e-mail, instead of on the phone, more money is saved and the call center agent is free to spend more time on sales calls. (A more detailed examination of the economics of migration transactions to low-cost channels and integrating channels for better cooperation are outlined in greater detail in the Special Section: Paying for Change—The Economics of Multichannel Selling at the end of this chapter).

Customers are applying pressure as well. They are becoming increasingly "schizophrenic," demanding the convenience of buying through multiple channels, and the choice to freely migrate between channels during different phases of the selling process. One Boston Consulting Group/Harris Interactive study found that 50 percent of online purchases were checked out first in a retail store. Hewlett Packard found out that 15 percent of their prospects preferred to buy online while 85 percent wanted help from a local business partner.

These cost and customer pressures are forcing larger enterprises to combine these call center and electronic channels with traditional field sales, retail, and distribution partners into multichannel selling systems. In the year 2000 most organizations were selling through about 3 channels (an average of 2.75 per company) according to a survey by IMT Strategies of 50 Global 2000 organizations. The study went on to show that at that time, traditional channels remained by far the largest portion of the revenue stream, with electronic channels representing less than 5 percent.

This will probably change. The chart below compares the difference in channel growth rates that the 50 Global 2000 companies are experiencing. The greatest expansion of effort centers on

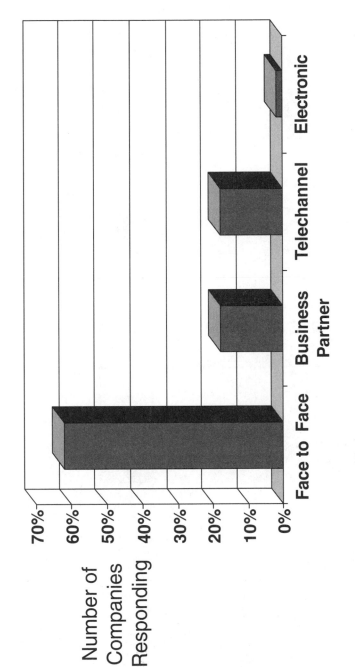

Figure 5.1.   Overall revenue mix of selling channels.

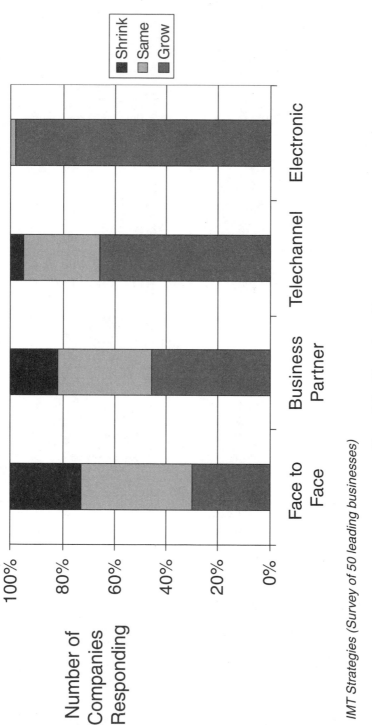

IMT Strategies (Survey of 50 leading businesses)

Figure 5.2.   Channel transition.

retooling telephone (tele-rep) call center operations and electronic commerce. This should not be surprising, as these can support both direct selling and indirect selling (for example business partner networks or Web affiliate networks). In many cases, in industries such as personal insurance and wireless communications, expensive face-to-face and partner selling channels are being downsized, (or, more appropriately, "right-sized") as marketers shift resources to align the value these can deliver with their higher selling cost.

A recent Boston Consulting Group (BCG) study shows that 62 percent of online retail volume is now generated by multichannel merchants. This means the lion's share of the online sales are being made by brick-and-mortar retailers and catalogers who sell through the Web as an additional channel. BCG estimates, moreover, that these multichannel retailers will account for 85 percent of all online revenue in five years.

Short-Term Strategy: Finding Ways to Make Many Channels Work Together to Improve Overall Sales Performance

Managing many sales and marketing channels is a lot like coaching a soccer team. Coordination and teamwork require a well-trained set of disciplined professionals, passing the ball to the player in the best position to score.

Compaq Computer is working hard to build a "multichannel sales and marketing system" that outperforms its competition. Compaq's goal is to find ways to make the many different channels they use—including high-cost face-to-face reps, over 30,000 indirect partner channels, and low-cost tele and electronic channels—work together for maximum business impact. One of their more successful pilot programs demonstrates how effective this strategy can be when it works well. Compaq consolidates leads generated from a variety of marketing programs in a special call center responsible for lead qualification. This provides Compaq the ability to control, manage, and measure the performance of these marketing campaigns and optimize the distribution of these leads. At this call center, representatives use a CRM software application to access customer data necessary to qualify the inbound leads. The best leads are enhanced with useful customer information and customized promotions to make it easier for business partners to make the sale. Once a lead is qualified by the call center, it is passed to the right business partner using an electronic channel, dubbed the Compaq Partner Network, for follow-up. When the pilot project was reviewed, it was found that leads that went through this "hybrid" process had a 50 percent close rate with average transaction sizes increasing to $45,000. This initiative generated over $230 million in new business for Compaq.

Think like a soccer coach: come up with a new game plan

If multichannel selling is like soccer, then world-class selling organizations will have teamwork that resembles a World Cup Soccer team. In reality, when organizations first try to combine many different selling approaches, the efforts look more like a bunch of screaming and enthusiastic six-year-olds chasing the ball around the playground in a cloud of dust. Everyone is trying to kick the same ball.

In sales this behavior is a little less fun. It translates into conflict between selling channels, lost sales leads that fall through the cracks, and gaps in market coverage where potential customers are not serviced.

Executives challenged with managing more than two selling channels first need to shift their focus, from building channels—whether that means opening new stores or adding an e-commerce Web site—to integrating channels. When they do shift focus, they generally find that the existing structures, policies, and goal measurements in most selling businesses do not support cooperative efforts across channel lines.

Any business that starts to sell through many channels can expect certain problems will arise:

1. Salespeople in different channels will compete for the same business;
2. Leads might not be efficiently distributed and followed up on;

3. Customers may complain about inconsistent service across channels;

4. And productivity improvements might not be realized because of poor channel coordination.

Addressing these critical issues is different and harder than simply building and automating channels. For example, Hewlett-Packard's (see case study, this chapter) early attempts to integrate third-party sellers with Web marketing are a good illustration of how one company managed to defuse competitive conflicts, fine-tune sales and service issues, and move ahead on its sales performance goals.

Most organizations have little experience with integrating "new technology" channels, simply because such multichannel systems have not been around very long. The best—organizations like Fidelity, Schwab, Dell, and IBM—have been at it only five to six years at the most, and they are only starting to get it right.

To be successful, managers have to begin by taking the initiative: defining task roles for specific channels in the selling process, and then dividing the work of selling so that each transaction can be placed in the most efficient, most cost-effective channel. And they must try to define new kinds of boundaries that make sense to staff, to manage and mitigate the conflicts that can arise. Ultimately, senior management must explore new incentive plans that encourage people in different channels to work together.

Managing many channels is a new game. To play this game well requires new rules, new scorecards and new playing fields. In soccer, a good coach begins to organize a team of players by assigning positions (tasks or roles) and responsibilities for covering zones (channel boundaries). The team soon learns to play together. For example, the ball-hogs learn the value of passing the ball (customer) to another player (salesperson in another channel). Coordination of efforts results in goals, and everyone shares in the win.

This is a simple analogy but it underscores the importance of approaching multichannel selling by first making staff understand that they will be learning a new game and that there will be new rules. Coming up with a new game plan involves two things:

1. Laying out the playing field—with a market coverage model that articulates new channel strategies;
2. Defining new rules—channel policies to outline the new rules that encourage cooperation and speed up channel integration.

I. Lay out the playing field with a market coverage model

To make many different sales and marketing channels play well together, organizations need to develop a unified, clear picture of the playing field. This means that everyone on the selling "team" has an understanding of what products are to be sold through which channel to which specific customer segments. In many cases, a "market coverage model" can be an actual picture or graphic rendition that shows who and what goes where.

This sounds as simple and obvious as having the coach stand up at the chalkboard and lay out assignments for his players. In business, drawing this picture is harder because there are many coaches in a typical selling organization. Politically, organizationally, and structurally, most organizations cannot create this picture easily because "market coverage" decisions are made in a variety of independent departments.

Even the most sophisticated organizations have not figured out how to plan across departments very well. The dot-com and direct marketing departments of one highly popular computer hardware manufacturer, for example, are constantly battling over who is a "Web customer" and who is a "direct customer." As a consequence they maintain independent (and overlapping) customer databases and execute their own marketing plans without considering the actions of the other. Yes, this is foolish—and far too common.

A market coverage model will help you determine not only the right mix of channels for today, but how that mix will likely change in the future based on changing customer needs, selling economics, or market shifts.

This sample market coverage model (see Figure 5.3) illustrates the basic relationship between what channels carry what products to which customers. In this model, sales reps are dedicated to the

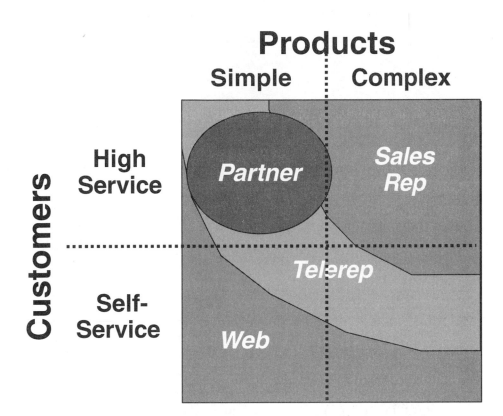

Figure 5.3. The market coverage model.

sale of complicated, high-margin products to high-maintenance customers. Business partners who are able to offer face-to-face support at a lower cost are a logical choice to sell simpler products to those high-maintenance customers who demand handholding on even the simplest purchase. The Internet channel is an excellent choice for fulfilling orders of simple products, particularly when the customers are sophisticated. And tele-reps working in call centers can fill in the coverage "gaps" between channels, based on their ability to sell reasonably complex products and respond quickly to finicky clients.

Consider creating a market coverage model that graphically portrays how a hybrid selling system will help meet growth objectives. This model can also help identify where each channel can create the most value in the company's overall selling approach.

A market coverage model helps define:

How big does each channel need to be?

What roles (lead generation, sales, service) does each channel play?

How will each channel fit in with other channels?

The model can help with designing investment and making an action plan. This information helps answer more important questions of market coverage.

What channels must be built or improved?

What market segments (or customer segments) will each channel cover?

What products will be sold in each channel?

What is interesting about this exercise is that when most companies start to fill out a coverage model, they quickly find out they must rethink the way they segment their markets—that is, the way they divide the work of selling their products.

For example, when IBM laid out a new marketing initiative based on a service plan, the company discovered it did not have enough field salespeople to cover their largest accounts. They decided the solution was to add more Web and telephone reps to effectively service these "named accounts," which can have hundreds of different buyers inside of them.

Organizations need to figure out what channels are best suited to service customers and what service levels they require. For example, Hewlett Packard estimates that most of its small business clients will require high levels of service. As a result, these customers were designated to be serviced by local value-added resellers on a face-to-face basis, where service issues are more easily addressed.

In another example, a custom printing company decided to build an electronic channel to help service their customers. When they laid out a coverage model they realized that most of the products that needed servicing were printed order forms (purchase orders or human resources forms) that were reprinted when clients ran out. So they created a digital catalog of all of the forms and print jobs they had already run for their customers. Then they allowed customers to access their forms online so they could reorder electronically. The digital catalog cost a lot of money to set up, but the coverage model provided management with information that showed the selling efficiencies would justify the retooling.

While developing a market coverage model, companies must start thinking about resegmenting their products by channel, rather than simply by model or price tag. Essentially, this is segmenting based on "product channel readiness" (see Chapter 1). For example, when the Herman Miller office furniture company launched its first Internet channel, it identified specific furniture models, such as computer workstations, that would be attractive to the "small office, home office" (SOHO) market segment. This became the main target customer for its Web site.

Hewlett-Packard: Fitting Business Partner and Web Channels on the Coverage Model

When Hewlett-Packard created its first Web site in the late 1990s to support its regional distributors, it moved cautiously to determine what benefits and pitfalls would occur. On this site, prospective buyers of, for example, printer products, could gather information on HP printers. But in deference to thousands of HP distributors, they could not buy a printer online, at first. Instead, Web site visitors were given contact information and links to the Web sites of third-party business partners (i.e., regional distributors) that were geographically close to the customer. Most distributors posted their product prices on these Web sites, so a prospective buyer could compare prices among the various distributors within his region.

The HP Web site's first week was pure chaos. On a certain printer product, the posted prices might range from $400 to $800, depending on which distributor's Web site was viewed. Customers viewing the sites might immediately see that by driving perhaps

25 miles out of their way, they could get a substantially better price on a printer.

Hewlett-Packard created perfect "price transparency" for its printers—making its distributors' pricing naked for the world to see. And no, HP's distributors were not pleased that customers could enjoy this benefit of transparent pricing information. The distributors were angry because a margin-friendly advantage had been removed. In the past a customer wouldn't know if a store-front down the road was selling the same printer product for $400 less. A customer would have had to drive five hours, or spend an hour on the telephone, to gather all the pricing information now viewed instantly on screen.

Hewlett Packard and its distributors gained valuable experience in online marketing, but it was very painful for the distributors in the short term. Within a few short weeks, posted prices for that printer settled down to a median $450 across all sellers. While buyers gained in market efficiency, some of the distributors lost margins. And some saw their customers migrate to other distributors that were either geographically closer or offered additional services or materials for the same basic price.

One of the most valuable bits of information HP gained was finding that while 15 percent of its customer base shopped online, 85 percent still preferred to buy "in person" through local distributors. To the distributors as a group, the possibility of losing customers through direct selling online was no longer seen as a revenue threat and source of conflict. This opened the door later to direct selling by HP to certain customer segments, and accelerated the adoption of more sophisticated online programs for distributor sales support.

HP now estimates that 15 percent of its customers overall fall into the "buy-now" segment, which includes customers who are more apt to buy over the Web and require little assistance. As a consequence, HP redefined its "Market Coverage Model" and plans to migrate a full one-third of its product line to the Internet channel.

For its business partners, programs now include "HP Select Express," which lets resellers offer clients superior fulfillment by direct shipping orders at short cycle delivery times for a price premium. An extranet initiative called Electronic Solutions Now improves key account integration by allowing resellers to serve large HP clients directly through secure key account Web sites.

2. Defining new rules to encourage cooperation

Rules are needed because making several channel organizations work together is politically, organizationally, and structurally difficult. These rules must address three critical needs: they must establish staff, customer, task, and product boundaries for each specific channel; they must accommodate conflict between channels; and they must be designed to foster coordination across channels.

Boundaries. These rules define what role a particular channel plays in the selling cycle. Are the main tasks to engage customers? Conduct transactions? Fulfill orders? Or provide service and support? The boundary rules a sales and marketing executive will create should also dictate what products and services are the responsibility of which salespeople in each channel, and what customers they are expected to cover, with the implicit understanding that some overlap will occur, and "passing the ball" will be expected.

Conflicts. Because customers will migrate across channels for their own convenience, these rules create the territories, measurements, and incentives that force staff in individual channels to either "stay in their own lane," act as a unified team, or compete intramurally as separate "channel teams." In the latter case, all channel conflict policies need to define an "optimal" level of overlap (or competition) between channels, one that recognizes that a tolerable level of friendly competition between channels may improve overall sales.

Coordination. These rules must provide a clear direction on how specific activities, transactions, or client situations will be handled across channels. Such rules might specify, for example, the amount of time permitted to lapse before passing along leads, or the recommended response time to any customer inquiry. Covad, for example, was able to use technology to enforce rules that would ensure that partners actually followed up on the leads sent them.

Clear rules, and making sure everyone knows the rules, can minimize problems of customer coverage and prevent harmful and embarrassing gaps in customer service.

Channel Conflict Is a Necessary Evil

It is important for managers to remember that some level of channel conflict is not bad—rather it is necessary for efficient selling and airtight market coverage. A sales force without conflict may be happy, but is probably not selling up to its potential and letting lots of leads fall through the cracks. The Roman Emperor Julius Caesar once said, "Let me be surrounded by men who are fat" because he felt fat men were contented and represented little threat to him. Caesar may have been a good emperor, but he would have been a lousy sales manager. Hungry channels are efficient channels. Sales and marketing executives need to be careful not to confuse conflict with chaos. World-class soccer players bump into each other a lot in the game. If they did not make contact some of the time, they were probably not trying to do their job.

Long-Term Imperative: Changing the Scorecard to Measure Goals and Performance

The object of a game is to score points. The object of an efficient sales force is to improve market coverage and increase revenues. Unfortunately, the traditional sales "scorecard" doesn't provide enough incentive for the teamwork that is required to integrate multiple sales channels.

For example, traditional sales quotas (revenue per representative) may not adequately reflect the performance of a sales rep collaborating with several other parts of the selling system. A new compensation system may reward reps for "passing the ball" when appropriate, while performance measurements assure that poor follow-up does not penalize the wrong player. (For more on this, see "Six Ways Organizations Are Changing the Scorecard," below.)

Yes, it is scary to change the scorecard. In practical terms, rewriting an established compensation plan can be a difficult change for a selling organization to make. But once a market coverage plan has been redrawn, and lower-cost selling channels are recognized for their worth, the rationale for changing commissions and other compensations may be easier to put across to the members of the selling team.

Some changes may include:

Modifying sales territories, compensation, and skill (personnel) requirements to recognize the value added to direct sales by other channel partners;

Providing incentives to encourage channel migration and integration ("passing the ball");

Establishing measurements for the value of the various smaller parts of a transaction that occurs during the sales process. This can better identify performance levels and could be trackable through extensions of the sales cycle (i.e., customer lifetime value).

As organizations find advantages to resegmenting both customers and products by channel, old methods of measuring sales activity may fall by the wayside. While it may still make sense to calculate efficiencies in cost-to-sell by simply measuring the weekly, monthly, quarterly, or yearly revenues per sales representative, it is ludicrous to count calls-per-day when a savvy salesperson can fire off 10,000 e-mail pitches in an instant.

The current method of measuring sales by making different sales channels (retail, partner, tele-channel, e-channel) compete with each other also remains flawed. Measuring performance in terms of an outgoing expense/revenue ratio for each channel does not take into account shared benefits (such as enhanced brand awareness caused by a Web channel) and the long-term effects of short-term but expensive investments in infrastructure for a new call center, extranet, or automated customer reponse management.

Six ways organizations are changing the scorecard

1.   Split or Double Compensation: This involves paying two commissions (one for each channel) for a single sale to motivate salespeople in both channels to work together. Typically this involves giving account reps credit for any Internet transactions that occurred in "their" account.

2.   Team Selling: This involves team-based compensation and bonuses for groups of many different channels that support a single account. For example, field account reps and their telesupport teams at large accounts can have a shared bonus pool based on account penetration.

3.   Removing Products From Play: This involves redesigning sales quotas in a way meant to force expensive field sales reps to stop selling the easy stuff that can be sold on the Web or by phone. Instead, compensation might only be given on high-margin, big-ticket sales that require face-to-face selling and sophisticated negotiations. (To ease the pain this causes, try combining this with #5.)

4.   Revenue Attribution: This involves splitting up credit among the many parties involved in the sale using a prearranged formula or ratio. For example, a telemarketing rep who "qualified" a lead and passed it to a regional sales rep would get a percentage of the credit if the field sales rep closed a million-dollar deal.

5.   Migration Incentives: These can be special bonuses paid to a human sales force, often in the form of a one-time bonus award, for convincing their customers to conduct certain types of low-margin business (spare parts, supplies, etc.) online.

6.   Profitability Compensation: In this case, credit is given on transaction profitablity or customer lifetime value. This involves calculating sales quotas over time, on actual account or transaction profitability instead of "booked" revenues.

Bottom Line

It's not how many channels you have, but how well they work together.

Special Section: Paying for Change—The Economics of Multichannel Selling

The economic benefits of making many sales and marketing and service channels work together are compelling. In 1999 a study by the Boston Consulting Group showed that the total marketing costs of "clicks-and-mortar" companies tend to be far lower than dot-coms who lived (or died) by a single sales channel. The study showed that the average e-commerce Web site spent 75 cents on every revenue dollar on marketing. Even the best-performing Internet companies only narrowly approached the marketing efficiency of the average Global 2000 organization. At Amazon (25 percent cost of marketing) and CDNow (35 percent cost of marketing), marketing costs were comparable to the biggest spenders in the United States in the packaged goods or pharmaceutical industries.

By contrast, the BCG study found that "clicks-and-mortar" firms using both online and offline selling channels together averaged a 13 percent cost of marketing. This gap in marketing effectiveness between single channel and multichannel sales and marketing systems is enormous.

To put it in perspective, that means that the average dot-com got $1.25 in revenues for each marketing dollar spent, while their "clicks-and-mortar" competitors were getting closer to $7 for every marketing dollar they invested. Shrinking ticket sizes and increased levels of customer interactions are two of the top reasons this situation exists.

Well-managed multichannel selling systems can create significant competitive advantage by reducing selling costs and increasing channel capacity. Specifically:

> The average company spends between 15–25 cents of every revenue dollar on sales and marketing. These organizations can reduce these sales and marketing costs dramatically without sacrificing revenue growth by getting many different channels to work effectively together.

The number of business transactions and customer conversations necessary to conduct business are growing. Getting many channels to work together allows organizations to handle a greater volume of customer interactions without adding to sales staff or expanding call centers.

Hybrid selling systems share three fundamental economic objectives: channel productivity, channel migration, and channel integration. They apply in varying degrees to different companies. These objectives provide a basis for return-on-investment (ROI) targets and are also the basis for performance measurement.

Channel Productivity

To make specific selling channel resources more productive, managers must automate low-value tasks, while enhancing both the efficiency and effectiveness of each customer interaction.

Tactics to employ in driving channel productivity include:

Automate mundane (i.e., low-value) selling tasks.

Focus selling resources on the best leads and prospects.

Provide more and better customer information to selling resources.

Provide tools that improve effectiveness and responsiveness (e.g., product configurators, marketing encyclopedias, proposal generation templates).

Improve sales performance reporting to management.

Application of these tactics will begin the process of improving ROI for each channel.

There are a number of enabling technologies to help you in this process, including operational Customer Relationship

Management (CRM) packages such as sales force automation, contact management, field service, and call center automation packages. Channel management and measurement tools go by the name of opportunity management, lead tracking, and reporting applications.

As a concrete example, it might cost a company up to $400 to sell a business machine through a fact-to-face sales representative. If through sales force automation tools that representative could become more effective, that transaction would cost the company $350 instead of $400. This savings, when played out over thousands of transactions, can have significant impact on the business.

Figure 5.4, a chart on productivity economics, illustrates the desired evolution in the selling process.

Channel Migration

As we have seen, organizations are currently shifting low value-added tasks (such as order tracking), minor transactions, and certain customer interactions to lower-cost channel resources such as call center and electronic channels.

Since a selling system may conduct millions of sales and service transactions a year, task migration allows a greater percentage of these to be handled at lower cost. Ideally, they may be done on a self-service and fully automated basis. When considering the fully loaded cost of sales (e.g., inclusive of mail, sales support, printing costs), this can make a material difference in overall selling costs.

The tactics to drive channel migration include:

Simplify certain transactions so they can be performed on the phone, Web, or via self-service.

Integrate operational CRM applications and automate work flow to communicate and transfer tasks to lower-cost channels and self-service interfaces.

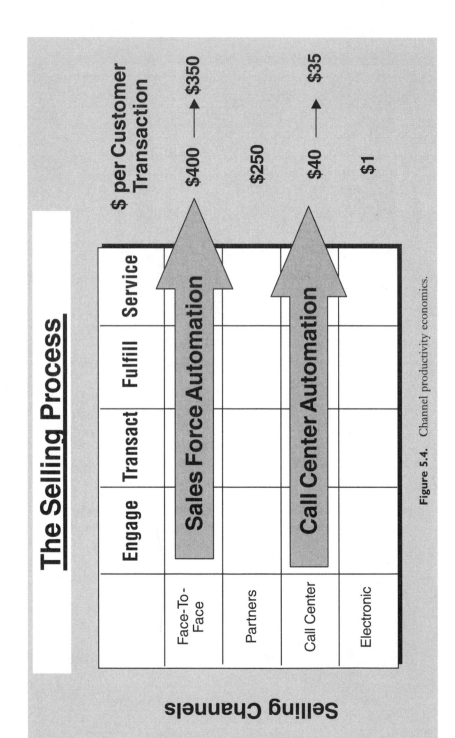

Figure 5.4. Channel productivity economics.

Create a central, shared customer data source that all customer-facing employees can access, including transaction histories, segmentation, buying preferences, and personalized service requirements.

Establish incentives for salespeople to move their customers into low-cost and self-service channels when appropriate.

Enabling technologies in this area include "CRM suites" and point applications that connect and communicate across multiple channels (e.g., sales, call center, field service, support, and electronic channels) and a wide variety of customer interfaces (Web, e-mail, voice, ATM).

Returning to our earlier example, if a company can push down or migrate the sale of a business machine from face-to-face to the call center, then the cost of sales tumbles from $400 (or $350) to $40. In addition, the sales rep is free to make a bigger sale. This more than justifies the investment and effort of improving channel productivity and migration initiatives.

Channel Integration

Getting multiple sales and service channels to work more closely with demand chain partners (retailers, third-party resellers, marketing and promotion partners or independent media) helps reduce overall selling costs, improve speed and quality of service, and maximize market coverage. The objective is to make the sales and marketing mix work together as a single, highly efficient selling system that delivers seamless service, rapid growth, and reduced selling expenses.

The tactics for driving channel integration include:

Use business analytics and reporting tools that can generate more detailed sales performance measurements to

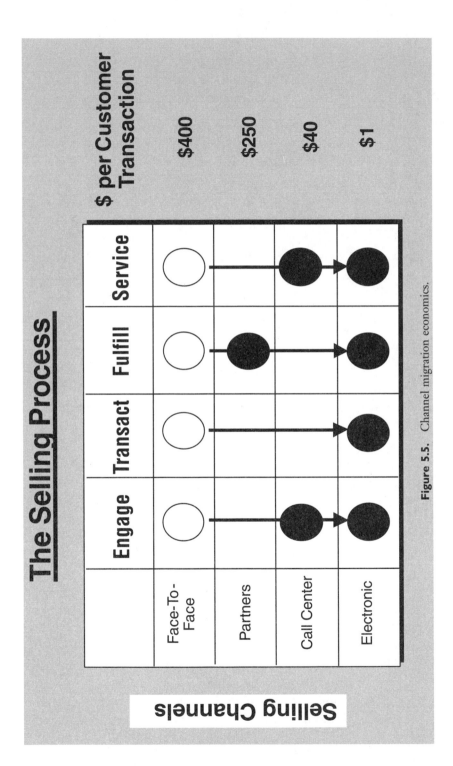

Figure 5.5. Channel migration economics.

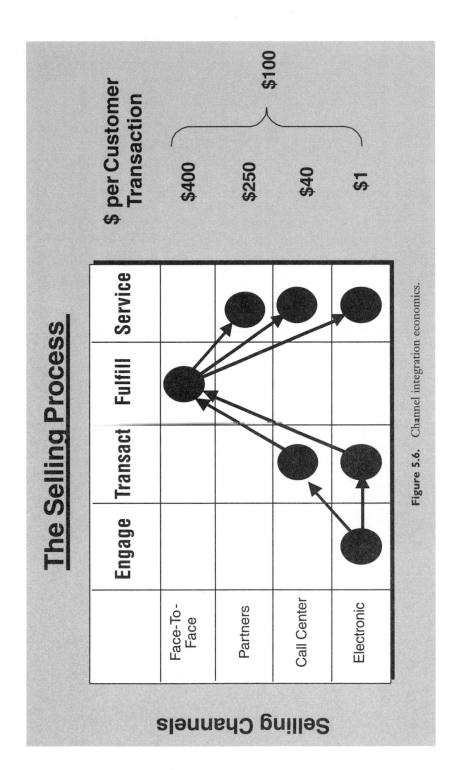

Figure 5.6.   Channel integration economics.

manage sales performance and calculate incentives across channels.

Build or purchase lead flow management systems that automate, track and intelligently route leads based on business logic and dynamic market conditions.

Establish analysis and reporting methods that measure system-wide performance

Use marketing automation systems that integrate campaign development, management, and measurement into the overall selling process.

Enabling technologies in this category include applications for lead flow management, partner relationship management (PRM), and integrated business process performance data marts and measurement systems.

Visiting again the example of a machine sale, if a company can successfully integrate its selling channels, then the "blended" cost of a sale across all channels can be significantly lowered and yield far greater ROI for the entire selling organization.

By having the best channel resource at every step of the selling cycle the average cost of sales can drop to $100 from $150, with an obvious impact. This concept is illustrated in Figure 5.6.

Adding Value to Sales:

Helping Field Sales Forces Take Advantage of Technology

W HEN TECHNOLOGY IS APPLIED TO SALES, THINGS CHANGE FOR SALESPEOPLE. In most cases, instead of being more productive, salespeople find themselves running harder to pay off expensive technology investments, such as sales force automation, and still compete with low-cost Internet channels.

Field sales executives are on the hook to fix this problem. Most have tried different ways to improve the value delivered by salespeople relative to their cost, from hiring people with new skills, to refocusing on more expensive products, to the drastic step of downsizing field sales staff. These are all sound ideas, but alone they are not yielding enough results to pay off expensive investments in selling technologies. For example, most organizations end up disappointed with their sales force automation efforts. Insight Technology (which conducts an annual survey of 122 sales force automation projects) reported that less than one-third of these firms had realized significant improvement by the year 2000.

This chapter will show why promising CRM and e-commerce technologies can cause the field sales channel to go "out of alignment" with cost and performance expectations, and what sales managers can do about it. There are two hidden roadblocks to success. The first roadblock is the need to change sales processes to create better teamwork across selling channels. The second roadblock is even harder: a reluctance to change existing performance measurement and compensation plans (commissions, bonuses, even salaries) so they will support and not undercut the team effort.

These roadblocks are real. They are both scary (changing compensation could make the salespeople really mad) and complicated (the right compensation measurement systems will take management, money, and time to build). But the bottom line is that without new and better measurements, most organizations will not get a return on their investments in selling technologies. Help from other parts of the organization will be required, but sales and marketing executives must take the leadership roles. The following story is a good illustration of why changing processes and compensation will be so critical to success.

Hitting the Roadblocks to Improved Field Sales Performance

Bob Linn is the CFO for a financial services conglomerate. Six months ago his company acquired several insurance, banking, and financial services companies. The Wall Street analysts seemed to think it was a great idea: they were looking for greater share of wallet, maximized customer lifetime value, and cross-sell campaigns. Bob, on the other hand, was looking for antacid.

The way Bob viewed things, his company had bought two piles of stuff. One big pile was "products" and one big pile was "sales channels." The product list was long. It included life insurance, personal insurance, mutual funds, trusts, brokerage services, and financial planning. But his problem was the other pile. The distribution numbers were huge: 10,000 feet-on-the-street in the form of agents, independent distributors, brokers, and financial advisors. Factoring in Web sites, call centers, and branch offices, they had the globe blanketed.

This was not comforting; it was scary. Any way he sliced it, he added up to hundreds of sales compensation plans and different sales specialties. How were they going to get all these salespeople working together as a team without killing each other?

Bob asked Matt, one of his star analysts, to calculate a "cross-selling" model to estimate what would happen when the piles were combined.

"The good news is that if our 10,000 salespeople sold every product we had, the company would grow ten times faster than the rest of the industry," Matt reported later. "The bad news is the compensation math is too hard."

Actually, thought Bob, it would be a nightmare. "All the sales managers out there are still calculating these commissions on spreadsheets or on the back of envelopes." Bob was already routinely "rounding up" commissions by 3 percent to build in a fudge factor in case these managers got their numbers wrong.

"There's something else, too," Matt pointed out. "We spent $50 million on Customer Relationship Management systems in the past two years. When you count that sales force automation system, the equipment, and the new customer database, that comes to roughly $5,000 per sales rep. At our current level of selling profits, we will need somewhere between $50,000 to $100,000 of extra sales from each salesperson to justify these investments."

"Well, it's a goal to shoot for," sighed Bob. "Luckily we do have quite a few high-margin products."

Matt handed over his report. "If we can get our sales agents to sell stuff like those insanely complicated insurance annuities that nobody understands, we can make a lot of money and probably have a shot at paying off that bill. But if they continue to sell too much of the easy stuff, like those mutual funds, we will lose money."

"And more and more customers are buying mutual funds online, and not even seeing a sales agent," Bob groaned. "If we cannot get the salespeople to sell more of the hard stuff, they won't be pulling their weight."

How Technology Is Changing the Role of Field Sales

The experience of Bob Linn is not uncommon. A recent IMT Strategies survey of 50 large organizations that sold through many channels found that field salespeople still brought in more than 60 percent of sales. Keeping these expensive selling resources happy and productive is very important.

But once field sales is combined with less expensive selling channels as part of a "multichannel selling system," it becomes apparent that, relative to low-cost channels such as telemarketing and Internet self-service, a human salesperson may not always deliver enough value to justify his or her expense. When a well-trained and highly paid salesperson sits down to have a cup of coffee with a client, it costs about $300 to $400 in selling costs. If the result of that chat is a $2000 personal computer sale, the profits from the sales will not even pay for the cost of the coffee. But if that transaction was executed online, the profits on that particular sale would be substantial. This means that unless a big deal is being drawn up on a napkin, or a potentially valuable new relationship is being formed, the conversation was not paying off in dollars and cents.

The key to making this technology-enabled selling work is "human and behavioral change." Such "human change" is hard for someone who is used to being a solo superstar, given credit for bringing home the bacon and scoring big numbers. But to fit with new players on the selling team (like Web-enabled call center reps and client-specific Web sites) these stars may find themselves playing a new position, and having to become more of a team player overall.

Playing Chiropractor: Sales Force Realignment Is a Strategic Priority

A modern selling system is a lot like the human spine. This is because most selling approaches today are made up of a lot of parts—Web sites, call centers, third-party business partners, and field salespeople. To get the job done, these parts must work together—and pull their weight—just like the many vertebrae in the human spine.

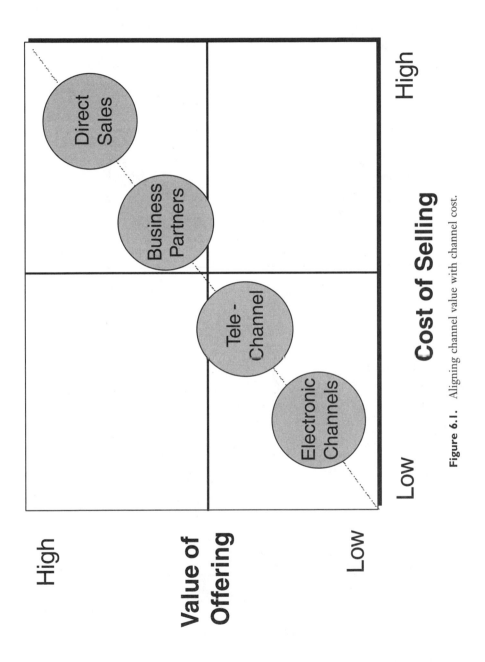

Figure 6.1. Aligning channel value with channel cost.

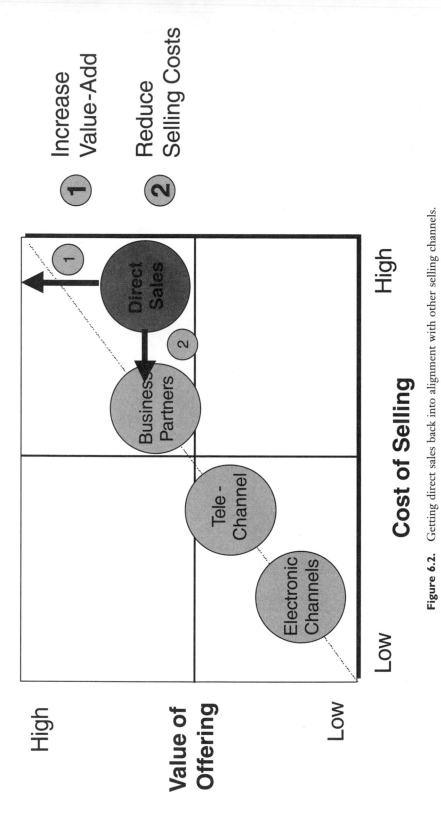

Figure 6.2. Getting direct sales back into alignment with other selling channels.

Like a spine, the load has to be "balanced" across all the parts. Each bone has to carry its share of the weight. But if one vertebrae goes out of alignment, useful activity is diminished. What happens when part of the spine is not in alignment? A lot of pain. It becomes a liability, not an asset to the body.

Field sales tend to fall out of alignment whenever the products they sell and the markets they sell in experience a rapid change. Suddenly, the value of the sale is not equal to the cost of the sale. As an illustration, consider the ubiquitous cell phone. When these portable telephones first appeared on the market, the average monthly service fee was $600 and the average phone sold for $200. Now you can pick up a phone for $50—unless you obtain one for free as part of your service fee. At only dollars per transaction, the selling margin on cellular service can only support the least-expensive selling channels: tele-rep or regional distributor.

An early study by Conning Life Insurance Distribution Strategies showed that customers themselves are often likely to perceive the value of face-to-face (in this case, the independent agent sales channel) as not worth the cost. In 1985 over half of customers surveyed felt an insurance agent added more value than cost (versus 25 percent who felt the cost of this channel was already too high). By 1998, a full half of respondents thought the agent channel did not add enough value to justify the cost.

In the short term, sales and marketing executives must give their field sales staff the technology tools to do their work faster and more efficiently. At the same time, they must begin to look at ways that take certain selling tasks off the salesperson's desks— or certain customer interactions or certain product lines—out of the salesperson's bag, so they can be given over to more efficient, lower-cost channels. The finality of a surgeon's knife may not be required: just perhaps the forceful readjustment a chiropractor deploys—a thoughtful manipulation of the individual vertebrae to help realign the spine.

By matching the right transaction with the right channel at the right time, organizations can realize selling productivity gains. That low value-added customer service inquiry is more efficiently delivered through a tele-channel (at $40) or a self-service Web site (at $1) than a field sales rep (at $400).

Selling channels that work together can sell more at lower costs. Fidelity Investments is one example of a selling business that appears to offer its customers the choice of a handshake at a branch office, the soothing voice of a tele-rep, or a middle-of-the-night, self-service Web transaction. What it is really doing is managing different kinds of client interactions over multiple interaction points. Every time it makes it easier for customers to do their less-important transactions through the least-expensive channels, Fidelity can manage a lower overall selling cost than traditional service companies, where human salespeople carry the burden of service and support, in addition to sales, for their Rolodex of customers.

Short-Term Strategy: Nine Sales Value Adjustments to Fix the Problem

There are nine basic "adjustments" sales executives can make to get the sales force back in alignment. Most of these are not new: selling organizations have been experimenting along these lines for the last decade. Though names and flavors may vary, they probably cover many of the sales performance improvement programs and initiatives currently underway in your organization.

Adjustment I: Improve Selling Processes

"Re-engineering" the selling process has great potential when the process is examined as thoroughly as a factory assembly line. Efforts to measure sales utilization ("face-time" analyses) typically will show that sales representatives spend less than half their time interacting personally with clients. The rest of their time is eaten up by account administration or lesser value-added tasks, for example, telephone follow-ups to see if a delivery deadline was met.

Re-engineering helps streamline the steps that make up the selling process and can redefine the role of the salesperson in a way that makes sense in the light of technology investments. Inadequate sales and marketing process change was highlighted as the top business risk factor determining the success or failure of CRM initiatives by project managers running best-in-class CRM programs, according to an IMT Strategies survey.

Productivity measurements will need to be taken before and after task migration to make sure the behavioral changes are positive to the bottom line. For example, if a redesigned sales process generates 10 percent more free time for a sales rep, how then can sales executives ensure that time is not spent on the golf course?

Adjustment II: Channel Migration and Integration

The development and maturation of hybrid selling systems continues apace. A recent IMT Strategies survey demonstrated that the average selling organization uses close to three selling channels; two-thirds of respondents had already automated both their field sales and tele-centers with automated Customer Relationship Management (CRM) solutions. One-fourth planned to add an Internet channel by the end of 2001. IBM (see the case study in Chapter 8) was able to migrate 72 percent of its millions of customer interactions away from field sales staff to tele-coverage reps in a call center. This freed up the field staff to acquire new accounts or penetrate deeper into existing ones, and is just one good example of how integration of Internet channels can improve field sales.

To be successful, these projects will require the input of field sales representatives to identify which transactions can be automated or migrated without hurting the chances for a new sale. A qualitative measurement of transaction economics, (e.g., knowing the cost and profit margin of particular transactions) needs to be established to identify and separate low-value versus high-value transactions. Clear rules will be required to enforce the distinction of tasks into channels. Split commissions or shared bonuses may be considered if the field force balks at "lost" sales.

Adjustment III: Add Sales Force Automation

Operational CRM solutions reduce the time field reps spend on low value-added tasks and help them better manage their sales pipeline. In the last decade, most selling organizations have put laptop computers into the hands of their sales forces, with varying results. Giving salespeople instant Internet access to customer sales data, inventory, and delivery schedules works best when field staff are provided incentives as well as training.

Most sales force automation programs are still struggling to reach 100 percent adoption rates with salespeople and achieve uniform entry of the most basic account data for pipeline and opportunity management reporting. The IMT Strategies survey showed that 72 percent of sales organizations will automate their field sales channel by 2001 with an operational CRM solution. Getting results from these initiatives has proven more difficult. Insight Technology, which conducts an annual survey of 122 sales force automation projects, reports that less than one-third of these firms have realized significant improvement to date.

One danger is programs that cannot generate reliable information people will trust for their compensation and performance reviews. Generally, it will be several years before these software applications mature to deliver robust reports of sales productivity, transaction economics, or incentive compensation.

Adjustment IV: Right-Sizing Sales

Reallocating resources and capacity to the most efficient channel can reduce selling costs. "Inside" telemarketing, business partners and Web channels carry more weight in this model. As a result, many sales organizations are demanding premium strategic selling skills in their field sales force, and are actively pruning "order takers" from their sales department payroll. Some industries, such as financial services and small electronics, are phasing field sales out of the selling process altogether. One recent IMT Strategies study of Global 2000 companies found that 22 percent had plans in place to downsize their field sales channel, and another 43 percent planned to keep investment in field sales flat while putting more money into other channels.

For sales management, this is where the real pain lies. Outside of the 10 percent of the sales force who are acknowledged stars, it can be difficult to decide where and how much to cut. Establishing downsizing priorities and fairly managing the process requires a clear understanding of total selling costs, rep productivity, and account profitability.

Adjustment V: Improve Performance Measurement

It is necessary to adjust incentives as well as performance measurement to get meaningful changes in sales rep behavior. Many executives fear this path because changing sales goals and incentive plans is difficult, risky, and not currently viewed as strategic by upper management. Compensation schemes that "share the wealth" are still the exception and not the norm.

In the IMT Strategies survey, improving sales performance measurements and incentives are ranked as the lowest priorities in the eyes of CRM program managers. Further, when asked to rank the importance of 22 business priorities for their large CRM investment, the business issues that ranked as least important to these organizations were improved incentive structure (#22), developing customer-based incentive systems (#21), and developing new sales coverage models (#20).

Significant economies may not be discovered simply because the information to run these programs is in itself expensive to collect accurately. Technology will not be of much help in the near term. Insight Technology reports that 44 percent of sales organizations feel the forecasts generated by their sales force automation programs are often inaccurate.

Adjustment VI: Deploy Value-Added Tools

Tools that enhance self-service by customers, such as product configurators and knowledge bases, also increase the efficiency of salespeople. The example of building customized Web sites (sometimes known as key account extranets) specifically for larger clients makes it easier to manage account coverage and service. A recent Mercer Management survey of sales representatives reported that Web sites saved about three percent of their work time. The task most often migrated to the extranet was conveying basic product information, which might be anything from complicated technical specifications to availability and delivery schedules. Sales reps also reported the time saved was most likely reinvested into deeper account penetration or product training.

Adjustment VII: Hire for Top Skills

Educating salespeople in strategic selling, account development, and how to best leverage available sales technology is a priority, although most sales managers can only expect that one to three percent of staff time can be dedicated to formal sales training. Hiring strategic sellers can be expensive; motivating employees to uniformly adopt automated selling aids continues to be a challenge.

Sales managers can only expect to have field sales reps spend between 1 percent and 3 percent of their time in formal sales training. Much of this structured time is eaten up learning systems such as sales force automation. Increasing sales training beyond these levels may be strategic, but demonstrating and justifying the return on this increased investment will be difficult to prove to management. Technology has the potential to provide training through distance learning, information distribution by computer, and self-help tools.

Adjustment VIII: Create "Value-Added" Products

Introducing higher-value products requires more sales interaction but can yield larger commissions. Putting more "thoughtful" and customizable products into the salesperson's bag is a sound strategy. However, new product development is largely out of control of sales management. Further, shortened product life cycles, global outsourcing, and increased levels of information are challenging organizations to create world-beater products faster than ever. More than ever, it has become more difficult to develop products that can sustain competitive advantage and maintain high margins over a longer period of time. Adding service to products to create added value, or packaging existing products into "portfolios" attractive to specific customer groups can be one way to add value to products without altering a single nut or a bolt.

Adjustment IX: Change the Market Coverage Model

Redraw the product and market coverage plan to deliver sales-people to the most important customers and highest-margin products. Developing a master market model is necessary to develop clear roles for each selling channel in a hybrid selling mix. It may be difficult to refocus field sales on the highest value-added tasks without a consensus understanding how partners, tele-reps, and Internet will pick up the slack. (For more on building a new coverage model, see Chapter 5.)

The IMT Strategies survey illustrates that channel strategy and market coverage planning are not yet top management priorities. When asked to rank the importance of 22 business priorities for their large CRM investment, using that information to develop new sales coverage models was ranked third to last (#20).

Getting better results by changing market coverage models may require drastic changes in compensation and incentive plans. For example, sales behavior may have to be changed by taking away named accounts and increasing account quotas to focus more on account penetration goals or changing the mix of products a particular rep can sell to focus them on the highest-margin transactions. These alternatives must be modeled on a fully loaded basis to understand which alterations in incentives will yield the greatest impact on sales productivity, before they are used to frame new compensation schemes.

Taking the lead

It is clear to most experienced sales executives what to do. Most organizations have one or many sales performance improvement programs and initiatives currently underway that generally map to the nine sales value adjustments outlined above, though names and flavors may vary. The question is why doesn't it work well.

The reason most of these solutions don't work very well is that they are usually applied as a Band-Aid, not the full-system chiropractic treatment required to get the whole sales spine in good form. Because of the teamwork and cooperation involved in improved sales performance, sales management cannot go it alone. To achieve the desired results, sales leadership must get the rest of the organization to help. As a first step, sales leadership should get the key sales, channel, marketing, and service constituents in their organizations to agree on three things:

1. What are we doing to improve the performance of field sales?
2. Where do we expect results to come from?
3. What programs and activities are getting results, and which ones are not?

If they take the time to go through this exercise, organizations will generally find:

> They are doing many things that can improve field sales performance, but were not fully aware of all of them;
>
> They don't agree on where and how value will be created;
>
> They are probably not getting great results if they are measuring them at all.

This last answer sheds some light on the key "roadblocks to success." Changing sales processes and sales incentives will prove to be the key dependency between success and failure for most of The Nine Sales Value Adjustments. Without incentive adjustments to create behavioral change, none of these actions are going to effect significant results. And it is not an issue that sales management can successfully tackle alone.

Armed with this information, sales management can make the case that sales performance measurements and processes be treated as a strategic issue. Help from other parts of the organization, most notably those under the watch of the chief financial officer

(CFO) and the chief Information Officer (CIO) is needed in tackling the problem.

Some companies have figured this out. For example, Hewlett Packard views sales performance measurement as a strategic imperative. Carly Fiorina, Hewlett Packard's CEO, initiated action after the company missed third-quarter sales forecasts, despite the launch of a strong new product line (UNIX servers). Ms. Fiorina attributed much of their disappointing results on inadequate sales performance management and poorly aligned compensation systems. Without strategic management of sales performance measurement and incentives, the nine strategies for increasing sales value are not likely to achieve very large results.

Long-Term Imperative: Breaking Down the Roadblocks to Success

The biggest reason "technology-enabled" selling does not get better results is that most selling organizations will not come face-to-face with the roadblocks to success—changing process and compensation. The bottom line is that without new and better measurements your organization will not get a return on its investments in selling technologies. The keys to getting more revenues from salespeople are rewarding complicated teamwork across channels and compensating changes in human behavior. Without measurement and compensation change to back up technology and process innovation, most selling organizations will not come close to getting field sales to reach their full selling potential.

Managing change in a field sales force requires a lot of coordination with other departments, the guts to get over fear of change, and a long-term vision. Pitfalls of the past have included not changing measurements fast enough to keep up with the rapid evolution of selling systems, and not modeling or testing proposed changes first—to make sure the desired behavior can be produced in the field staff, and the results justify the pain of changing.

To break down these "roadblocks" and achieve the desired results, sales leadership must focus on four keys:

1. Change how you manage and measure field sales performance;
2. Model and measure for results;
3. Get out of your silo;
4. Look to automation to manage complex compensation plans.

1. Change the Way You Manage and Measure Field Sales Performance

Compensation plans and commission structures must be redesigned to encourage cooperation between the field sales force and the other channels. If a large "name" account wants to use Web channels (such as a dedicated and customized extranet) to place one million dollars in repeat orders, sales management has to place the responsibility and the commission in the proper channels. Solutions might include double-crediting sales back to the original account manager, as a reward for cutting the cost of these future sales. Another option might be to take transaction credit away from the field sales rep covering that account, and instead credit sales to the Web channel only. Another plan might credit everyone in a team-based, split compensation scheme that the Web channel and field rep both respect and trust.

A major impediment to success is a fear of changing sales measures at all. Some executives fear that changing sales measures will put their quarterly revenue numbers at unnecessary risk. Others fear that change will lead to miscalculating commissions in the financial statements. There is also some consternation that any changes in sales measures would anger the top sales performers.

For example, "Assists" may count in basketball and hockey statistics, but salespeople still like homeruns. Teamwork measures are very hard to put in place, but "attributed" revenues are always subject to debate. And very few salespeople are compensated on more evolved "customer-centric" measures. It is hard to find commission plans that heavily factor in customer profitability, lifetime value, or "share of wallet" you read about in books.

Another hurdle to jump involves the increasing complexity of measurement systems that span several channels or different departments. In order to understand selling costs across a mix of channels, sales must be measured by the transaction and ultimately, at the individual customer level. This would need to be done for different channels and in the end will create better models—highly useful models—of true selling costs.

2. Model and Measure for Results

Efforts to align sales cost with value are hamstrung by vague information. To effectively measure field sales, sales managers will need to better understand the true economics of selling. This means they must quantify all of the sales and marketing costs involved in a transaction (not just revenues) to understand true selling economics. To do this, they must build "cost-to-sell" models that track true selling costs and transaction margins. These models will become critical to optimizing selling systems and "tuning" the role of direct sales as part of that system. Selling organizations will benefit from these models with faster and truer dynamic costing. In turn, they will be more competitive in dynamic auctions and trading. Cost-to-sell models will become essential tools to sales executives who are attempting to learn how to better manage selling performance over time by defining better-aligned sales plans, compensation tests, and proof of concept pilots aimed at demonstrating the effectiveness of the nine sales adjustments outlined in the short-term strategy.

These models will factor in "total" selling costs like executive resources required to close; channel and marketing support such as Web sites; volume pricing agreements (VPAs); custom catalogs; ongoing sales support/tele-coverage resources; discounts and "one-offs;" product mix; product margins; and expediting fees need to be factored in. To do this, organizations will have to use the same activity-based costing approaches used to manage production costs for years.

Over time increasingly sophisticated sales measurement systems will start to incorporate customer data into operational measures. In the long term, this will allow selling organizations to shift to performance measures and incentives that are built around each and every individual customer. (See Chapter 11.) Organizations will be able to build compensation schemes that take into consideration customer factors such as share of wallet, customer lifetime value, account profitability, and customer loyalty. Needless to say, such compensation plans will favor salespeople inclined to long-term commitments and strategic selling, and this is turn supports investments in a smaller, but high-quality and turbocharged field sales force.

Using sophisticated models like these to manage field sales will lead to competitive advantage. Building them will be complicated and take a long time. There are five strategic actions that sales managers can take today to jump-start the process of building performance measurement and incentive systems that will be required:

1. Better understand your organization's selling economics by identifying and calculating all of the major costs that occur during a sale or transaction.
2. Build a "cost-to-sell" model that illustrates the impact of any of the nine sales performance adjustments on those selling costs.
3. Work the model to rank the best alternative sales performance adjustments based on business impact and revenue growth.
4. Use the model to define new measurements/incentives; create pilot tests and define business requirements for new measurement software and systems.
5. Figure out how software and systems are going to help make the task of modeling/measuring easier and more reliable over time.

3. Getting Out of Your Organizational Silo

Sales departments cannot change measurement and incentive systems alone. They must get help from other parts of the organization, specifically finance, human resources, and IT.

Selling organizations will benefit from these models with faster and truer dynamic costing. This is reason enough for a CFO or finance executive to become involved in changing measurements and incentives. In the faster-paced business environment created by Internet selling, cost-to-sell models will become essential tools to organizations attempting to manage selling performance over time and on-the-fly, for example in dynamic auctions and trading.

As discussed earlier, migrating tasks means changing job descriptions, adding human bodies in some places, as well as reducing the body count elsewhere. Much of the value of sales will depend on selling teams that combine a variety of sales/marketing resources. For example, a key account team could be made up of an account executive supported by several designated business partners, tele-coverage reps in a call center, and a customized "extranet" interface designed specifically for that account.

Team selling is hardly a new concept: what is new is that there are no "lesser" positions in the team. The ideas of "staff" and "line" can begin to fade. In a hybrid selling system, there is only "line." All the vertebrae count, because there is only one spine. Communicating new cooperative goals will go smoother with the cooperation of human resources departmental support.

The Pressure to Pay for Expensive CRM Technologies

By 2001, the size and scope of customer relationship management initiatives will grow to the extent that the economics of simple sales force productivity will not be sufficient to show a return on investment. CRM systems will increasingly expand across the enterprise (see Chapter 11) with best-in-class organizations anticipating CRM spending in excess of $10 million over the next three years. These ambitious "enterprisewide" CRM initiatives (projects that cross the entire company) will seek to automate the sales, marketing, and service functions; collect vast sums of customer data, and manage customer interactions across several media. The scope of these projects, coupled with the expanded use of low-cost Internet and tele-channels, will force Global 2000 organizations to pursue productivity gains for all sales and marketing resources. At this point, most organizations will hit a wall.

Realizing value from these investments will be complicated, requiring significant management and measurement change. Pressure to realize returns will force selling organizations to take "multichannel" selling approaches that can effectively integrate and manage many selling channels at reduced selling costs and coordinate much more with other parts of the organization. (See Chapter 5, Multichannel Selling Systems). These systems will allow direct sales representatives to migrate low-value-added tasks and transactions to less costly channels. On the whole, organizations can expect to coordinate more effectively with other parts of the organizations, business partners, or cross-functional teams in order to deliver higher levels of service.

4. Look to Automation to Manage Complex Compensation Plans in the Long Run

The folks in the IT department deserve a nod as well. Traditionally, sales departments have not relied on systems to develop, measure, and provide incentive for sales. Most commissions are still calculated manually, or offline on spreadsheets. Modern sales incentive systems will become increasingly complex and the information needed to develop selling cost will be soft and subjective (e.g., people and commissions make up most of direct selling costs). One company administers eight plans for its sales force of 500 reps, and their finance officers are not confident they can accurately calculate commissions within 3 percent. They suspect there may be certain errors that exceed 10 percent.

Current software solutions may need to be linked to manage complex compensation programs. While a small number of Enterprise Relationship Management (ERP) systems can generate reliable sales cost data to support measurement systems, operational CRM solutions are focused on pipeline and opportunity management—not sales productivity or incentive compensation. These solutions providers are beginning to offer nominal sales incentive packages but remain several years away from delivering financial cost to sell data. A second systems issue is that true "cost-to-sell" models require assembling data from many places, including ERP systems, CRM systems, sales commission spreadsheets, activity-based costing models, payroll, and employee timesheets.

For example, NEC Technologies, a leading computer peripherals manufacturer, took on several initiatives to improve the performance of its direct sales. Their goal was to motivate field sales to sell only the highest-margin products. To accomplish this, NEC management strove to focus on selling higher-value-added products, automated the sales force, and redesigned parts of its sales process to speed up commission payments.

NEC's sales compensation approach was complicated and labor intensive. One hundred direct sales reps could sell a wide variety of high- and low-margin products. The sales channel generated over 35,000 monthly transactions, and team selling meant these transactions had to be attributed to multiple representatives. The sales reps were using an Operational CRM solution from Siebel Systems, but commissions were still calculated using a homegrown compensation system understood by one lone individual in the finance department.

NEC management chose to deploy Enterprise Incentive Management (EIM) software solutions from Incentives Systems to streamline sales incentive calculations in the short term. Managers were able to give their sales representatives feedback faster by reducing the cycle time for calculating commissions from five days to two days. They also had a new capability to deliver commission checks on the same day they generated and gave out commission statements. This benefit went a long way towards giving field staff a reason to applaud the new compensation plan. Because commission checks were in their hands sooner, it became less of an issue that compensations were spread around differently than they had been before.

Ultimately, sales management, the CIO, and CFO must work agreeably toward a target for when sales and finance can abandon the spreadsheet approach to rely on a coherent system for sales measurement/compensation.

Bottom Line

The role of field sales will have to be radically changed to ensure they continue to contribute value as role players in these new selling systems.

7

Mastering Networks of Partners, Media, and Middlemen to Effectively Reach the Market

M ANY BUSINESSES, PARTICULARLY IN MANUFACTURING, PACKAGED GOODS, AND THE INSURANCE INDUSTRY, DEPEND HEAVILY ON NETWORKS of third-party agents, distributors, and middlemen to sell their products. Marketing and communications professionals also rely on a broad mix of independent media for support—to create market awareness, drive traffic into stores, and distribute promotions to the customer.

Advances in network technologies—such as the Internet—are changing the way we communicate with our business partners and customers. Controlling customer relationships through third parties becomes more difficult when electronic channels and relatively unregulated new media like cellular telephones come into play.

This is important to sales, marketing, and communications executives because all businesses will have to contend with and learn to manage an expanding number of third-party distribution channels, communications media, and partnerships or risk losing access to their markets.

This chapter will outline how sales, marketing, and communications managers can adapt their approach to adjust to this changing landscape. A good example of what to expect can be found in the music industry, where one innovator transformed the product distribution landscape dramatically by taking advantage of the networking ability of the Internet.

Napster: The Renegade as Distributor

For decades, the music industry has been accused of wielding an unfair control over market forces, with record companies and large retail chains holding an iron grip on distribution channels. Then along came Napster. Invented by a college student in his dorm room, this system allowed users around the globe to share music files freely in a digital data format known as MP3. Virtually overnight, Napster became one of the Web's most popular services, with millions of computer users paying nothing to assemble vast libraries of their favorite tunes. Not surprisingly, the music industry acted with great alarm and in knee-jerk mode. Many large record companies rallied to sue the burgeoning service. What was surprising is that many more record companies, most particularly medium and small organizations, simply sat back.

But the distribution genie is out of the bottle. The music industry may have found a way to deal with Napster, but other similar services will be even harder to manage. Napster's Achilles heel was the centralized directory on a server hub that supported "peer-to-peer" swapping. The next generation of services such as Gnutella and FreeNet are totally decentralized, based on free software that users download with built-in intelligence to form a self-aware network with no central server. Thus, lacking any clear locus point, these services can be virtually impossible for a music company, court, government, or other body to ever rein in.

Eventually the music industry has come to realize that file sharing represents more of an opportunity than a threat, just as videotapes, once feared by the film industry as a destructive force, opened up billions of dollars in new revenue for that industry.

Notably, research from Cyber Dialogue indicated that 55 percent of Napster users made purchases of new CDs after first hearing the music for free. In the midst of a landmark court challenge, the record industry took a new tack of if-you-can't-beat-them-join-them, with a consortium led by German media giant Bertelsmann proposing to transform Napster into a subscription service. Sony, Vivendi, and others are now launching their own versions of peer-to-peer digital music exchanges. These will not be free; the small fees charged to users will help underwrite the development of what is now seen as a new avenue for music product promotion.

Managing the Balance of Power: Coverage versus Control

Innovators like Napster are taking advantage of emerging networks like the Internet to disrupt the existing "balance of power" between marketers and their third-party distribution partners in many industries. To stay ahead of this trend, marketers must first understand the nature of this "balance of power" in their own industry.

Many industries—such as insurance, food, and manufacturing—rely on third-party partners to sell and distribute their wares. What all these third-party networks have in common is that they are large and independent. Independent agents and sales reps work for themselves, and do what is best for their own bottom line. State Farm's independent insurance agents, for example, "own" the most important information about their customers, and do not pass on much of it to Allstate's marketing department. Technology companies like IBM and Hewlett Packard sell through tens of thousands of "value added resellers" to get their hardware and software sold and installed into businesses. Marketing managers at packaged goods companies like Green Giant do not own the thousands of retailers and convenience stores who distribute their cans of peas and corn.

Managing these third-party networks is a constant tension between getting maximum coverage with high levels of control. Often these goals are mutually exclusive. For instance, when placing media, marketers can put ads on every bus in town, but they cannot control where prospects will look for product information and what they choose to find credible. Using independent insurance agents allows manufacturers to stretch sales budgets and have a "branch office" in every town. But these manufactures cannot force these armies of distributors to march in formation and follow orders. This makes it hard to adjust to market conditions.

Successful marketers and third parties strive to strike a healthy balance. Marketers get the market reach and management control needed to meet their revenue growth goals economically. Independent third parties are allowed the freedom and autonomy to run their businesses as they see fit. Marketing dollars can help manage this balance as well. Indirect trade spending in the form of slotting allowances, co-op advertising dollars, and product placements serve as a lubricant when friction arises between marketers and third parties.

Why the Internet is creating a distribution dilemma

The number and variety of third-party channels and media is expanding. The way products and information flow across them is changing in ways that marketers cannot control. The pathway between seller and buyer is being overrun with a variety of "networked" and peer-to-peer information sources and distribution outlets.

Losing control over distribution of product, or the distribution of product information, creates serious problems for sales managers. Channel conflict will occur between captive channels (people who work for you) and independent, third-party channels (people who do not work for you) fighting for the same piece of business. It can be more difficult to gain "mindshare" with busy trading partners and get them to pay attention to your products.

Losing control might mean being cut out of the loop by a new player who decides to bypass traditional middlemen. Marketers might lose access to valuable customer information when a distributor decides not to share it anymore, or demands a high price for data that was once casually shared.

Less control also means less predictability. If marketers cannot make distributors do what they ask, they cannot count on the results. This will make meeting sales targets and quotas more difficult than it already is.

Linear/Hierarchal Communication

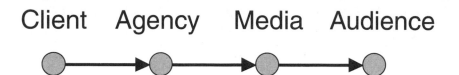

Networked Communication

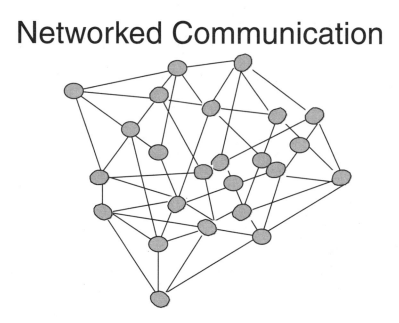

Figure 7.1. The shift from linear to networked communications.

Perhaps most importantly the ability to add value will become a moving target. For example, stockbrokers once created value by giving free advice, but got paid (captured value) with thousand-dollar stock commissions. When the online brokerage company e-Trade came along and stole those stock transactions away for under $30 each, stockbrokers were stuck giving good advice to clients without any way of getting paid for it.

In the automobile industry, a new set of online "middlemen"—such as Autobytel, Microsoft Car Point, AutoSite, and Autoweb. com—are giving car manufacturers like GM headaches by unbundling their pricing packages and economics so customers can force dealers to sharpen their pencils or make apples-to-apples comparisons on competitive brands.

Metcalfe's Law and Marketing

Electronic commerce is said to have changed the nature of business in the past five years. However, the "networked effects" of Internet communications suggest that by comparison, the Internet's impact on communications has been far larger. This may be evidenced by the fact that the "network effects" of the Internet are measured by the number of users squared, while the impact of electronic commerce on the economy is measured in fractions of user buying power.

The impact that the Internet has had on global commerce can be measured as a tiny fraction: under 1 percent of the value of all global trade is done online. By contrast, the impact of the Internet on global communications has been logarithmically large. In the space of a decade the number of people communicating online went from thousands to hundreds of millions.

This is because communications have a multiplier effect. The value, power, and effectiveness of the Internet communications network grow with the number of users. Bob Metcalfe, the founder of 3Com Corporation, articulated the power of networks in Metcalfe's Law, which states that the value of any network is equal to the number of users of the network squared. In the last decade, the global population of Internet users grew from a few thousand to over 197 million. That still accounted for only 60 percent of U.S. households, a pathetic ratio compared to the reach of telephone, television, and the U.S. Postal Service. When one considers that this number is expected to double to 372 million by 2003, the effect of the Internet on how communication occurs will be logarithmic compared to the growth of electronic commerce.

Six ways networks will change things

In the past, marketing information flowed in a mostly linear fashion—from point A to point B to point C. For example, an advertising agency (point A) would generate an advertisement, which was distributed through a newspaper advertisement (point B) to the consumer (point C). This provided business managers structure and control over their ads and messages. There were natural choke points in this process, like newspaper editors and media buyers in place, where business managers could exert control. For example, if a public relations firm wanted to control a story, they called in favors with a handful of key editorial contacts at major newspapers. Likewise, a well-heeled marketer like Coca Cola might spend enough money to control all the billboards in town with one phone call, not leaving any room for another point of view (or cola).

These information "hierarchies" made it easy for organizations to influence or control via public relations or mass media advertising. The open, interconnected nature of the Internet is replacing this linear information chain with a large and disorganized information network that has no place to grab on and control.

For example, peer-to-peer communications is impacting the way we sell, as more customers prefer to rely on peer reviews of what works rather than the advice of professionals (such as industry analysts or movie reviewers) when making buying decisions. For marketing and media professionals, buying a raft of trade magazine ads to encourage favorable trade press won't cut it anymore. The dialogue about your industry, and about your company is already taking place online, among your customers, employees, key journalists, critics, regulators, and every other constituency that matters.

The Internet is forcing change on third-party networks in six fundamental ways:

1. Quality and authenticity will be self-regulated.
2. Information volume will continue to grow.
3. Media sources will continue to proliferate.

4. Centralized information control will continue to decrease.
5. Communication will become more efficient.
6. Collaboration will increase.

In response to these changes, marketing and communications professionals are scrambling to lead the conversation and build technology platforms to help "good" information flow faster and easier. Unfortunately, these forces are largely beyond the control of a selling organization. Running faster to keep up with these changes will not work because there are enough people to "cover" these expanding channels or money to buy them.

New approaches will be needed to manage an expanding number of third-party distribution channels, communications media, and partnerships. Adapting will require a better understanding of how change is happening, and this is described in greater depth in the special section at the end of this chapter.

Short-Term Strategy: Navigating the Shifting Third-Party Landscape

New forms of media and new flavors of business partners require new strategies. Media relations professionals must now shepherd messages through hundreds of thousands of online and offline media outlets to reach influencers, prospects, and legislators. There are over 300,000 major print, broadcast, and Web media outlets, according to Media Map. For example, there are 4500 publishing sites whose primary business is placing advertisements for marketers, according to the Internet Advertising Bureau.

And "word-of-mouth" channels have appeared. The Internet has "amplified" word-of-mouth communications in the form of employee-to-employee communications and viral marketing, and self-publishing assures that millions of alternative communications agents exist. By the middle of the decade, wireless devices worldwide will exceed one billion and surpass laptop computers as the means of peer-to-peer Internet communications. Over 100,000 chat groups exist, discussing meaningful business issues and over ten Web properties now reach over 50,000,000 people monthly. Marketers will struggle to balance the risks and rewards of abandoning existing distribution relationships in favor of tantalizing new forms of customer access.

These include:

Electronic distributors that eliminate middlemen and sell directly to customers

Aggregators of product, content, and pricing information for buyers

Online marketplaces that create demand and match buyers and sellers

Trust communities and portals that serve as one-stop information and recommendations

Online publishers, advertisers, pundits, and newsletters that influence customers

One way to understand how the demand chain in your industry is evolving is to create a "map" of the demand chain from a customer's perspective. Once the broader outlines of an the demand chain are visualized, there are two key steps to take:

1. Identify the key sources of credibility and influence.
2. Find opportunities for partnering with online intermediaries, including "independent" online media.

1. Identify the key sources of credibility and influence

The sources of influence and credibility are not as obvious today as they were in the recent past, when mass media outlets were the predominant source of news and information for most of society. The Internet has given voice to powerful niche communities, for it offers a simple means to rally a global audience around issues that once were deemed irrelevant by mainstream media. These new trusted sources of online information are also often not simple editorial publishing bodies, but equally significant new types of resources, including discussion communities, search "portals," self-rating guides, and more.

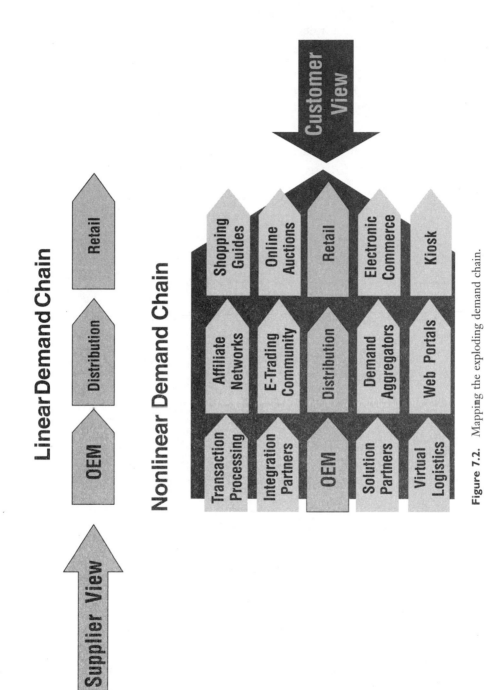

Figure 7.2. Mapping the exploding demand chain.

Some online examples include:

Open source reviews and ratings who vote on what is good or bad and post detailed comparisons of products and prices (BizRate.com, Internet Movie Database, Amazon.com)

Meta content analysis and content aggregators that assemble content and products from different places into bigger and better offerings (eMarketer, Yahoo Movies, Bulldog Reporter)

Relevant user group communities where people with common interest share information, make decisions, and make recommendations (Usenet, Yahoo!Groups, Topica)

Complaint and feedback sites where people and employees freely disseminate sensitive internal information and unvarnished opinions. (Epinions, Complaints.com, AirTravel-Complaints.com, PissedOff.com)

Trusted intermediaries and information-trading communities where people of like interest build a community dialogue that can influence markets, sell products, and make or break brands (Motley Fool, iVillage, WebMD, Intuit)

Online newsletters, gurus, and evangelists that sling gossip and make recommendations to their loyal constituents (Matt Drudge, Michael Tchong of ICONOCAST)

Employees of your organization and the organizations you deal with who use electronic mail and similar technologies to communicate with each other, with family, and friends.

Open Source Theory

The sharing of critical business data finds its model in the "open source" movement. Traditionally, the software business had been a one-way channel, where corporations employed teams of programmers who developed proprietary software, released those products onto the market, received feedback from customers, and repeated the cycle with subsequent new versions.

Even prior to the establishment of the World Wide Web in 1994, amateur computer programmers were using the Internet to share software coding that worked on proprietary designs. Known as "open source" development, this might involve hundreds or thousands of independent programmers who collaborated on creating a publicly posted code. The benefit of the process is that it often allows for more creativity in design and more thoroughness in quality assurance.

One of the earliest examples of this approach was Apache, the leading Web server application that still powers 60 percent of all Internet sites. Most open source applications, including Apache, are still available for free, though in many cases large software firms adopt a version of the software to distribute for a fee with value-added support, such as IBM in the case of Apache.

Notably, Linux is a powerful new network operating system developed freely as open source code. It was chosen as the "official" Internet operating system for the People's Republic of China, and now poses the most serious challenge to Microsoft's control over the OS market, at least in the corporate and government networking arena. Inspired by the success of Linux and similar initiatives, major software publishers are experimenting with open source programming, including Netscape, Macromedia, Sun, and Nokia.

Mapping all the potential third-party relationships your organization needs to reach customers (or constituents) helps size the problem and allows executives to answer some important questions using facts instead of fear:

Just how many online distributors serve our markets?

Where are people "voting" on what is good and what is bad in our industry?

> Who reviews our offerings and posts our prices for comparison?
>
> Who is combining our offerings into bigger solutions and selling them for more?
>
> In just how many places are people chatting about us and our problems?

Answering questions like these will provide a sense of what the risks are and which opportunities need to be addressed. This information will also help justify changes and new resources needed to cope. For example, if it turns out your products are being reviewed in over 500 online media outlets, it is logical to use e-mail updates to keep them all informed of your lastest developments.

2. Find opportunities for partnering with new online intermediaries

Leaders will actively reposition themselves on this exploding demand chain and make partnerships with information and product-distribution intermediaries that may re-establish some degree of control. Even "independent" online media provide opportunities for corporate partnerships, such as the affiliate programs and brand sponsorships of online content described as brand-builders in Chapter 3. As in the old days, once money changes hands, selling organizations can earn the right to onscreen presence if not respect. Online marketplaces described in Chapter 2 are another arena for partnering and may be developed into viable selling channels for the multichannel selling mix. As that chapter discusses, there are many pros and cons to consider before adding this kind of electronic channel.

Before making any major moves, executives should look at the changes to the demand chain in their specific industry and answer several questions:

1. Where is value being delivered and where is it getting paid for? (These tend to be different and move around among partners.)

2. Where are we in danger of being cut off from our customers?
3. Where are the potential value-added solutions and partnerships?
4. How should we redefine our market coverage model and third-party partnership priorities?

Answering these questions will allow organizations to identify the top risks and opportunities and prioritize where they must invest in change and find ways to exploit these peer-to-peer networks. For example, computer resellers were forced to adapt when direct online selling by manufacturers began hurting business. When Cisco, Dell, and the rest of the industry started selling off-the-shelf computer hardware like servers, routers and PCs, Microwarehouse and other resellers were reduced to the status of order takers. Margins shrank and many resellers folded tents. Microwarehouse survived because it refocused itself to become an active partner with PC makers, providing logistics and inventory management services.

Manufacturers will need to find ways to adapt their networking strategies to exploit "peer-to-peer" networks. Makers of high-tech software products have been earlier adopters and offer some solid ideas. For example, the Internet has allowed Intuit—a software company—to remake itself into one of the most attractive partners in the financial services world.

Intuit started by selling a software program, Quicken, that helped millions of people and small businesses keep track of their finances. Over time, these loyal Quicken users began to use Intuit's Web site forums to discuss other ways to control finances, such as advice about how to get a lower interest rate on loans. Intuit ran with this and used its customer trust levels to gain the power to recommend third-party services to its user base.

Aggregating these information seekers on a network on the Intuit Web site has given this small company the power to refer large numbers of customers directly to bigger business partners. Financial Services giants like American Express, Citicorp, and Allstate insurance are still beating a path to their door. Amazon.com does a great job of using third-party networks to their advantage. For example, Amazon.com is the 800-pound gorilla in affiliate relations. It has inbound links to its online retail store from 450,000 sites with specialized content. A bird-watching enthusiast site can sell books about birds online through a storefront set up by Amazon. Bird enthusiasts can get specialized books in one click, and the Web site gets a commission.

Amazon.com also uses "key word search" and "search engine optimization" as well as anyone to blanket the many media outlets on the network. This is smart because most heavy online buyers rely heavily on search engines when shopping (as opposed to other marketing tools). Amazon makes it easy by placing ads and recommendations that are triggered by search terms on both search engines and third-party partner sites. Affiliate networking and search engine optimization are emerging as a powerful medium for creating demand and dispersing information. (For more information on affiliate networks and search engine optimization, see Chapter 3.)

Long-Term Imperative: Five Ways the Mind-Set Must Change

In the long term, to succeed you have to have systems in place to rethread your demand chain confidently through the maze of new media and new flavors of intermediary third parties. This involves changing the way you think about and execute your business. This will take a while because it involves new models, new skills, new processes, new capabilities, and even new software.

These strategies can provide a structure to ease control issues within a selling organization:

1. **Find ways to extract value from information;**
2. **Redefine your role from gatekeeper to gateway;**
3. **Get faster and/or get out of the way;**
4. **Anticipate channel conflicts from network disruptions;**
5. **Experiment with new intermediaries.**

1. Find ways to extract value from information

In many situations, more value can be derived from extracting value from information the network generates than by stuffing more information into the network and trying to rise above the noise. Marketing and communications professionals need to shift the focus of their primary work from providing information to learning from it. They must use online tools to recognize the momentum of new trends as they emerge, and use this marketing intelligence to create product messaging that speaks to the trends in a timely way. For example, as an adjunct to reading three or four business newspapers daily, the communications leader may employ Web-crawling "spiders" that search out and deliver company product mentions or product-related issues throughout the Internet.

2. Redefine your role from gatekeeper to gateway

The sooner marketing professionals accept their loss of the ability to control information, the sooner they will begin to master what power they do have to influence the dialogue going on. Upper management must also accept that the most effective way to deploy the communications department is not as "gatekeepers" of corporate information, but open "gateways" that stimulate, nurture, and host open communication around the issues that matter most to the company. In the realm of crisis management, the emphasis will be less on protecting secrets than on ensuring the accuracy of what is reported.

At its heart, the Internet is about communications. So is, by definition, marketing. Yet, although "communication" implies a give-and-take dialogue, corporate communications has traditionally been a monologue.

The new information economy requires that companies engage in two-way conversations with key constituents, including customers, media, critics. and the public at large. Best-in-class communications professionals will focus on redefining processes and adopting new technologies that focus on generating immediate and value-added feedback, such as the viral marketing strategies discussed in Chapter 3 and interactive messaging tools described in Chapter 4.

3. Get faster or get out of the way

News cycles are shrinking towards zero. The time between juicy news scoop and brazen headline has been reduced to a few mouse clicks. Access to information is increasingly the least of the media's worries. When encountering slow, uncooperative, or ill-informed corporate communications professionals, media and other constituents seeking information have ample alternative sources of information, including direct access to employees and management, self-service resources, third-party analysis, and your competitors.

Using an e-mail management system to inform customers during a crisis is a given. Moving faster means looking beyond repaving cow paths with automation that speeds existing (linear) processes. Nonlinear, exponential strategies for getting accurate information out in a short time can use the entire arsenal of online communication tools, from inoculative viral marketing to content syndication of news stories.

Marketing professionals must find ways to migrate messaging to self-service or low-cost online channels. They can also assist in creating content that will be used directly in online selling channels. This may be the creation of value-added information resources that will boost visibility in an online marketplace, or the knowledge bases and FAQs on Web sites that can be used to help manage customer complaints and service issues.

4. Anticipate channel conflicts from network disruptions

In the multichannel selling system, sales channel conflicts may be inevitable due to the looser control of information and products through third parties. For example, a promotion designed to boost sales in retail locations may get a mention on a popular and heavily trafficked Web site. The amateur poster may not mention retail at all, just the name and contact data for his favorite reseller, who happens to be the one distributor who never wants to participate in co-op ad campaigns. The retail sales team may feel hurt and dismayed, but they will really be steamed if they feel they are losing significant sales volume to the reseller. An even worse scenario might be a Web posting that directs enthusiastic buyers to *only* the online sales channel; retail sales may pale compared to online purchases, but the retail team may clamor for its piece of the commission pie.

Having procedures in place to settle turf wars and encourage team selling across channels can mitigate the internal problems caused by uncontrollable developments in the demand chain. (For more on procedures, see Chapter 5.)

5. Experiment with new intermediary partners

Early participants in online marketplaces may gain the advantage of useful experience. One of the early lessons of the online marketplace trend, as described in Chapter 2, is that participants who arrive bearing "value-added information," in addition to product or service offerings, can enhance their positions to gain a competitive edge.

On the Internet, even a casual conversation or random act of Web surfing occurs just a mouse click away from the point-of-purchase interaction. Relationships with third-party partners are not restricted to affiliate relations payments; they can be sweetened with the offer of extra information, in the same way traditional partnerships are enhanced with co-op advertising dollars.

Keeping an ear to the ground under one's constituency can provide clues to which kinds of information will be most valued. Independent insurance agents, for example, are routinely deluged with offers of online link assistance to "make it easier to sell our product."

Bottom Line

As third-party intermediaries proliferate through online channels, selling organizations should try proactive experiments in peer-to-peer online networking, polish up their awareness of online media, and review existing third-party relationships to see where potential opportunities or channel conflicts may arise.

Special Section: Six Ways Networks Will Change Third-Party Marketing, Communications, and Distribution

Networks like the Internet have triggered a basic shift in the way people communicate with each other and the way companies can communicate with them. This has important consequences for the way organizations share and distribute information with their customers and prospects.

These networks are changing entire industries. Take, for example, the publishing industry. Networks have changed the publishing industry by shifting $10 billion in advertising and promotional spending from traditional media like newspapers onto the Internet. Publishers must now distribute content through both online and offline media. They must contend with content "aggregators" who repurpose their content and combine it with many different sources into new magazines that compete for the same audiences. And self-publishers, in the form of thousands of independent news groups and newsletters, create noise, blur standards of quality, and steal niche markets by representing thousands of independent viewpoints.

Information networks are breaking apart traditional business models in several specific ways. Forces of change such as the "open source" movement, the sharing of files across the Internet, and the development of trust communities will break down traditional business approaches. Also, the democratic and open nature of the Internet is giving voice to the disgruntled employees, the man on the street, and independent Internet pundits.

The "open source" movement has implications for products beyond computer software. Think of the thousands of software programmers worldwide who collaborated for free to develop a software operating system—Linux. They did it just to make a software program that works better than the one made by Microsoft, because they thought they could do

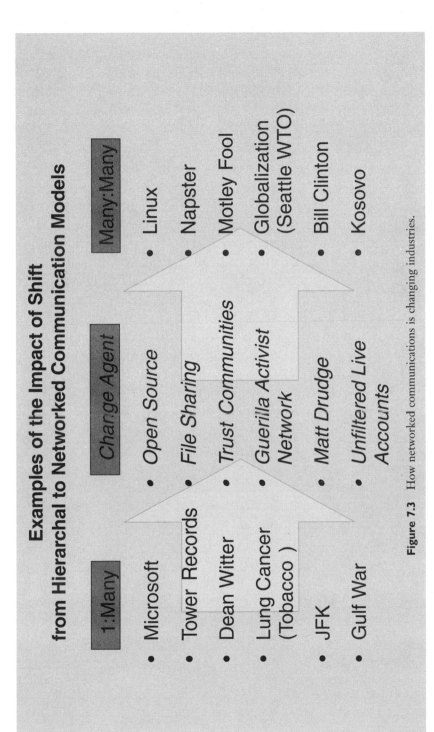

Examples of the Impact of Shift from Hierarchal to Networked Communication Models

1:Many	Charge Agent	Many:Many
Microsoft	Open Source	Linux
Tower Records	File Sharing	Napster
Dean Witter	Trust Communities	Motley Fool
Lung Cancer (Tobacco)	Guerilla Activist Network	Globalization (Seattle WTO)
JFK	Matt Drudge	Bill Clinton
Gulf War	Unfiltered Live Accounts	Kosovo

Figure 7.3 How networked communications is changing industries.

a better job. In the case of Napster, a college kid turned music product distribution on its ear when he amplified typical dorm room behavior with the Internet, allowing people to trade music on a global scale through file sharing of digital music.

Groups of like, but independent-minded people have built communities of interest, where trust and collaboration bind people to a cause better than current institutions, public relations, or brand advertising. For example, In the 1980s, an investment services company Dean Witter ran several commercials portraying busy rooms falling silent with anticipation when someone mentioned the financial advice they had received from that broker: "When Dean Witter speaks," ran the tag line, "people listen." The message was clear: this organization was the single best of source investment advice. Today, one of the leading sources of advice about investment is an online service whose very name mocks that old stiff-shirt pretense of anyone having a monopoly on wisdom: Motley Fool. Their business takes advantage of the democratic nature of the Internet. The Fool takes as its governing principle that the aggregate behavior and opinions of large numbers of people is a better source of insight than any single person or elite organization can lay claim to.

The power of the Motley Fool is the community discussion boards, where thousands of amateurs and professionals alike use collective wisdom to outsmart the market. More importantly, the Motley Fool has significant influence and power to make or destroy brands. Financial services giants—like Dean Witter—cannot replicate this type of trust no matter how much money they spend on TV ads. And Motley Fool cannot be bought (for now) because it cannot afford to sully its hard-earned reputation and independence by hawking other wares.

Independent activists connected by networks were able to take the world stage away from the well-funded and organized World Trade Organization in the Seattle Conference in

1999. In 1998, self-published Internet pundits like Matt Drudge rudely lifted the veil of media relations and spin control at the White House to shed light on a president's scandal, something even J. Edgar Hoover could not pull off in 1961. And private citizens in Kosovo were better than the Pentagon at telling us how many of our bombs actually hit the target.

The six ways networked communications will change things

The dialogue about your industry and your company is already taking place online today, among your customers, employees, key journalists, critics, regulators, and every other constituency that matters. If you're not already leading the conversation and building the platforms to help information flow faster and easier, you will become less effective with these third parties over time.

Marketing leaders have to recognize that the Internet is forcing change on corporate communications in six key ways:

1. Quality and authenticity of information will be self-regulated.

In the famous words of Abraham Lincoln, "You can fool some of the people all of the time, and you can fool all of the people some of the time, but you can't fool all of the people all of the time." In the Internet age, this axiom means that people will vote with their mouse clicks as to what sources of information they trust most, which in many cases will *not* be traditional media outlets.

The law of large numbers and the power of word of mouth are granting unprecedented influence to many small-scale, semi-amateur sources of information, such as the political gossip site the Drudge Report, the reader reviews of books and music on Amazon.com, and the phenomenally popular greeting cards index Blue Mountain Arts.

2. Information volume will continue to grow.

There are over 300,000 major print, broadcast, and Web media outlets, according to Media Map. And new "word-of-mouth" channels have appeared as well, in the form of employee-to-employee e-mails, viral marketing, and self-publishing. Millions of alternative communications agents exist. Any parent with teenage children chatting all night long on AOL's instant messaging can confirm this.

Print publications, radio, television, telephones, fax machines, cell phones, pages, e-mail, Web sites, discussion boards, instant messaging, wireless PDAs, videoconferencing, online kiosks, networked appliances—there is no end in sight for the diversity of information sources making their way into our everyday lives. The so-called "information glut" will perpetually increase across more communications channels for the foreseeable future.

3. Media sources will continue to proliferate.

Online publishing and data distribution costs are already near zero. While revenue models for online publishing remain dubious in the short-term, many more small and medium-sized online publishers will use the new media to make their voices heard.

This new paradigm that, at least temporarily, seems to favor economies of small scale has resulted in a proliferation of media sources that shows no signs of slowing anytime soon. And while the largest online publishing operations may continue to be dominated by large media conglomerates such as Bertelsmann, AOL Time Warner, and Viacom, many smaller online publishing operations will reach important audiences and wield influence far beyond what their size might indicate, such as JTJ.net (Hollywood gossip), Speak-Out.com (political activism), and Geek.com (technology resource).

4. Centralized information control will continue to decrease.

"Information wants to be free" was the rallying cry of early Internet evangelists. Given the value information commands in today's "information economy" and the simplicity with which everyone can disseminate it, the notion that information can be easily controlled, let alone sold profitably, is crumbling. For evidence of this, one need look only far as the "news leaks" from within some of the previously most secure sources of information in recent years, including the White House, national defense facilities, and major tobacco companies.

Corporate public relations departments could once effectively decide what information was to be released to the media and what information would be kept confidential. That control point is rapidly disappearing. Disgruntled employees, public records, and other alternative sources of information are too easily accessed by reporters and other curious constituents. Corporate communications departments cannot realistically expect that there is much information they can prevent from ever being released freely.

Data Leaks Are Everywhere

White House news correspondents once famously gauged the urgency of a foreign affairs crisis by noting the number of pizza deliveries made after midnight by White House staff.

Similarly, stock prices have been affected at the Motley Fool Web site's discussion boards, where thousands of amateurs supply tips for their fellow investors. In one example, the manufacturer iOmega experienced a stock run when Motley Fool faithful went so far as to monitor and report weekend activity in the parking lot of the company's Roy, Utah manufacturing plant, as a measure of the firm's prospects in the competitive industry of data storage hardware.

=====

5. Communication will become more efficient

On the surface, today's information explosion sometimes seems overwhelming. In truth, however, humans are nothing if not adaptable, and we instinctively make order of this cacophony of communication. As rapidly as the volume of information increases, so do tools to manage it, including data mining, neural networks, data warehouses, search engines, e-mail filters, caller ID, privacy policies, and so on.

As these tools mature, individuals and organizations are rapidly gaining skills in research, knowledge management, and value extraction from information. From the overnight ubiquity of the latest political joke and personalized, permission-based marketing techniques to online medical records and emergency roadside assistance by cell phone, technology is enabling all of us to communicate more efficiently than ever, a trend that will only increase with time.

6. Collaboration and peer-to-peer communication will increase

Businesses need to realize that the much-vaunted idea of "one-to-one marketing" is a two-way street. The open nature of the Internet has empowered individuals—be they customers, critics, analysts, or media—to expect that their voices will not only be heard but also answered. E-mail to the Webmaster, feedback forms, opinion surveys, discussion boards, customer service real-time chat, and other collaboration tools are increasingly popular on commercial sites. While key constituents may be old hands at venting their opinions through online forums, the real difference is that corporations are finally interested in what they have to say.

Many companies are still unprepared to deal with the volume of direct electronic communications their customers and constituents suddenly demand online. But there is no putting that genie back in the bottle, so companies must turn to automated assistance (such as the e-mail response management software) and figure out best practices for collaboration fast. If constituents do not get satisfactory answers from the horse's mouth, they will seek a sympathetic ear elsewhere online, including peer-to-peer industry discussion groups, public chat rooms, critic corners, and more responsive competitors.

CHAPTER 8

Putting the Call Center at the Center of the Action:

Turning the Call Center into a Strategic Sales and Marketing Asset

THE CALL CENTER IS BEING TRANSFORMED FROM A UTILITY FOR ANSWERING PHONES TO A STRATEGIC SELLING ASSET. To take advantage of its potential to grow sales at lower costs, the best organizations are putting the call center at the center of the action.

Tele-reps can do more than help keep customers happy, or smooth over the problems that may occur with Web site selling. They can do a lot of the "heavy lifting" of sales so expensive field salespeople can go after the big clients. In the best cases, tele-reps are used to initiate profitable "cross-selling" opportunities, and put promising leads into the right hands that can turn this information into real sales.

Sales and marketing executives are taking a new look at call centers for another reason as well. It turns out that technology-enabled selling programs like Customer Relationship Management (CRM) and Electronic Commerce don't work very well without the support of human call center agents.

Unfortunately, most call centers to not report to the sales, marketing, or distribution management teams. Most call centers today report to a customer service manager who is paid to treat it like a factory that handles customer complaints and questions at low call costs; its job is to produce high customer satisfaction ratings instead of leads and selling opportunities.

Organizations that can transform their call center from an "untapped asset" to a revenue growth machine capable of turning inbound online and offline customer questions and complaints into sales dollars can build an unstoppable competitive advantage. And yet in many organizations, sales and service executives still view the call center only as a cost center. The experience of Wally Hogan underscores these tensions and the need to evolve the role of the call center.

The Challenge of Making the Call Center Part of the Selling Team

Wally Hogan runs the call center organization for a consumer electronics company. His tele-reps answer customer service calls for catalog buyers; they also handle customer support for retailers and manage returns. But Wally is not having a good day. In particular, he is unhappy with Bob Eran, who runs the dot.com operation that just started selling DVD players and video games online. So when he runs into Bob in the coffee room, he can't help but vent.

"Bob, your Web site is killing me! Shut it down until you can figure out how to answer those e-mails yourself."

"What do you mean shut it down?" Bob sniffs. "The Web site launch is a home run! We're getting 2 million unique monthly visitors and we sold $100,000 of stuff this month."

"Well, I got 10,000 calls complaining about how your shopping cart doesn't work so well and asking questions about delivery options. And the e-mails are stacking up like cordwood. My people can't type and talk at the same time . . . and besides, phone calls are not free. Your $100,000 in sales just ate up $250,000 in staff time responding to inquiries. Let's not even mention how we're pissing off a lot of customers we haven't gotten to yet."

Now Wally's phone is ringing. It is Jeanne Cohen, the charismatic West Coast sales manager. She can sure get her field sales reps worked up to a fever pitch and she always beats her quota. Wally knows what she wants. One of Wally's "tele-coverage" agents actually took some initiative and generated some business in one of Jeanne's accounts that wasn't very active. Both Wally's agent and Jeanne's star salesperson that "owns the account" want credit for the sale and both want the cash commission.

"You're taking food out of my people's mouths!!" Jeanne screams into the phone. "Stay in your lane," she warns, "and I will stay in mine." Wally will have to dole out double credit to both people and make nice to keep everyone happy for the time being.

"It's expensive for me, but it beats having two salespeople pout instead of sell," he tells Jeanne. "Why can't we just work as a team? There's plenty of business out there."

"The answer is pretty simple, Wally," confided Jeanne. "You run a good shop and I am a team player, but until the day we figure out how salespeople can get paid to play nice with your tele-reps, we are likely to have this conversation again."

Why the Call Center Needs to Become a Strategic Business Asset

This organization—a fictional one based on many real examples—isn't going to fully capitalize on the potential of tele-channels until its management stops thinking about the call center as a cost center, and starts to view it as the engine of sales growth. To grow sales at lower cost, the Wallys of the world (and their bosses) will need to start managing the call center as a sales channel, instead of a labor-saving utility.

The problem is most of the world does not see things this way. The best sales and marketing organizations are transforming their call centers from customer service utilities into strategic selling channels that play traffic cop for a variety of online media and telephone communications. For companies like IBM it is the glue that allows organizations to manage large volumes of customer interactions seamlessly across a variety of channels and media. Others, like Dell and Fidelity Investments, have used the call center as a low-cost/high-value channel that can manage sales, service, and lead generation activities at low cost and high levels of customer responsiveness.

Leaders are investing in their call centers because a strategically managed call center is critical to effective sales growth for many reasons:

It is a "traffic cop" that helps manage and coordinate complicated multichannel sales and marketing (e.g., direct sales, partner, phone, direct response, and Web channels) as outlined in Chapter 5;

It is perhaps the best place for organizations to apply and manage advances in technology to enhance the efforts of hundreds of customer-facing employees and make thousands of customers happier;

It is an asset on the corporate "balance sheet" that includes a high percentage of the people and technologies that touch your customer;

It is the cradle of sales and marketing change where the greatest amount of sales and marketing process investment and innovation will occur in the next several years.

The call center as traffic cop

The call center currently sits at the intersection of many trends. Web, telephone, and electronic commerce technologies are merging. New media, from Internet, e-mail, to cell phones and kiosks are in mass use. And customers are schizophrenic and will want to use all of them . . . all of the time. Call center managers have a choice: either become a traffic cop or accident victim.

Customers increasingly prefer to use a combination of telephone and Web channels to do business instead of retail, catalog, or face-to-face interactions. For example, an Arthur Anderson Survey shows that over the last three decades, customers have grown to prefer the immediate response of the phone to a face-to-face sales call. Over 20 percent of the U.S. population regularly does business on the Web. Most Web customers will want some phone support. For example, IBM's electronic commerce organization discovered that even this tech-savvy audience of Web customers wanted access to humans over 70 percent of the time during e-commerce transactions (see IBM case study, this chapter).

As of the year 2000, people sent almost three trillion e-mails. That is five times as many e-mails as paper letters, or, to put it another way, 54 e-mails for everyone on the planet. Several billion cell phones will inevitably deluge organizations with voice or Web requests, stock trades, or orders for spare parts. Making the call center the hub of all this activity may simply be the most efficient way to manage all this traffic.

To manage the growing volume and mix of customer contact, the emphasis of call centers will shift from the "telephone" to managing a variety of "points of interaction" such as e-mail, Web, voice, and others. These souped-up call centers are commonly called the "customer interaction center" or "tele-web" channels.

Applying technology to the call center

Advances in telecommunications, the Web, and database technology are dramatically changing the call center. Call center technology is becoming more sophisticated. The switches and computers that run telephone systems are becoming much better at helping agents be more responsive and productive, and keeping customers happier. Unfortunately, like all technological advances, this does not come without buzzwords and confusion. Telephony, in particular, is a veritable alphabet soup of acronyms such as ACD, IVR, CTI, and SBR. These are confusing but useful developments.

On a practical level, certain of these technologies help send inbound phone calls to an available agent, or even better the right person to answer the question. These are called automated call distribution (ACD) and Skills Based Routing (SBR). These will help manage and route calls to the right resources, or allow callers to help themselves. This is vital when call center reps are being made the "default" or "back up" resource to support customers struggling to complete electronic commerce transactions.

Other technologies will allow self-service by letting callers give orders and retrieve information without talking to a human. These are called Interactive Voice Response (IVR), Computer and Telephony Integration (CTI).

And over 80 percent of call centers will have a customer relationship management (CRM) application (like Siebel Systems, Clarify, or Onyx) in the next few years that helps manage, coordinate, and store customer interactions. The META Group anticipates that these three capabilities will likely be combined into product bundles tailored to the call center in a three- to five-year time frame.

Despite this consolidation, we can expect a steady stream of new capabilities that allow customers to interact with sellers through new types of media or across combinations of media. For example, the online stock broker Ameritrade advertises on television how their agents use "shared white board," a technology that allows brokers and prospects to work together on building a stock portfolio as they view a Web screen that both can see and tinker with at the same time. A sampling of these are profiled in the Special Section: An Inventory of Tele-web Tools, at the end of this chapter.

Putting call center assets on the balance sheet

What if you managed a sales operation that:

Represented over 20 percent of your corporate technology investment?

Controlled 50 percent of the conversations and interactions with your customers?

Managed most of the "customer-facing" employees?

Would you think it was important? Well, this is your call center.

For the average company, the call center is out of sight and out of mind. Senior sales and marketing executives often don't notice how many resources are tied up in call center operations, because all of these agents and technologies don't actually sit in one place. Typically, call centers are based in remote locations such as North Dakota, where there can be economies in square footage and salary costs. And smaller companies may outsource their call centers to third parties.

Waking senior management to this "hidden asset" is easier once someone takes the time to do the math—to recognize that call centers *already* make up a significant percentage of "customer-facing" employees, technology assets, and customer contacts.

Less affectionately, call center agents are known to management as "cheeks in seats." They represent all customer-facing employees who are not traveling—and they may not even be your own employees. At the turn of the century, Global 2000 organizations spent $25 billion outsourcing call center services. That number could double by 2005.

The call center is becoming the modern focus of technology investment. Yet this makes perfect sense: organizations that in the past turned to automation technology to reduce costs of manufacturing are now, logically, applying technology innovations to reduce cost-to-sell.

The Call Center is the Cradle of Sales and Marketing Process Change

Like a volcano ready to erupt, a number of forces are putting the call center at the center of sales and marketing process change. In particular, several of those outlined in this book are putting the call center in the spotlight. Sales and marketing executives can make a good business argument for expanding the role of the call center and making it the centerpiece of a technology-enabled revenue growth engine.

In particular, a strategically managed call center is critical to:

1. *Helping Field Sales Add More Value:* A well-run call center is a great way to free up valuable field sales capacity and make sales force automation investments pay off in a big way. The IMT Strategies survey of 50 top organizations showed that over two thirds of organizations have automated both their sales force and their call centers with CRM software. Smart managers will connect these dots.

Organizations typically start by corralling poorly organized and underutilized inside sales employees and putting them into a well-run call center organization. Once there, these call center agents actually use all that expensive sales force automation technology (laptops, networks, synchronization) to tether themselves to field sales reps so they can communicate and work as a team. Smart organizations will use this connection to "offload" more and more tasks from overburdened and more expensive field sales reps. For example, IBM was able to "offload" 70 percent of its field sales workload onto call center agents.

At first, the call center takes away the low-value sales that field staff tend to ignore. Over time, call center agents start taking on responsibility for covering and hand-holding existing or small customers and eventually selling them more things. "Tele-coverage" teams, assigned to field staff, can support account penetration and handle subsequent business in named accounts (restocking, scheduling upgrades or maintenance visits, etc.). This frees up the field staff to concentrate on new business.

2. *Managing Complicated Multichannel Sales and Marketing Systems:* The call center will emerge as the perfect "traffic cop" for managing hybrid selling systems. This means screening, prioritizing, and routing leads from clients. This could include handing off hot prospects to the right field sales person or logging a service request with a field sales organization. It also means playing backup on service calls and bailing out Web channels when transactions go bad.

A well-equipped call center agent has access to a variety of technologies. For example, many CRM software packages have business "rules" that automate the decision of who gets what lead or what phone call. Workflow programs automatically tell all relevant people of an opportunity—instantly letting spare parts billing and a technician both know of a breakdown so they both arrive in the same place.

Channel integration technologies allow different channels to share information and networks to keep different channels in communication. E-mail response packages (such as those from Kana Communications or e.Gain) use artificial intelligence to sort inbound leads for you and route them to the appropriate resource.

3. *Getting Results from CRM Programs*: The call center is a logical home base for CRM technology and relationship management programs. It is the place where most customer questions and service calls arrive. It is a place where a high percentage of customer-facing employees work. It is an easy place to enter data about customers and gain access to database. It is the place where Web, CRM, and telecommunications technology can logically converge.

Most importantly, the call center is an excellent control point for execution of one-to-one customer campaigns and "service-driven" sales. Revenue growth will come from existing customers (upsell, resell, cross-sell). Traditionally, all support inquiries go to the call center, which will have the easiest access to customer records. As most retention and penetration opportunities are driven by service and support calls, it makes sense to create ways to enhance these selling opportunities.

The call center should also be home base for targeted, cross-media campaigns designed to stimulate product demand. Today's typical cross-media campaigns (e.g., see an ad on TV, check the Web site, call the toll free number) follow noticeable patterns of buyer behavior.

For example, IBM found that about 40 percent of prospects that received their direct-mail promotions were checking the Web site first before calling the toll-free 800 number to buy. For the promotion to be successful, the direct-mail offers had to be posted on the Web site, and the call center agents needed to know about the offer as well. In this and similar promotions, IBM has experienced a 30 percent revenue "lift" on personal computer Web transactions that originate on the Web and close in the call centers when customers use "Call Me" and "Chat Online" connections on IBM's Web site. Catalog retailers with phone order-takers have long reported similar "lift."

4. *Building Customer Care Systems That Manage Many Points of Interaction*: The call center is the most logical point for administering customer care programs. In a single year, for instance, IBM was able to migrate 99 *million* post-sales service transactions to self-service. While moving such a degree of service and support interactions to a lower-cost channel can be a good move, this tends to drive up call center volumes, and nearly always requires adding new technology or additional staff.

Short-Term Strategy: Building a Tele-web Command Center

Eventually, all the human and technology capital tied up in the call center will show up as a major item on the balance sheet and someone will notice. When executive management does the math and counts the hundreds of customer-facing employees and stacks of technology assets, they will ask two questions:

1. How do we leverage with these technology assets, infrastructure, and bodies?
2. How do we specialize enough to manage this complicated mix of customer interactions and channels?

Managers must find ways to leverage expensive call center assets while at the same time creating specialized processes for serving customers better. They already have the job of managing human and technology assets that include thousands of call center reps, big telecommunications switches and networks, phones, computer terminals, and expensive CRM databases. To make all of this work better, organizations must develop selling processes, create functional specialties, and motivate high levels of teamwork to coordinate customer interactions across different media such as the fax, mail, e-mail, voice, and Web sites.

Leveraging assets: Managing call centers means buying and maintaining phones, computers, and routers. Building a global call center network means coordinating many vendors, languages, locations, and regulations. Human resources are also difficult— finding, developing, and keeping agents in a business where turnover rates average 25 percent and training and development are on the rise. Performance measurements in call centers are rigorous and transaction volumes can number in the millions. Sophisticated measurement systems, strategic outsourcing, and the consolidation of operations wherever you can find the opportunity can help simplify things.

Specializing processes: Effectively mixing Web and human interaction and blending many selling channels will require a lot of teamwork and role-playing in order to come up with a more streamlined selling process. A good Web site and fancy voice recognition system cannot cover for a lousy set of procedures that doesn't pass the customer to the right team player.

Tasks, products, and customer segments will have to be broken down and rearranged into highly specialized job functions that may perhaps span more than one channel. The call center needs to eventually be populated by a group of role players that can adapt to changing customer needs and whims. Specialized processes will help keep things organized; this can also provide a framework for tracking, managing, and measuring activities so costs and service levels can be controlled.

If in the long run the more sophisticated (and educated) marketer wins the prize, then specialization is necessary. The long-term benefits of an investment in specialization are organizational learning, better customer data, better channel integration, seamlessness, and the development of more sophisticated and tailored programs for upsell and resell.

Facing the hard trade-offs: five questions to ask

Balancing leverage and specialization means leaders will have to make some hard decisions and trade-offs. Call center managers who are willing to transform their operations will have to gain broad management consensus on some tough questions.

1. Should our organization invest in call center technologies that optimize voice only, or many different media?
2. Should our call center emphasize transactions or relationship building?
3. Should we manage the call center as a cost center or a selling channel to get the most business impact for our money?
4. Are we better off measuring hard productivity measures or soft value and revenue measures in the call center?

5. Is it more strategic to measure and manage call center assets or selling processes?

The guidelines to answer these questions can be found in your call center's current level of activity, in the kind of product you sell, and what profit margins you expect. For instance, if your organization receives over 500 online inquiries a week, it probably makes sense to consider adding "tele-web" capabilities to the call center outlined in the special section at the end of this chapter.

If your average transaction size is under several thousand dollars, it probably makes sense to emphasise tele-rep efficiency and migrate more transactions to the Web. If the lifetime value of each customer is high (say over $20,000) or you service large accounts with hundreds of independent buyers inside of them, then a customer relationship management system (CRM) should probably be considered. These systems will give reps the information they need to give personalized service to good customers and keep track of many small buyers as part of a "tele-service" role.

If you sell relatively simple products to many small customers, then it may make sense to give your call center reps a role as a selling channel with a real sales quota (say $400,000 of component sales to small businesses). If your customers are part of a selling team that coordinates with sales reps, resellers, and service organizations, then "softer," team-based measurements make more sense.

If your customers have low lifetime value (say under $400) and your call center gets a large number of low-value transactions, then it makes sense to focus on asset utilization. If call center representatives are becoming a critical part of a selling team and serve many different roles, an investment in process integration would be justified.

Long-Term Imperative: Evolve the Role of the Call Center

Call center managers cannot simply react to sales and marketing process changes that are going on in other parts of the organization. They must take a leadership role and actively force answers to these questions from executive management. By not being proactive, the call center managers risk becoming garbage collectors—constantly picking up the pieces for direct marketing, sales, and electronic commerce organizations as they expand into interactive marketing, permission e-mail, and other multimedia promotions and campaigns.

Call centers will stumble if they are the last to know when a new marketing program is launched that will land leads, inquiries, and complaints at their doorstep. Over time, as customer support and inbound tele-reps struggle to keep up with new customer interaction flows, they will be paralyzed by undercapacity and will remain in constant "catch-up" mode. Customer satisfaction will suffer from this overload, particularly in online channels and new media, which have not been properly planned or resourced.

Unfortunately, existing measurement systems will fail to sound alarm bells. Current staffing and return on asset models, if unchanged, will not justify the additional investment in technology and resources needed to make a difference.

Three long-term strategies emerge for managing the changes:

1. **Plan the evolution of call centers;**
2. **Change how call centers are measured and managed;**
3. **Invest in incremental technologies that improve selling performance.**

I. Plan the evolution of the call center

Traditionally, most call centers handled customer service and support phone calls. For example, electric utilities have had large customer service centers for decades to handle complaints, billing issues, service installations, and emergencies like power outages. The exception was catalogers and publishers that had more sales-oriented call centers staffed not only with inbound telemarketers responding to customers but outbound tele-reps hunting for new business.

In the early 1990s, call centers started evolving from cost centers to sources of revenue growth. They evolved first in industries with low "customer switching costs" and high levels of competition. Credit card companies like Citicorp, long-distance telephone companies like MCI, and GEICO in car insurance used the call center as a weapon to acquire new customers and create incentives to keep existing customers. These organizations raced to build large call centers so they could bother consumers at dinner with a special offer.

Over time, business-to-business marketers in technology, office supplies, payroll services, and telecommunications started using call centers to sell. Companies like IBM, ADP, and Sprint used these telechannels to reach their small business clients, selling low-margin products that were too small for field sales. Call centers also serviced geographically remote customers. These call centers were supported by investments in more sophisticated phone switches and equipment to help route, dial, and manage calls more effectively.

The smartest organizations have figured out that call center agents can help grow revenues in retained accounts. "Tele-coverage team members" can respond to inquiries and questions at much lower costs. Customer relationship management software (CRM) systems from suppliers such as Siebel Systems and Clarify can be used to manage these account relationships and coordinate attribution with field reps and team staff more easily.

Organizations have learned that Web channels do not work very well without human support. As a result, call center managers have created special job functions like e-care, and e-mail response specialists emerged with nontraditional skill sets such as interaction management, speed typing, and privacy policy management. When the volume of Web transactions get too large to handle, these specialists will be supported by technologies that help connect and integrate Web and voice channels like "click-and-connect," text chat, and mail response capabilities. Other organizations will consolidate global call centers into "centers of excellence" to create leverage and share best practices. These centers of excellence will have specialties in Web response and multilingual support. Some may even be set up as labs for testing the effectiveness of new relationship technologies and marketing programs. Investments in training will increase to spread best practices across the organization.

Over the next several years, call centers will continue to add tools and capabilities that allow organizations to communicate with customers though new points of interaction. It will take many years for measurement systems to mature to the extent that managers can track these transactions more easily as they flow into and out of the call center. And the technologies of telephony, CRM, and electronic commerce technology will mature to the extent that these capabilities can be combined into useful bundles that allow agents to handle more and different types of customer interactions.

2. Change how call centers are measured and managed

Of course, none of this works well unless revenue attribution for sales made by other channels, and revenue "lift" for incremental sales, are figured into compensation and incentive plans. As call centers will evolve from cost centers to tele-web operations that grow sales and profits, new measurements must be put in place to define channel boundaries and motivate agents to work across selling channels.

Traditional call centers focused on customer service are some of the most tightly measured organizations in the company. This is because all of the data concerning what agents do on the phone sits inside the phone switch. Benchmark data that allows one call center to compare itself to another is readily available and freely shared between companies. Agent productivity is almost directly related to call volumes. The typical call center has a scorecard that measures calls per agent, average call time, cost per call, speed of answer, the number of calls resolved on the first conversation, and many other hard numbers.

When call centers start playing a role in selling, value is created in new and different ways. But it is much harder to measure this value. Things get confusing. For example, is revenue per call a better measure than length of call when it comes to a telemarketing rep? Are lead referrals more important than first-call resolution in team selling?

Smart organizations will create incentives for:

Channel migration by offloading work and tasks from more expensive field sales representatives;

Channel integration by coordinating sales and service efforts with other selling organizations and channels;

Upselling and cross-selling to existing customers in response to inbound customer service calls or prospecting calls to existing clients.

Measurements in a tele-web channel get "softer" because it is cumbersome and expensive to get the hard numbers. Unfortunately, hard performance numbers will be needed to justify the strategic value of continued investment in the call center. In the beginning it may take full-time employees from both finance and human resources departments just to calculate these complicated measurements.

Everyone laughed in the year 1900 when "productivity engineers" showed up at the factory with their stopwatches and cameras. But the cost benefits of better measuring things eventually became apparent as production costs dropped steadily and manufacturers were able to streamline their production processes. In the short term, most organizations will feel the view is not worth the climb when it comes to call center metrics. This means they will either settle for soft measures that do not paint the complete picture, or even abandon the effort to learn and measure altogether. In giving up, organizations will sacrifice valuable learning and experience that will ultimately separate the winners and the losers.

3. Invest in incremental technologies that improve selling performance

There are any number of useful enhancements to basic call center functions, including technologies that will help make things easier by recognizing your voice and translating foreign languages on the fly. As marketers add new points of interaction, call centers are adding new tele-web tools that allow agents to communicate through them, or add electronic commerce to their responsibilities.

One example is delivering customer service online. IBM put "call me back" buttons on 500 Web pages. But when marketers put up Web sites with "help" signs and invitations to chat, call centers have to be able to have access to existing customer information to respond correctly. Having prewritten scripts and hiring agents with good typing skills is also needed.

Another way to boost the productivity of call-center selling is event-triggered marketing. Smart direct marketing departments are starting to automatically alert call-center agents to a buying event based on a customer's past history or script a "real-time" personalized offer based on a customer's interests. For example, a company targeting direct consumer sales may offer a discount on a birthday, or a business-to-business vendor might offer a product upgrade on the expiration of a service contract.

Calculating the cost of change: the ROI of new tele-web tools

Making rational decisions about where and when to add new technologies to the call center is difficult given the range of choices. These technologies should create significant improvements in sales and marketing effectiveness. Put another way, any new parts in the sales and marketing engine should dramatically improve gas mileage or miles per gallon. Making good investment decisions will require experimentation and disciplined performance measurement. Some facts to consider:

The call center makes up over 20 percent of IT investment in most Global 2000 companies when you factor in the phones, switches, networks, databases, software, and electronic commerce capabilities needed to support a call center.

Added up, it can cost an average of $5000 to $6000 to outfit a call-center agent with only the basic equipment needed to do business (phone, switch, personal computer, workstation, headset, etc.).

Add to that training and salary costs of between $5000 to $18,000. Figures are actually higher when compounded by staff turnover; turnover rates in call centers average 25 percent or higher, according to Purdue University. Training costs are rising with increased functional specialization, the need for cross-training and typing skills, and the addition of new Web interaction and CRM technologies to the call center. And there will be hundreds of potential add-ons available to improve the productivity of call-center agents.

Adding flashy new capabilities (such as an operational CRM package, IVR, mail response management, and call-me-back buttons) adds costs of $250 to $1200 per agent. Getting a return on investment of these incremental capabilities depends on how much productivity and selling leverage you get from them. The large up-front expense mandates that they dramatically show that they can improve the "miles per gallon" from existing sales and marketing dollars.

Measuring that return is difficult because there are so many different types of software supporting the agent and so many different channels taking credit for having a hand in a sale. Creating ways of attributing revenue to the agent and specific technologies will remain an ongoing battle.

On the whole, given the breadth of investment alternatives out there, and the complexity of measuring returns, if an incremental technology does not deliver 100:1 productivity, it probably does not make sense. A 100:1 productivity gain means that a $250 shared e-mail response system that costs $250 per agent should allow that agent to generate $25,000 in cost reduction or incremental margins (which likely means more like $200,000 in extra revenues).

Here is an overview of just some of the agent interaction capabilities that will help connect the "tele-channel" to the Web channel. All call centers will add these and others to their shopping list in the next few years. As new points of interaction emerge and technology matures (remember when the fax was new?) you can count on many more alternatives.

Bottom Line

An integrated call center can be expensive, but it also creates value by cutting costs and improving opportunities to sell more to existing clients and new clients.

An Inventory of Tele-Web Capabilities

Capability	What It Does	Technologies That Make It Happen
Click and Connect	Allows an agent to offer customers various options for assistance.	These are Web-based interaction agents that let online customers connect with agents. These include Web-based agents (or hot buttons) that offer Call Me later, Call Now Features. They also include tools that allow agents and customers to collaborate in real time (either using text chat or shared whiteboard) or actually talk over the Internet (Voice Over IP).
E-mail Integration	Allows an agent to respond to, manage, and track e-mails from customers.	These are agents that respond to online inquires automatically (for example inbound e-mail acknowledgment) or distribute messages to the right person (parsing, routing tools) or use "artificial intelligence" to auto reply (for example, auto reply modules that are programmed using either business rules, pattern recognition, or neural nets).
Online Chat	Allows an agent to interact with customers with text chat.	These are chat features similar to AOL instant messaging that let customers chat individually with a rep (using buddy lists or one-to-one chat features) or in a group (such as chat room, or discussion list).
Application Integration	Passes along information about the customer to the agent during a call so they can better sell and serve them.	These provide call-center representatives with access to customer profile information and the current state of the customer (for example, IP address, what URL they are looking at).
Agent Console	A dashboard that routes calls and provides agents guidance and scripting to help them better help customers and respond quickly.	This tool helps agents become more productive by managing their workload and routing inquiries to the right person. They include skills-based routing, scripting agents, queuing.
Application Sharing	These are software interfaces that allow agents to share information with customers.	These are tools that allow both parties to share information such as push-pull co-browsing technologies.
Self-Service Knowledgebases	Allows customers to access proprietary information and databases available for self-help from behind the firewall.	These self-help capabilities include self-help databases, Frequently Asked Questions (FAQs), and exclusive extranet access to protected files.
Web Campaign Management	Manages the execution of outbound e-campaigns.	These are available from software providers who make e-mail engines, marketing automation, direct e-mail campaigns such as Responsys, MarketSoft, and Kana Communications.
Speech Recognition	Authenticates the identify of the caller and responds to voice commands.	Emerging speech recognition technologies and speaker verification are becoming viable self-service alternatives for online customers.

Figure 8.1. Tele-web tools chart.

Special Section: How IBM Built a
$8.6 Billion Tele-web Channel

International Business Machines (IBM) is a 88-billion-dollar organization that sells technology to large and small businesses as well as directly to consumers. For decades, IBM built a stellar selling culture around highly trained "blue-suit" sales representatives selling multimillion-dollar mainframe computers and systems. For such sophisticated products, it was not unheard of for a selling team of eight people (engineers as well as salespeople) to make customer calls as a group.

Things changed.

As the number of IBM products offered through electronic channels grew to exceed 18,000 and the average product price tag shrank to under $20,000, these field sales representatives grew less effective. In response, IBM had to transform its sales and marketing processes.

Call centers played a major role in this transformation. In the last decade, IBM has expanded and evolved their call centers to the point where IBM now owns a very sophisticated 8.6-billion-dollar tele-web channel. IBM integrates the management of the telephone and Internet channels to provide seamless service to customers. This tele-web channel—named **ibm.com**—generates over 11 percent of sales and is an engine of revenue growth for other selling channels. By the year 2000, this growth engine was generating:

4.5 million Web visitors a week

10,000 e-mails a week

95 phone call inquiries a minute

1 qualified lead per minute

$38 million in revenue opportunities a day

$46 million in sales transactions a day

Over 99 million self-service transactions a year

The economics of this channel are compelling. Sales through ibm.com are growing at a rate of over 50 percent, and tele-web channel costs are 40 percent less than traditional sales channels. Also, by migrating millions of customers to self-service, IBM saved over $1.86 billion dollars in support costs in 2000.

This transformation did not happen overnight. During the first 10 years, IBM added call centers globally to the point where they had 130 call centers serving 150 countries and had over 5000 agents on the phones. While the tele-channel grew in size, IBM saw the need to leverage and specialize. By the late 1990s, it had consolidated these agents into 25 consolidated call centers.

How did it learn where and how to specialize? IBM assembled a team that researched and recorded best practices from all of their call centers and identified performance standards for the consolidated and specialized centers of excellence, where a particular call center had built a leading-edge capability. For example, a major North American call center has built a specialty in Web response, while a top European call center became a center of excellence for multilingual support.

At the same time, IBM was building a multibillion-dollar electronic commerce channel. And ibm.com (as well as thousands of dot.coms) started to realize the Web couldn't stand alone as a selling channel for sophisticated products. In particular, they found that 70 percent of Web customers wanted access to people. In addition, as IBM sold more products online, the number of online shoppers seeking assistance had doubled and call-center volumes increased.

IBM figured out it made sense to manage tele-channels and electronic commerce as an integrated channel. By connecting Web sites to customer support call centers, it became easier to convert browsers to buyers. The call centers also provided around-the-clock "live" support to online marketing efforts, and answered e-mails in less than four hours.

After a series of over 10 organizational changes in six years, IBM arrived at an ibm.com organization that treats telephone, Web, and e-mail as an integrated channel, although this will continue to evolve as IBM exploits new technologies and customer demands change. During that period of time, the call center moved from being part of the direct marketing organization to becoming an independent tele-channel to an integrated tele-web channel. This integrated channel approach provides seamless service and dramatically improves selling leverage and market coverage while reducing channel costs.

IBM attributes the success of ibm.com to their focus on sales and marketing leverage and speed of execution. Internal selling and evangelism got the concept off the ground with executive-level management, sales channels, and customers who were used to doing things a certain way. Once senior management bought into the concept of tele-web, resources were shifted to quickly operationalize the concept of "tele-web" channels with real measurements, ROI programs, and management systems. Equally important to IBM is the effort it took to manage learning curves and get its 6500 agents operating at high levels.

IBM sees several keys to future success. They will continue to:

Balance leverage and specialization

Change the way they run call centers as needed

Invest in new technologies with the potential to create selling leverage

Take a disciplined approach to measuring results and learning.

Align incentives and management systems with field sales operations.

The considerable resources required were leveraged by consolidating call centers globally. This required additional investments—for example, a two-years-in-the-making CRM program to have all marketing resources run off the same customer database.

IBM was not afraid to make fast changes in the way it was running its call centers. First, the company marketed the channel aggressively to customers to make them aware of this alternative to business partners and field sales. They also changed measurements and incentives to encourage channel migration from field sales and foster better integration between channels to deliver seamless service and lower costs. They enhanced agents' skills and training. Perhaps most importantly, they got many channels to work together as a team to redefine their selling processes to satisfy customers and provide around-the-clock support for a variety of Web marketing programs and applications.

IBM invested and tested new tele-web technologies and capabilities to understand where technology could provide the greatest performance improvements. Some of the specific innovations at IBM.com include the following tele-web programs:

5000 large and medium-sized accounts have dedicated tele-coverage reps within the tele-Web channels available for servicing and penetration.

500 large and medium-sized accounts have their own customized Web sites, called "e-sites." These provide personalized information, custom pricing, and direct access to order information, plus one-click access to the dedicated IBM.com tele-web support team familiar to the account.

IBM supports online inquiries from all IBM marketing Web sites with 24-hour support and delivers four-hour response time to e-mail inquiries and two-hour response times on "call-me-back" Web inquiries.

Six-hundred Web sites are experimenting with "click and connect" technologies such as "call-me-back" buttons, shared white boards, and online chat. Some 73 percent of IBM customers have used these features.

To determine which incremental "tele-web" capabilities offer the greatest selling leverage, IBM has designated one of its call centers to include a Teleweb Laboratory. Given the large number of potential tools and capabilities that can enhance the performance of the tele-web channel, IBM has established a return-on-investment hurdle to screen which new capabilities get rolled out and deployed across the company. Given that almost any software package costs at least $200 per agent, each application needs to prove it can deliver over 100 times its cost in reduced selling expenses, improved productivity or increased margin contribution or new revenues. This ensures that every new investment improves IBM's selling costs.

IBM has also been a leader simply by taking a disciplined approach to measuring results. What they learned is this: if you integrate tele-web channels and put more self-service on the front and back end of the buying process, then involve humans more in the middle—when they are buying—you reap dual benefits. By migrating the front end (product consideration) and the back end (post-sales service) of the buying cycle to online self-service, IBM has freed up agent time and saved millions on its cost to sell. Getting agents more involved in the middle helps with conversion rate and cross-sell and upsell opportunities. This gets results. IBM has found that when a call-center agent gets involved in a Web transaction, the average order size is 30 percent higher than Web-only transactions.

Reorganizing Around the Customer:

Transforming the Organization to Get the Most Value from CRM Investments

TODAY, MANY MARKETERS ARE SPENDING MILLIONS ON CRM SYSTEMS AND "ONE-TO-ONE" MARKETING PROGRAMS. They hope these investments will lead to more intimate relationships with customers and better sales and marketing performance. But building these expensive customer relationship management "machines" is not going to be enough. Somebody will have to run these sophisticated sales and marketing systems and make sure customers are actually getting happier.

If marketers want to extract big returns from their investments in CRM technology and customer data, they will have to find ways to refocus their organizations on customers (instead of products and business units).

In the end new job titles, organizational structures, and skills will be needed. Traditional job titles like "product manager" will give way to newer specialties such as "customer segment" managers or "customer care" managers.

This will not be trivial. Some have compared the process to making elephants dance on the head of a pin—balancing the weight of a whole organization around the individual customer. This often involves making painful, wholesale changes to the status quo and altering the job descriptions of most employees involved in sales and marketing. Cadence Design Systems, for example, had to reorganize its entire selling system around the customer before it could take advantage of its technology investments and grow more efficiently.

Cadence: Creating a Customer Focus

In the early 1990s, Cadence Design Systems, the tenth largest software developer in the United States, was struggling to meet the demands of its rapidly changing customers. Cadence went from making a $55 million profit in 1992 to losing $13 million in 1993 and saw its stock drop over 36 percent in one day.

To correct the situation, Cadence decided it needed to "customize" its selling approach to match the way their customers liked to buy, instead of giving them a catalog of thousands of individual products to choose from. To accomplish this, Cadence switched to a strategy of selling more customized product and service "solutions" and invested in technologies to improve the selling process.

However, the real story was how Cadence made the painful organizational changes necessary to succeed. A shift from a "product-focused" to a "customer-focused" organization helped Cadence to double its revenues in the next four years.

On the product side, Cadence changed itself from a company that sold over 3000 different software products to a business that offered software with value-added services in product packages tailored to the specific needs of specific customers. By "resegmenting" the product line with a customer focus, Cadence found it could drop certain less profitable products. It would bundle others, and improve some product offerings by adding services.

On the selling technology front, Cadence invested in an "intranet" to give salespeople the information they needed about many different products and services their customers needed. 500

sales reps were outfitted with a sales force automation system that could easily "configure" client solutions from the thousands of components and full range of services Cadence had to offer.

The hard part was redefining its selling processes. By looking at how customers used their products, Cadence came up with several customer-defined buying processes called "technology flows." These "technology flows" processes had names like the "Deep Sub Micron Flow," "Chip Assembly Flow," "High-Speed Board Flow," "Logic Verification Flow," and "Architectural Level Design Flow." Arcane as they sound, these processes made sense to customers because they were consistent with how they bought and used the product in their own operations.

To shift the focus of marketing from products to the customer, product specialties were eliminated. Cadence broke apart their many product divisions and reorganized into "segment management" organizations that were responsible for "portfolios" of products that matched the technology "flows."

To sell this level of customization, Cadence had to make some changes in their sales force as well. For example, before the change, salespeople were experts in specific product lines. This motivated them to push their particular product on customers instead of giving them what they needed. This hurt margins as well because the sales force would often give away discounts or services to make enough sales to reach their product sales quotas.

Now these savvy tool specialists would become consultative sellers, focused on assembling the right solution for the customer. Cadence gave salespeople account responsibility and defined selling processes for salespeople to follow. It provided the skills they needed by training them in target account selling (TAS) and value-based selling (VAS). Giving salespeople customer responsibility and a clear process to follow forced them to use the sales force automation and knowledge-base software they were provided with, to coordinate on accounts and share information across the organization.

Getting the rank-and-file to sign on to these changes was critical to success. Without marketing, sales, and delivery management working together like a team, Cadence would not have gotten the same results from its strategy and CRM technology investment.

Driving Growth with Customer Data

Many companies like Cadence are leading a wave of investment in customer databases and automated tools that are commonly referred to as customer relationship management (CRM). In 1990 only a handful of very sophisticated marketers had built large databases about their customers that exceeded 1 terabyte of information (a terabyte is one trillion bytes). Customer databases that size are now common. By the year 2000, a full third of Global 2000 companies had built customer databases that exceeded a terabyte, according to the META Group.

Executives at these companies rubber-stamp these multimillion-dollar CRM investments because they truly believe that better customer data will be a pivotal factor in growing revenues and building a competitive edge. Already, many "early adopter" companies in the financial services, high-technology, and telecommunications industries are putting the finishing touches on their long-term CRM projects that consolidate customer information in "data warehouses."

This data is the gasoline that fuels personalized products and "one-to-one" promotions. Armed with better data about customer buying patterns, service-level requirements and—ultimately—profitability, organizations can build better products and design more relevant promotions. This data will also allow organizations to rebuild their selling processes around their most profitable customers. For example, companies like Cadence and Fidelity are using this information to break down their customer bases into smaller and smaller segments that can be "managed" better. Large financial services supermarkets like CitiGroup and Bank of America are using this information to design "cross-sell" and "upsell" marketing campaigns that identify products customers might like from other divisions (for example, offering car insurance to customers who have just taken out a car loan).

When CRM systems start coming online, most companies learn the hard way that getting a return on these investments requires process change. A recent Economist Intelligence Unit survey of Global 2000 companies found that while only 18 percent of the surveyed businesses are currently organized around "customer type," nearly 50 percent expect to be reorganized along those lines by 2002. Additionally, most (76 percent) of the responding executives foresaw that within five years, a high degree of integration between sales and IT functions would become commonplace in their organizations, and 27 percent report that such collaboration exists today.

Even Microsoft—a company famous for great products—has reorganized around its customers. The company was formerly structured along product and technology lines. For example, Windows 2000 was first introduced as a single solution for all consumer and business needs. It is now "customized" for four customer-focused groups: consumers, corporate customers, home office and telecommuters, and software developers in its own industry. The big shift is an acknowledgment that even top companies have a better shot at growing and retaining customers through superior customer relationships, even with a killer product like the Windows operating system.

Short-Term Strategy: Identify and Inventory Key Customer-Oriented Functions and Business Activities

Most companies are quick to become enchanted with expensive "black box" CRM technologies and solutions that promise more sales and happier customers. But sales and marketing executives should not rely too heavily on software applications to create business value. It is also a mistake to put CRM "in place" and *then* turn to the task of making necessary, and possibly painful, changes to organizational structures, management systems, and customer communications controls.

This is putting the cart before the horse—or the elephant before the ringmaster. Some thought needs to go into just who they are going to put behind the wheel of this expensive CRM machine they are building, and what skills are needed to run it well. In other words, if your CRM program team is spending millions to build the marketing equivalent of a jet aircraft, and all your marketing team knows how to drive is a car, you may have some problems. Even the best race-car drivers in the world will not be very good at flying a jet aircraft unless they have the skills to fly it.

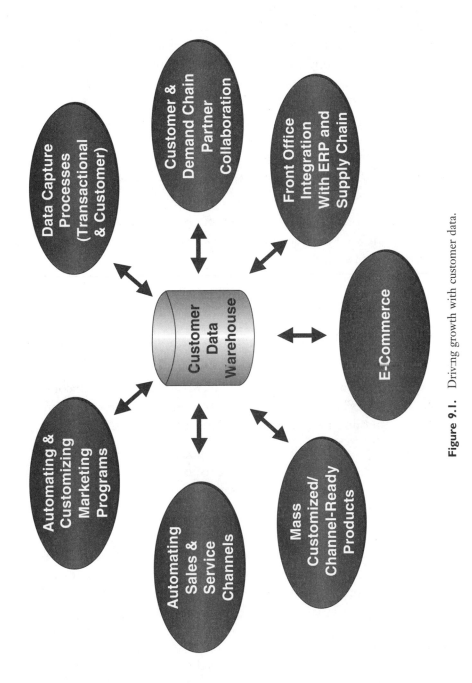

Figure 9.1. Driving growth with customer data.

The immediate challenge for executives is to determine whether they have the people and procedures in place to extract real value from the technology. A first step is to identify and inventory the top customer-oriented functions and business activities that are currently underway within your organization.

Executives can assess how ready their organizations are to "fly the CRM machine" by asking themselves the following questions:

Who in our organization is (or can be) responsible for:

> Managing the input, output, and quality of customer data into the critical and expensive customer database we just built?

> Picking products and services off the rack to deliver "mass customized" and personalized products to our highly targeted one-to-one customer segments?

> Creating the market segmentation, customer profiles, and data models necessary to build and run sophisticated targeted marketing automation programs and customer data warehouses that have something to do with how you go to market and sell?

> Managing and supporting the performance of "key account Web sites" and affiliate networks that are the focus of our extranet and interactive advertising investments?

> Actively monitoring and managing the profitability and satisfaction of each customer regardless of the organization, sales channel, or point of interaction they are dealing with on a day-to-day basis?

> Establishing business requirements to direct ongoing CRM investment that factors into your businesses' market coverage and growth strategies into business requirements for the CRM investment plan?

The answers to these questions often point to the need for new job functions and skills. For example, if your organization just spent millions of dollars to collect data about which customers pay the most and which customers complain the most, then someone is going to have to analyze the information to figure out what actions to take based on that information. While there is plenty of popular software to do this (from SAS or SPSS, for example) the analytical skills needed to interpret and act on it are in short supply in most marketing departments. Some new job functions will be needed to fill these gaps. Job titles like chief customer officer, market segment manager, CRM program manager, online channel managers, and direct marketing analysts are becoming more common as organizations struggle to find the right people to run their CRM machinery.

One new function that will emerge to meet these needs include the e-care executive (or the chief customer officer). These positions typically enter into the corporate lexicon as soon as "conflicts" occur between the Web channel and the sales force, or the CEO gets a phone call from a client complaining about SPAM (unsolicited commercial e-mails) from the marketing department, or a business reporter writes a feature about how your customers' e-mails have gone unanswered for five months.

The role goes far beyond simply being a customer advocate. Some organizations designate a vice president, from Microsoft (worldwide customer care) to Agilent technologies (e-care and privacy) to wrestle with how they will administer privacy and permission e-mail policies and customer contact rules across business units. Digital Think, an online education company, created a chief customer officer role to oversee all customer-facing functions including sales, customer service, and business development.

Another area of need will be the CRM program office. As organizations assemble cross-functional teams to develop customer relationship management strategies, someone will have to run the show. For example, a large printing company assembled a cross-functional CRM team that included inside sales, the head of marketing information systems, and the head of the e-commerce business division. On the IT side of the table sat the help-desk manager, who was getting complaints from frustrated salespeople, the manager of the sales force automation technology, and the customer data warehouse manager. Keeping all of these people happy and working together will take strong project management, diplomacy skills, and a solid understanding of technology.

Once a Web site is built, it does not run itself. *Online channel managers* will be needed. In the late 1990s, most organizations had "special" Web operations like interactive marketing or an e-commerce Web site. These were regarded as infant sales and marketing channels, to be incubated until organizations figured out what they were good for. For a while it was vague as to whether these folks managed marketing or had sales quotas, or just had special titles, wore cool clothes, and drank lots of Starbucks coffee.

As online channels and media mature, these experimental programs are being pulled back into mainstream marketing operations. Online channel managers will ultimately be held accountable for sales quotas and productivity to electronic commerce sites, online marketplaces, affiliate networks, or key account extranets. They will either grow in the role or be replaced with people who know their P (profit) from L (loss).

Some traditional roles like *direct marketing analysis* will become more important parts of the team. For customer information to do any good, it needs to be used by marketers and executives. As customer information becomes a strategic asset, and more marketing programs require business analytics to run, the direct marketing discipline will need to be extended beyond the direct marketing organization into mainstream marketing management and even general management. In some organizations, this role has also been elevated to a vice president position. Examples include Bear Creek Corporation, a mail order catalog company that sells fine fruits, confectioneries, roses, and orchids. First National Bank created a VP-level position to manage and mine marketing information across over 6 million customers and 18 million accounts.

The chief customer officer: the symptom or the solution?

All the forces of gravity suggest that the chief customer officer needs to exist. As companies build increasingly complicated selling systems with more and more ways for customers to interact with the organization (such as e-mail, the Web, interactive kiosks, ATMs, call centers, expanded selling partner networks, and outlets) they will be forced to manage these expanded contact points on a companywide level.

Someone must be placed as the advocate (or at least the dispassionate observer) of the newly empowered customer. New program management positions, such as chief customer officer or e-care executives, may be created to coherently manage the profitability of customer relationships as they are spread over many different selling channels and affect each phase of the selling process. Much like Ford's "Quality Is Job One" program in the 1980s elevated the importance of quality as a differentiator against stiff Japanese competition, the chief customer officer is a call to action for organizations to pay attention to customer processes, policies, and service levels. The primary difference between today and the customer service management frenzy 15 years ago is that customer relationship management involves more complicated cross-functional business process channel systems with many customer touch points, and expensive technologies that must be justified.

If the chief customer officer function actually existed (a few really do), they would have a job description that included some meaningful objectives like:

> Defining customer service and contact management standards, including customer data privacy policies for the entire company;
>
> Identifying cross-functional business processes;
>
> Deploying and integrating customer relationship management solutions;
>
> Bringing a voice of the customer to the organization;
>
> Defining and administering customer-service-based incentives and measurements.

The job as currently described is largely an omnibudsman function with a lot of symbolic value. This is vague and lacks teeth in the form of budget and line responsibility or executive-level influence. In the entrenched, product-focused mentality still common to global 2000 organizations, there is considerable upper-management reluctance to give broad powers to a customer surrogate. To ignore the issue risks losing advantage to "new economy" competitors who can beat you with a stronger customer focus.

A third alternative, and perhaps the best option, is to cast the role of chief customer officer as a transitional organizational figure that is part of the path to defining the next generation of customer service executives. In this scenario, effective chief customer officers would retire themselves.

Long-term Imperative: Four Actions to Become a More Customer-Centric Organization

Executives looking to get out in front of the competition should focus their longer-term attention to four key areas of organizational evolution:

1. **Create a new breed of executive;**
2. **Shift to customer segment management;**
3. **Create highly segmented distribution systems;**
4. **Define marketing-driven customer data architecture and policies.**

1. Create a new breed of executive

The weight of multimillion-dollar investments in electronic commerce and CRM programs will force companies to find or develop a "new breed" of executives who can bridge the many departmental communities involved in CRM systems.

Much like the segment managers at Cadence Design Systems, these executives are being given functional responsibility for getting the builders of these systems to work more closely with the sales, marketing, and service organizations that use them. These managers will need to be diplomats that can get many different departments to agree on things. In particular, they must be excellent at getting IT and marketing to work together effectively.

Marketing and IT folks are meeting for the first time on crossfunctional teams for CRM and e-business task forces. In a study of 50 leading CRM implementations, marketers reported they were actively involved in CRM projects 77 percent of the time. The goal of these teams is to combine marketing strategy with

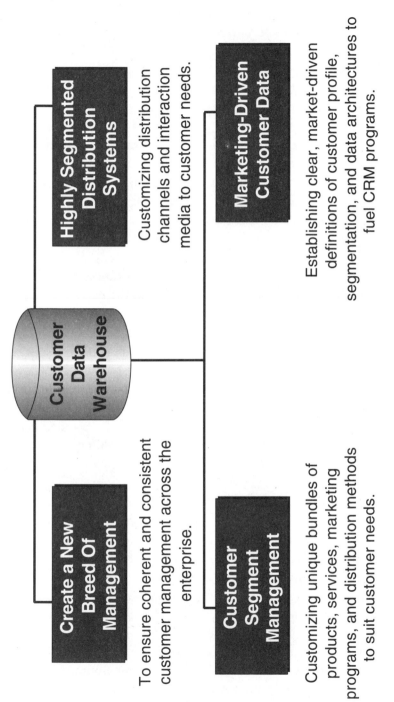

Figure 9.2. Four key actions to creating a customer-centric organization.

technology strategy. Working effectively requires the two departments to find a common language and develop a common planning process.

Common language is important because despite their best efforts to work together, IT and marketing organizations speak entirely different languages and have very different incentive plans. For example, "strategy" to the CIO means "electronic systems architecture," while to sales and marketing executives, "strategy" means a "sales growth plan." IT organizes around applications, infrastructure, and services, while marketing organizes around markets, products, and distribution channels.

Measurement and incentives are another bridge these new executives will need to cross. Measurements for IT are largely internal and cost-based, while marketers are focused on external benchmarks like market share, growth targets, and customer satisfaction. Typical CIO yardsticks include day-to-day reliability of data and systems, while marketers focus on longer-term performance, such as meeting quarterly or other periodic revenue quotas. Probably most significantly, the IT department measures return on investment in terms of total cost of ownership, while a marketer's scorecard looks at costs in relation to revenue and share growth. In the survey cited above, when asked if their CRM initiatives were successful, the IT folks who installed it claimed it was a success, while marketers were hard pressed in 80 percent of the cases to come up with math that justified the investment in the first place.

Finally, these "hybrid executives" will have to build a common process for many organizations to work together. For example, the marketing department and customer service department don't work together much. Marketers are good at writing letters and developing ad campaigns that drive calls to the telemarketing department. However, they have no easy way to give customer service ideas on how to turn inbound customer questions into sales. This is why after years of lip service, most large banks are still pulling their hair out trying to execute "cross-sell" and "upsell" campaigns in the customer service department. Doing so means the marketing and customer service (and IT) departments must work more closely on a day-to-day basis.

Marketing, sales, and IT are not used to planning budgets together. Marketers tend to plan from the top down, breaking a revenue goal into its component parts and distributing the work out. IT tends to deploy first and learn later, just to stay ahead of the technology curve. At the end of the day, both sides of the house need to find a way to link the revenue growth plan to technology and software selection criteria to succeed. This will take some relationship coaching in the near term.

2. Shift to customer segment management

Historically, in strong consumer marketing organizations like Procter & Gamble and Gillette, the primary management focus is products or product lines. Traditional product managers' jobs have limited incentive and opportunity to personalize their offerings to the needs of a customer. For example, the primary task of a product manager for a hot dog is to find ways to sell 10 percent more hot dogs this year than last year. Likewise, the product manager for canned beans needs to sell 10 percent more beans. If a prospective customer does not like hot dogs but enjoys franks cut up in beans at family barbeques, the product manager has limited opportunities to pursue this kind of customer. Unless a third "pork-and-beans" product manager exists, the two product managers don't have an incentive or resources to work together to fill this customized need. The opportunity falls through the cracks or gets tossed to new product development.

To better take advantage of the opportunity to personalize and target their marketing approaches, some companies are changing their organizations to focus more resources on "segment-based management" of products, marketing, and sales channels. This shift in management focus allows them to better integrate many different product and selling channel "fiefdoms" so they make more sense to the customer. It is an important step to instilling a corporate culture change from product focus to a customer focus.

As has been discussed earlier in this book, the practice of segmenting and resegmenting of products, services, marketing campaigns and sales channels will become a core management discipline for the modern sales and marketing executive. To make this happen, marketing management needs to create jobs focused on customer segments. Companies like Cadence saw sales grow 100 percent in four years when they started resegmenting product offerings with customer groups in mind.

Innovators like Fidelity and First National Bank have started to create "segment management" positions where managers are responsible for assembling "portfolios" of products, distribution channels, and service options that are tuned to the individual needs of groups of customers. For example, a segment manager for "the busy executive" market segment would understand that this customer valued time over money. The segment manager would avoid sending lengthy research or big investment prospectuses to these customers. They would instead package only the critical highlights of new products in personalized "e-mail alerts" that would encapsulate only the most important market information the customer would need to make decisions—or at least feel sufficiently updated with this heads-up. If these "busy executives" spend a lot of money, make decisions fast, but also don't have time to look up the password, the segment manager would make sure the account reps covering these clients could access critical pieces of identifying information and be empowered to execute the customer's orders quickly.

Those employed to be "segment managers" will manage these portfolios against more sophisticated measurements that reflect the business rationale behind CRM, which include improving "share of wallet," reducing "costs to sell," and increasing the profitability of each customer, either over time (lifetime customer value) or as a result of a particular campaign.

First National Bank: Mastering the Art of Segmentation

First National Bank invested heavily in consolidating customer data into a single customer data warehouse. The goals of this investment included better retention of customers in a competitive banking market, growing "share of wallet," and managing and measuring customer profitability.

This was a complex and expensive task, since the bank had over 6 million customers and performed over 75 million annual transactions that were stored in over 9 different data banks. The project team successfully consolidated this data into a single customer data "asset." Then it made the customer data more useful to sale and marketing by matching households and "clustering" the data to better understand customer behavior.

First National Bank took the additional step of forming a market segment management team that was responsible for using this data to grow customer profitability and improve service levels. They reallocated marketing staffers to serve as "customer segment managers" who used this data to create a "master customer segmentation" for the entire company that showed the behavior of how customers were actually buying the products and services offered by First National. This could be matched up with the bank's market coverage approach and growth plans.

Having a companywide view of the customer also allowed these segment managers to better redirect sales and marketing programs and resources to where they would do the most good and create the greatest top- and bottom-line growth.

For example, by examining customers' channel preferences, account balances, and product preferences across multiple organizations and product divisions, these managers could budget their marketing resources in a more effective way. This data was also used to design customized cross-sell campaigns targeted at the highest potential customers, and providing better training direction to the customer-facing employees who were responsible for making sales.

3. Create highly segmented distribution systems

As organizations expand the number of channels they use to reach customers (see Chapter 5), the number of "paths" a product can take to market tends to multiply. Sales and distribution managers will need to better manage how products move through these complicated distribution systems' organizations. This is because there are economic benefits of managing how a product moves through the system. "Transaction" costs and profits can vary dramatically depending on which "path" a product takes.

For example, Financial services companies, such as Schwab and Fidelity, and PC manufacturers, such as Dell, have been able to profitably sell products that are commodities or have small margins by placing them into specific distribution channels, particularly interactive media for self-service that have lower selling costs.

Also, customers are buying through different combinations of channels. Marketers in the automobile, brokerage, and computer hardware businesses have found that customers increasingly prefer newer Web sites, kiosks, ATMs, and automated telephone systems channels for certain types of interactions.

As a result, leading organizations are putting energy into segmenting customers and products in terms of which distribution channels they fit best with. They are building sophisticated management systems to support these multitier "paths to market" that blend a mix of selling channels, customer interfaces, and CRM marketing programs. These distribution systems will require clearly defined customer coverage models to line up the best product with the best selling channel resources based on the way customers want to buy.

Fidelity: Tracking Customers Through Many Channels

Fidelity, a leader in mutual funds management, enjoyed phenomenal share growth in the mid to late 1990s. But this growth had less to do with the performance of its funds—many other funds did as well—but more to do with Fidelity's skills in deploying existing customer information to configure its marketing messages and new product offerings to specific distribution channels.

Because Fidelity sold directly to customers, it could amass a great deal of primary customer data. It analyzed this data to create about eleven customer segments based on "customer buying behavior." And it began customizing unique "routes-to-market" based on how, where, and when customers wanted to buy.

For one particular investor segment, for example, Fidelity might build a customer relationship by attracting that certain class of customer with an appealing suburban storefront. The storefront representative would establish an online brokerage account for a customer, which the customer would use for day-to-day trading and reporting needs. A telephone hotline was also available. Subsequently, an affiliated independent agent could cross-sell more complicated annuity products when the customer seemed ready.

That is, when the customer's product history and account activity indicated the time was right for a prospecting phone call.

4. Define marketing-driven customer data architecture and policies

The significant investments in CRM technologies mean that the IT functions and business executives will have to get out of their respective silos and work together much more closely. It is often tempting to hand over the entire job of analytical data-crunching for CRM to the team that installed the technology, but responsible sales and marketing managers will err if they defer the critical job of defining and segmenting critical customer markets and demand chain processes to others.

In the current business environment, these strategic marketing tasks are increasingly prescribed by IT organizations, outsourced integrators, or "consultants" working with software solutions providers. It pays to remember that CRM vendor teams, as well as your company's own IT managers, have incentives to deploy predetermined "data models," reporting templates, or "canned" software vendor solutions because they speed execution and simplify integration. There are very few "one-fits-all" solutions.

Sales and marketing management must take the lead in defining which customer data will be the most useful to capture, well before the IT department goes shopping for software and gear. They must also have a voice to assure that this useful customer data can be quickly retrieved and compiled easily for the use of "nontechies" in the sales and marketing department. This is in keeping with sales and marketing as a whole assuming more responsibility for customer data assets. Executives should take the time to build protocols and procedures to ensure their continued input and control over programs that impact—or even track—core customer behaviors.

Line-of-business executives, including the "portfolio managers" of the newly restructured selling team, should shoulder, as much as possible, a functional management over the structure, input, output, and quality of customer data. They should be actively involved in the ongoing development of formal data policies and processes. They will probably have to spend a little time in the IT silo to gear up: CRM works best if everyone knows how it works, and what its benefits can be.

Bottom Line

Organizational structures will have to change, to focus more on the customer and house the new skills needed to run sophisticated sales and marketing systems.

CHAPTER

Building Customer Care Systems:

Extending Customer Service into Electronic Channels

Whenever selling organizations add channels, launch an interactive direct marketing program, or deploy CRM initiatives, they can expect dramatic growth in the number of online customer interactions. Corporate Web sites, around-the-clock online customer support, "e-tailing," targeted Web advertising, and e-mail direct marketing will open the door to hundreds and ultimately thousands of electronic customer inquiries weekly.

A Boston Consulting/Harris Interactive study showed that 51 percent of Americans bought online during the 2000 Christmas season. That same Christmas, 16 million more tried to buy online but failed. Depending on your perspective, this is either a customer service nightmare waiting to happen or a selling opportunity waiting to be harvested. To solve the problem, we will have to relearn much of what we know about customer service and invest in new approaches to delivering customer support.

Customer service is being reinvented to handle many different contact points and use information to improve service levels. In the short term, fixing online customer response problems can be critical. But the real rewards will go to those companies that stay focused on building customer care systems that add value to the customer experience. The strategy of online marketplace pioneer e-Bay provides a good perspective on what can be done to manage extremely high levels of online customer interactions.

eBay: Delivering Customer Care Without Phones

As late as spring 2001 you could still go to eBay's popular auction Web site and search high and low for an 800-number telephone link to the company. A telephone line for customer service simply didn't exist. Lack of traditional "phone support" wasn't simply hubris for this pure-play startup: it was a matter of survival.

Since its beginnings, eBay has struggled to keep up with its own success and match its online customer growth with online customer service excellence. The company amassed 3.8 million registered members in its first two-and-a-half years, and of course its online customer interactions grew just as dramatically. As a consequence, e-Bay has had to deal with volumes of online customer inquiries that are an order of magnitude greater than almost everyone else.

In its early stages, eBay received 200 e-mails each week with submissions, bids, or replies from buyers and sellers. They soon received 60,000–75,000 messages each week and now routinely pass the 100,000 mark. To handle this rapidly growing load of online customer interactions, the company built a customer service and support staff of 200 employees and 60 independent contractors. They invested in an electronic mail response management system (MRM) by Kana Communications (now part of Broadbase) that provided e-mail routing and tracking. Kana also helped eBay build a "knowledge base" of sales and support content that describes the rules and requirements for using the auction site services.

The combination of mail response management and knowledge base reportedly improved customer service representatives' productivity by more than 50 percent, as they learned to route messages to appropriate specialists and dealt with routine inquiries by invoking the ready-made content in the company knowledge base.

The knowledge base also allowed eBay to provide customers with a self-service alternative for frequently asked questions. Such a strategy was perfectly attuned to its customer base, a broad army of do-it-yourselfers who enjoy buying and selling in the comfort of their own homes. At last look, the knowledge base currently answered 200 questions every 20 minutes, without assistance from a service representative. (By way of comparison, the best live reps at IBM's state-of-the-art tele-web center manage 400 e-mails per day.)

Over time, e-Bay has created a variety of options for customer self-service within the site. One popular function is a "rating" service that allows customers to comment on the quality of their trade with another member (the best get gold stars). This kind of self-policing wards off customer problems and helps decrease the chances of an unsatisfactory trade. It's a form of "proactive" customer service that helps reduce complaints or error-related customer queries. Other online self help options include automated account management, item search engine, a suggestion box, and dozens of forums and chats in topic areas. eBay also has a standard e-mail customer service request form, but buried deep within its Web pages to encourage maximum usage of the automated knowledge base.

Factoring Electronic Customer Interactions into Service and Support Strategies

The challenge of delivering customer service online is not restricted to Internet innovators like e-Bay. As traditional "bricks and mortar" organizations blend electronic sales, marketing, and service channels into their selling mix, they will also need to reinvent the concept of customer service. Adding online channels means businesses will interact more frequently with their customers, and much of this interaction will be electronic. As companies mature through e-commerce adolescence, they will struggle to "plug the holes" in their customer service operations, so they can more effectively manage the increasing volumes of electronic inquiries and capture some valuable customer data. Managing a high volume of customer interactions over low-cost, online channels will become fundamental to business success.

But extending customer service into electronic channels goes well beyond investing in technologies that make self-service easier and automate electronic response management. Sophisticated customer care systems that can handle a mix of online and offline inquiries gracefully are proving to be fundamental to customer retention in electronic channels. It is an important part to building e-brand loyalty. It is a requisite to delivering seamless service to "schizophrenic" customers who want to move easily across a range of online and offline channels. Consistency is vital: a Price-Waterhouse Coopers study in 2000 found that half of online shoppers reported they were influenced by shopping they had done in brick-and-mortar stores and paper catalogs. And a quarter of store purchases and a third of catalog purchases were influenced by browsing online channels.

e-Pocalypse Now: The Coming Flood of e-Inquiries

As online marketing and customer intimacy efforts intensify in the next two years, e-mail and Web self-service customer inquiries will grow dramatically. For instance, 1997 was the first year the Americans sent more e-mails than "white mail." By the end of the decade, e-mail had eclipsed regular mail by a five-to-one ratio. Around the year 2000 a mature and successful electronic commerce site averaged e-mail volumes of 1000 to 5000 per week.

At the head of the pack, online stock traders Suretrade and Schwab receive well over 20,000 messages a day. Retailers anecdotally report that inbound electronic inquiries tend to double every month once they start offering merchandise online. Superb online promotions can boost the input even more. Victoria's Secret, for example, received 1.5 million Web site visitors after an online lingerie fashion show was promoted on the Super Bowl telecast.

Most established businesses are ill prepared to handle this increased volume of e-customer inquiries. Until recently, 95 percent of Global 2000 organizations reported they were receiving less than 1000 inbound electronic communications per week, according to a study by *Sales and Marketing Magazine* and Pittiglio, Rabin, Todd, and McGrath.

Yet most businesses are still struggling to respond to online customers within 24 hours. Many shopping sites can only manage an average e-mail response time of 48 hours, according to a recent Shopping.org study. Even "best-in-class" companies do not perform that well. An informal test in 2001 by *The Industry Standard* of the 10 most highly trafficked electronic commerce sites (as defined by Media Metrix) showed that:

> Only 7 of the top 10 were able to respond to a product availability e-mail inquiry in less than 24 hours.
>
> Only 6 of 10 provided personalized responses.
>
> Only 8 of 10 actually answered the question that was asked.

Response times for these "best-in-class" companies, all well-known brand names, ranged from 34 minutes to 73 hours. And as late as 1999, an informal study of Fortune 100 companies by Brightware, a software company, showed that more than three-quarters of the world's largest selling organizations did not respond to a simple e-mail request within a day. Ten percent did not respond at all.

Clearly, there is room here for many companies to set themselves apart from the herd with prompt, online customer service. As a point of reference, most established e-commerce companies average from 1000 to 15,000 electronic customer interactions per week. Bellwethers like Schwab and e-Bay manage more than 100,000 electronic inquiries per week. Less than 10 percent of "brick and mortar" enterprises currently receive more than 1000 customer e-mails per week.

But that number is expected to triple as Internet use expands: in 2001 approximately 60 percent of U.S. homes were wired for the Web. The past experience of early adopters suggests that ad-hoc customer response systems (such as those that bounce queries to traditional call centers) begin to break down as the volume of electronic customer inquiries grows to between 500–1000 per week.

Short-Term Strategy: Capture Inbound Electronic Customer Inquiries

To deliver adequate support to customers, most businesses will be forced to build coherent e-response management systems. This is critical to meeting customer expectations and establishing trust. These management systems will cleverly combine human interaction with technical solutions like electronic mail response management systems (MRMs) that can automatically deliver personalized responses and can be expanded easily to match rapid volume growth. To build these systems, senior management must focus on three near-term priorities:

1. **Reallocate sufficient resources to service and support e-response;**
2. **Add e-response and self-help technical infrastructure;**
3. **Establish a single point of management control for online customer care.**

1. Reallocate resources to e-response

Human interaction will always play a major role in customer response management. Real people are necessary to solve complex problems, respond to cries for help from the "e-frustrated," and intercede or "cover" events like Web site failures and other forms of error resolution. In the best scenarios, well-trained tele-web reps may collaborate online with customers (via shared electronic white boards, Internet chat, or voice over IP,) to sell, cross-sell, and upsell products and services.

How much should be allotted to supporting the needs of online customers? Customer lifetime value certainly enters in the equation here. Premium real-estate companies with Web sites may find it well worth their while to add a "live Web chat" with a sales agent if they stand to get a $20,000 commission on a $800,000 co-op apartment in New York City. In the direct-marketing industry, where customer lifetime values are measured in hundreds of dollars, catalogers like Land's End try to balance live telephone with online resources operators to serve online customers who buy products with much smaller price tags. For others like e-Bay, who must deal with small transaction fees combined with massive online inquiry volumes, it probably makes it economically impossible to offer full-scale phone support.

For some businesses, the solution may be to reallocate some of their outlay for call-center agents or customer service representatives to handle e-mail response. Companies can choose to build or buy this capacity incrementally. Some firms cross-train existing agents so they can respond to e-mail as well as phone calls. Others dedicate certain customer service representatives to e-response as a functional specialty or create "centers of excellence" as e-response utilities. Notably, ibm.com takes this approach and is able to respond to e-mails from customers within four hours, taking full advantage of a state-of-the-art mail response program that was pretty expensive. This makes sense because electronic customer response requires technical and writing skills.

This strategy worked for iGo, formerly known as 1-800-Batteries. The company caters to mobile professionals, selling portable devices, their accessories, and supplies. Traditionally, iGo relied on telephone agents to field customer calls. When it opened its e-commerce site in 1994, traffic mushroomed. E-mail began piling up at a rate of 100 per day, and it took two days before service representatives could respond to the gamut of online requests, which ranged from routine order status questions to whether the company carried batteries for cattle prods. As the process got out of control, it was later discovered that 50 e-mails even got lost in the shuffle.

This represented a serious customer service problem for a business-to-consumer electronic commerce company that was well aware that its tech-savvy customers could switch to the competition at a click of a button.

To fix the problem, iGo installed an e-mail response management system and hired a small group of people to serve as e-mail specialists at its call-center. Each of these specialists now handles 200–400 online messages per day.

Firms with limited call-center capacity can add independent contractors to handle an upsurge, such as event-driven (campaign-driven) spikes in e-response volumes. Many traditional retailers and virtual businesses simply outsource to grow capacity quickly. These firms are turning to a growing number of customer support service bureaus, cyber call centers, and low-cost, real-time chat-based customer support for answers.

All of the above are Band-Aid solutions, however. To handle the expected real volume of customer interactions that arrive via Web channels but do not require a complicated response, we must turn to machines, not humans.

2. Build an e-response and self-help technical infrastructure

To efficiently respond to thousands of electronic inquiries, businesses must turn to technology for leverage. This will require investments in two key areas: electronic mail response management (MRM) programs, and automated self-help systems that give customers access to product-related or sales-related "knowledge bases."

A good e-mail management response program (MRM) can enable a single call-center customer service rep to handle hundreds of inquiries daily, most with personalized responses, and many without any intervention at all. These software solutions basically use artificial intelligence technology to "read" and sort inbound inquires and respond to simple questions. For instance, mortgage brokers get thousands of online inquiries through Internet marketplaces like Lendingtree.com that let consumers comparison shop. MRM software would automatically answer the simplest inquiries (e.g., what interest rate do you offer?). If an inquiry is important (e.g., I am ready to lock in a million-dollar mortgage right now to the first person who calls me), the program would "escalate" the inquiry to a human who can take action right away.

These software applications can also be programmed with an organization's own "business rules" that stipulate when complex problems or large opportunities should be transferred appropriately to humans. More than 20 vendors have emerged in this area, including E.Piphany, eGain Communications, Kana Communications (part of Broadbase), and Brightware. META Group estimates that 75 percent of Global 2000 companies will have these types of applications in place by 2002.

Customer knowledge bases try to give customers the information they need to answer questions themselves. These can be as simple as FAQ pages (lists of answers to frequently asked questions) or as complicated as self-service libraries for diagnosing problems on personal computers or steam turbines. Such "technical support databases" can capture the engineering knowledge locked in the brains of designers and field engineers and offer it online to industrial customers. These can cost millions of dollars to develop and need to be cost-justified because only certain types of customers (the "Leave-me-alone-Larrys") will use them.

Online self-service transactions cost *pennies* compared to phone-based service approaches. A simple customer service call costs about $35 per call (to check order status or answer a simple question). A technical support inquiry can easily exceed $100 per call (for more complicated technical support questions).

To date, most companies are only beginning to stretch beyond basic self-service capabilities on their Web sites or customer extranets. The most common services are those perceived by the customer to add value; these include order tracking, part number look up, a complaint box, natural language search (a la "Ask Jeeves"), and the interactive chat mentioned earlier.

Most of these self-service capabilities mentioned above will soon be considered mainstream business tools. It is a perfect example of how the customer service bar has been raised. A growing number of consumer and business buyers now fully expect to be able to check their order status online at any time of day.

Building an interactive database to provide relevant information to customers, while technically feasible, can, however, be labor intensive. Not surprisingly, this, too, can be outsourced.

3. Establish a single point of management control for inbound electronic inquiries

Organizations need a single point of control to manage online customer inquiries and service requests effectively. A business that opens several avenues for customer communications and has independently managed e-business initiatives is creating the possibility of poor customer service.

Many e-business programs are still managed independently by individuals, by specific functions (e.g., advertising, direct marketing, product marketing), and sometimes through entirely separate organizations. Consequently, few Web sites are well integrated with customer service call centers, and many e-mails "fall to the floor" unanswered due to lack of coordination.

The solution in many cases is to create a position or a job function to handle customer service in online channels. Some of the traditional job descriptions, such as customer service manager or call-center manager, may fall within this purview.

The immediate tasks for these managers include:

> Taking inventory of all points of interaction (any place where customer can contact your company) where electronic customer communication can occur;

> Documenting trends and spikes in electronic customer interaction volumes;

> Establishing realistic estimates and targets for service levels and capacity requirements;

> Mapping how electronic interactions flow across a mix of many different sales, service, and support channels (like phone versus retail service center versus the Web).

This data, when gathered, will provide a foundation for managing and allocating resources for customer service in electronic channels. It can also help determine the level of investment in electronic mail management applications and other forms of self-service automation. Particularly if resources need to be taken away from other programs, taking the process apart and looking for bottleneck areas will help develop a business rationale to justify reallocating resources.

Long-Term Imperative: Building Customer Care into the Sales and Marketing Process

Responding to electronic customer inquiries is only a start. Marketing leaders will look beyond the immediate challenge of "e-response" to focus on ways to add value to customers through advanced customer care systems.

Marketing and sales managers will need to work more closely with service and technical support to find ways to use their customer care systems to increase revenue, not for damage control. To create competitive advantage, companies must integrate their online and offline service channels, anticipate service needs, and ultimately leverage technology to embed service in their product offerings to maintain a lasting customer relationship.

There are three steps these managers can take:

1. **Integrate service channels across the company;**
2. **Anticipate service needs to avoid costs and grow sales;**
3. **Embed service into products.**

I. Integrate service channels across the company

Headquartering customer service in the tele-web center is a good way to bring many "points of interaction" together in a single place. Call centers based on a single channel (i.e., the telephone) are being evolved into "tele-web" command centers that can manage multiple channels in one place. Tele-web centers (covered in greater detail in Chapter 8) will become hubs for all customer interactions including Web inquiries, e-mail, fax, phone, and other emerging media. This, in turn, provides a single point of management control over customer care processes, technology assets, and personnel.

Getting sales, service, and support organizations to present a "single face" to the customer can happen in several ways. By 2001 the stronger e-mail response management vendors (like E.piphany) were bundling many different tools into packages that can help customer service representatives manage and escalate electronic interaction across multiple online and offline channels and media. Alternatively, the major CRM suites currently in vogue (e.g., Siebel and Clarify) will eventually incorporate robust electronic customer collaboration applications like e-mail response management and Web personalization systems into their bundled packages of sales, service, and support applications. In addition, providing these call-center agents with useful CRM tools lets them use data about buying histories and other past customer behavior (see Chapter 11) to open the door to upsell opportunities from human salespeople.

Not everything can be automated, of course. Executive leadership must establish rules to govern customer collaboration, service quality, and lead flow, to avoid turf wars and encourage cooperation. Documenting interaction volumes, capacity, and customer migration across points of interaction is an important prelude to changing established rules.

2. Anticipate service needs to avoid costs and grow sales

An ounce of prevention is worth a pound of cure. Smart marketers no longer view service and support as a terminal stop at the end of a linear and transaction-oriented sales process. The leaders are using customer care as a way to retain and penetrate their key accounts. Here is the road map:

Forecast service needs ahead of demand. This will enable service and support management to effectively anticipate service volumes and issues and address or mitigate them before pileups occur.

Proactively push support solutions to customers. Businesses have the opportunity to apply relationship marketing and loyalty programs to cross-sell, upsell, and rebuy opportunities that are service-related. This will require the use of database marketing technologies (see Chapter 11) to proactively push service or service-related solutions to those who most likely need it.

Direct clients to more relevant and personalized information made available through lower-cost channels. It's not coincidence that a high percentage of advertisements, product packaging, and automated telephone systems urge the customer to "check out our Web site." The best way to serve customers when they oblige is accomplished by collecting and compiling better data about customers, the products they own, and their service history. Then Web personalization technologies can be applied to customize Web response to provide the exact information needed.

Proactive service models are hardly an innovation. The Book-of-the-Month Club set the standard for auto-replenishment. Receiving books and magazines by mail is one thing, but now, distribution innovation and one-to-one online technologies are making it possible for a wider range of companies like Drugstore.com and Peapod to offer "subscriptions" to groceries and sundry items. As obvious as this concept sounds, most organizations are unable to take advantage of these opportunities as much as they could because the service department head and marketing department head and the head of the CRM database probably sit in three different places in the average company.

Proactive service grows directly from what work companies have done to capture customer information in the service process. Amazon.com and 1-800-Flowers, two of the pioneers in e-commerce, originally started identifying and automating routine inquiries to minimize congestion in their help lines. Both companies figured out that a large percentage of post-sales service questions had to do with order tracking. By automatically sending online customers e-mails noting order confirmations and shipping status updates, they were able to keep customers informed and cut down on the traffic to their call centers.

Jiffy Lube, a chain of auto service companies, turned customer information into a sales tool. Based on a car's mileage noted at the time of a tune-up and information provided by manufacturers, the company projects when customers will be due for their next service and sends reminders via direct mail and telemarketers. When customers arrive at the Jiffy Lube location, service personnel enter license plate information and set off a process that touches on manufacturer databases and Jiffy Lube records enabling not only a quicker service recommendation but also a personalized greeting.

Pampers earns the good will of new mothers by sending a monthly e-mail newsletter from "the Pampers Parenting Institute" with tips and tricks on taking care of their babies (based on the baby's age). The newsletters offer "proactive" technical support by anticipating the mother's needs at each stage of life and are a platform for delivering advice and promotional offers just when the mother needs it most (e.g., teething solutions at five months, coupons for pull-ups in the second year).

Event-Triggered Marketing

Organizations that have invested millions of dollars collecting customer data are struggling to figure out how to use this information to grow revenues. Today the fastest-growing companies have already identified their most profitable customers through the use of CRM tools and are looking for ways to use service channels to extend the "lifetime value" of these customers. One good approach is called event-triggered marketing. This strategy uses customer database information to anticipate and automatically deliver promotions precisely when the customer is feeling pain or is ready to buy.

The trick is to identify the critical buying "events" in the customer life cycle. Smart marketers will resegment their revenues around events to figure out what events are associated with the greatest amount of revenues. For instance, 1800flowers.com, like its parent company, is fully aware that most flower sales fall on a few very specific events, including Mother's Day, Valentine's Day, birthdays, holidays, and illness in the family. Four out of these five events can be predicted with very little information. This online marketer seeks to "own" these events by collecting birthdays, anniversaries, and simple preferences and then hits customers with e-mail promotions with customized offers and coupons timed a week or so before the special date.

Simply being organized will get results in the short term. In many business-to-business operations, a large number of warranties and service contracts expire unnoticed. These are missed resale and cross-sell opportunities. These opportunities are termed "event-triggered marketing." In the future, marketers will get better at understanding the cause-and-effect relationships between events and buying to accurately predict when a sales opportunity is likely to occur. A CRM software model will notify salespeople when a customer's equipment is ready for an upgrade or a client is running out of cash and may need a loan.

3. Embedding service in products

Clever marketers will ultimately marry technology and service by embedding customer care into their products to add value to them.

Today, virtually every appliance—from a laptop computer to a refrigerator—comes with a service plan that can be purchased along with the product. Looking further into the future, companies will embed e-care in their products to enhance margins, increase the cost to the customer of switching to another vendor, and differentiate from the competition.

For example, software companies no longer sell static, isolated computer applications that sit on the computer. Intuit's Quicken is just one of many software products that features help-links built into the software, all tied to dynamically updated information on the Quicken Web site. Network Associates, a provider of computer network security solutions, allows its customers—home users and sophisticated network managers—to "subscribe" to a service that dynamically updates their "antivirus" software and helps them to ward off the latest computer viruses.

Computerized "help" networks are an obvious starting point, but advances in technology are creating opportunities to embed service into almost any offering. Microprocessors (chips) are small and cheap enough to be put into almost any product. Remote software programs like Java can run those remote microprocessors to diagnose or fix problems. New networks like wireless communications and the Internet are cheap and and pervasive enough to send back "real-time" information from the most remote locations.

Smart companies are already building services into products as diverse as train engines, elevators, and automobiles with the help of new technologies such as on-board diagnostics (which can tell how and when a product is broken). For example, GE Transportation Services installs 20 microprocessors in the locomotives they sell, to monitor engine parts and other critical train operations. If the cooling system is failing on a train routed to Pittsburgh, GE is able to warn the engineer of the problem and put in a work order to have it repaired when the train gets to its destination. Keeping trains healthy and running adds value to the locomotive product because the average train is out of service over a quarter of the time with maintenance problems. Otis Elevators does the same thing for their high-rise clients. The REMS (Remote Elevator Maintenance System) network monitors client elevators 24 hours a day. Appliance makers such as Whirlpool have

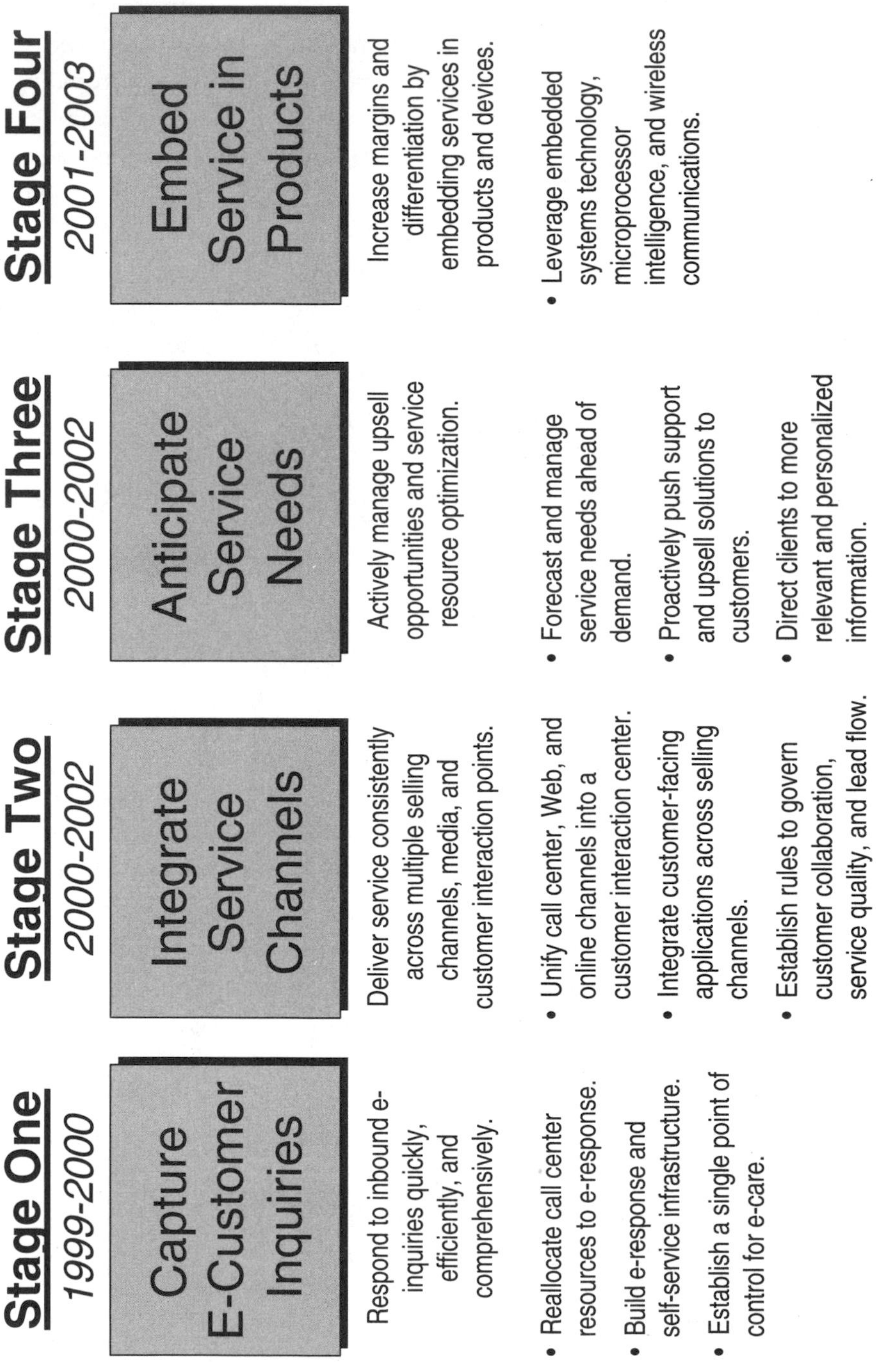

Stage One
1999-2000

Capture E-Customer Inquiries

Respond to inbound e-inquiries quickly, efficiently, and comprehensively.

- Reallocate call center resources to e-response.
- Build e-response and self-service infrastructure.
- Establish a single point of control for e-care.

Stage Two
2000-2002

Integrate Service Channels

Deliver service consistently across multiple selling channels, media, and customer interaction points.

- Unify call center, Web, and online channels into a customer interaction center.
- Integrate customer-facing applications across selling channels.
- Establish rules to govern customer collaboration, service quality, and lead flow.

Stage Three
2000-2002

Anticipate Service Needs

Actively manage upsell opportunities and service resource optimization.

- Forecast and manage service needs ahead of demand.
- Proactively push support and upsell solutions to customers.
- Direct clients to more relevant and personalized information.

Stage Four
2001-2003

Embed Service in Products

Increase margins and differentiation by embedding services in products and devices.

- Leverage embedded systems technology, microprocessor intelligence, and wireless communications.

Figure 10.1. The evolution of e-care.

shown prototype networked products, such as a microwave oven that can scan bar codes and communicate online with the makers of packaged foods to automatically handle cooking instructions.

One of the best early examples of embedded e-care is General Motors's OnStar system. OnStar takes advantage of cellular communication to provide customers with several safety and convenience-oriented services including roadside assistance, airbag deployment notification, and remote unlocking, directions, and concierge services.

"Subscribers" have the opportunity to talk directly with an OnStar representative or help themselves through a series of voice recognition prompts. Soon GM will offer OnStar customers "asset management services"—so GM can schedule maintenance and monitor the performance of the car remotely. The OnStar service itself is one of GM's rising brands and is changing the basis of competition in the luxury car market. Where once luxury cars differentiated themselves on the basis of physical product design, now online services are factoring into buying decisions.

Bottom Line

Customer service will be reinvented to handle many different contact points and use information to improve service levels.

Rebuilding Customer Exit Barriers with CRM:

Keeping Customers from Leaving

NEW ELECTRONIC CHANNELS ARE TEARING DOWN SOME OF THE TRADITIONAL BARRIERS THAT KEEP OUR CUSTOMERS FROM SWITCHING TO THE COMPETITION. Strong brands, good location, and being bigger are no longer as effective as they used to be in keeping our customers around.

Many organizations are investing millions of dollars in customer relationship management technology (otherwise known as CRM) in hopes of rebuilding these customer exit barriers. Marketers will be on the hook to make sure these expensive CRM systems actually keep their best and most profitable customers from leaving.

Understanding these technologies will be hard enough for most. But the difficult task will be to find ways to make the customer the "design criteria" for these expensive CRM systems. For this, marketers will have to look at the market through a different set of eyeglasses. This chapter will show how the best marketers are studying patterns of customer behavior to understand exactly where CRM can help in the buying process.

To be effective, marketers will have to think differently about the ties that bind buyers to sellers. Take the example of Anne Tesoro.

Customer Collaboration as an Exit Barrier

Anne Tesoro was born in the Bronx in the 1920s. She was the daughter of Italian immigrants and learned to shop on her mother's hip. Shop probably wasn't exactly the right word to describe it: more like haggle. Her passion was negotiating. To Anne, no price was fixed and everything was negotiable. When she would go to Arthur Avenue in the Bronx to buy fresh cheese, bread, and sausages from local merchants she would argue price and quality for hours with storefront vendors while live chickens were running around at her feet and her children cried. While shopping for suits of clothes at the open-air markets in the East Village of Manhattan, she inspected fabrics ruthlessly and argued for discounts based on shoddy workmanship, poor quality, and other factors real or imagined.

Anne always preferred a good fight to a good price. Her ongoing conversation with the merchants (in the form of haggling) was part of the shopping experience for her. This collaboration created a bond with the seller and was part of the "value proposition" for her. She remained loyal to these old neighborhood merchants even when she moved to the suburbs, even as large supermarkets and fancy shopping malls emerged in her new neighborhood. It wasn't so much the fresh mozzarella that kept her driving back to Arthur Avenue. In fact many of the old Arthur Avenue merchants shipped their fresh cheese to the local supermarkets and delicatessens in her neighborhood. It was the bond built through haggling and interacting that made her a loyal customer to the end. Collaboration was an "exit barrier" that kept her from switching to those other stores all those years.

Using CRM Technology to Build a
Wall around Customers

The concept of customer collaboration represents one of the better ways marketers can use technology to build walls around their customers so they don't defect to the competition. The image of building walls—or exit barriers—around customers is a practical way of thinking about customer loyalty. It implies customers have to break through a wall or jump over a hurdle (emotional or real) to get away from us.

Building walls around customers with CRM tools is important because the old exit barriers don't work as well any more. Advances in technology, notably the Internet, are eliminating many of the exit barriers companies traditionally relied upon to retain customers over the long term. Geographic "convenience," for example, is rendered meaningless by e-commerce. Barnes & Noble, Crown, and Borders financed their expensive stores on the premise that they would be the only place to buy books in a 10-mile radius. They did not count on online channels siphoning off a good portion of those customers. Once customers know you are not the only game in town—or a better price is just a click away—geographic location becomes less important.

Size used to matter too. Barnes & Noble and others built their superstores to offer greater selection than competing independent booksellers, and they had the cash to keep more books on the shelves. Again they did not count on the unlimited selection offered by online retailers.

Brand loyalty established in offline channels does not guarantee loyalty in online selling, where the empowered buyer is always just a mouse-click away from exploring the offerings of a new competitor. General Motors recently retired their Oldsmobile line because this once powerful, multimillion-dollar brand failed to keep customers loyal like it once did. People who define themselves as Ford, Chevy, or Oldsmobile drivers are becoming more rare. Instead, car shoppers now use online discussion rooms or online marketplaces such as Microsoft's Car Point to decide what kind of car guy (or gal) they are. The ease of comparison shopping over online marketplaces (both business and consumer are-

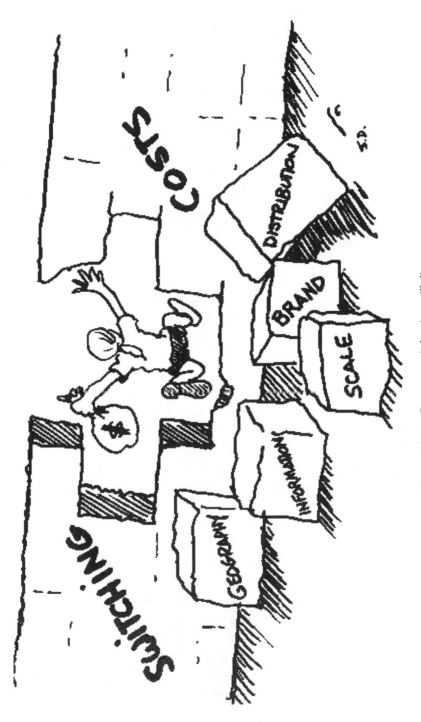

Figure 11.1. Customer exit barriers will disappear.

nas, as described in Chapter 2) means that customers are better informed, and more frequently informed, about alternatives and alternative pricing. And better access to information opens doors for customers to exit.

If technology is making it easier for customers to stray, then the name of the new game is to rebuild your exit barriers. Technology, in the form of a maturing set of Customer Relationship Management (CRM) solutions, can help in the process of rebuilding these walls.

What Is CRM and Why Is It Important?

What Customer Relationship Management actually means is subject to debate. Depending on whom you talk to it is a "strategy," a "marketing philosophy," or a software "package."

On one hand CRM is a strategy. Spending money to cultivate your best customers is regarded as good strategy for most corporations. This is because it is getting harder for marketers to distinguish themselves with quality, cost, or great new products. For example, most personal computers wind up having the same basic price and configurations. Despite massive innovation in the last two decades, most manufacturers use the same suppliers for parts. While PC manufacturers are fast at generating new products, good ideas are copied and on the shelves in less than six months. With products, quality, and cost basically the same, more organizations feel that improving existing customer relationships will be a more important factor in determining who wins business in the future.

Customer relationship management is also the philosophy of gaining a deeper understanding of your individual customers that can be exploited for future sales. Most marketers have embraced the idea of giving customers more personalized offerings and service makes sense. Direct-marketing budgets now exceed that of mass media advertising at most companies. Most larger organizations now have dedicated management in charge of their CRM strategy and are spending millions of dollars on CRM software solutions that promise to help them become more "intimate" with customers.

For all practical purposes, CRM is a marketing "buzz word" that stands for "customer relationship management" software. It was invented by marketers looking for a way to describe a variety of technologies that help improve the sales and marketing process. Specifically, these technologies are designed to automate sales and service forces, aggregate customer information into data warehouses, and create opportunities for collaboration with customers through electronic "points of interaction."

The IMT Strategies survey of 50 leading Global 2000 organizations showed they will be spending heavily—on average between $10 and $30 million—on these CRM programs over the next few years. CRM spending will ultimately reach many times this number for leading Global 2000 companies, as markets drive up the value of customer information and they realize how difficult it is to integrate these solutions into existing operations. For example, to date, only 60 percent of best-in-class companies have started to integrate CRM across channels, functional silos, the front and back office, and partner organizations. And organizations have been surprisingly slow in bringing their Web channels into their CRM programs (less than 40 percent of leading companies have even begun to do this).

The distinctions between CRM, "eCRM," "Enterprise CRM," and other software are not important. What is important about CRM software solutions is they represent some useful building blocks to help marketers build a wall around their customers.

CRM software is made up of about 30 to 40 basic building blocks. Unfortunately, buyers cannot get all of these blocks in one box. In addition, these blocks need to be assembled and glued together. Instruction manuals are hard to come by.

There are literally hundreds of software solutions that fall into the category of CRM. To simplify things, the universe of CRM software solutions breaks down into three basic categories—operational, analytical, and collaborative CRM.

Operational CRM: These are software solutions that make "customer-facing" employees like salespeople and tele-reps run faster and become more productive. These include software applications that automate the sales, customer service, and marketing functions. They have names like sales force automation (SFA), enterprise marketing automation (EMA), and automated customer service/support. This category also includes more specific technologies that help configure products, display product catalogs, and connect mobile salespeople to the factory.

Sales force automation software for field sales reps has been around for almost a decade. It is provided by companies like SalesLogix, Siebel Systems, and Saratoga. Customer service software to help call-center representatives is made by companies like Clarify (now part of Nortel Networks), and Pegasystems. Companies like Annuncio, Prime Response, and Broadbase provide Enterprise Marketing Automation software packages that help to streamline the way marketing campaigns are managed. There are specialized software programs for field service from companies like ASTEA that help service professionals order parts and arrange for support while driving a repair truck to a client emergency.

Analytical CRM: These are the brains behind "one-to-one" marketing programs. These applications help marketers store, analyze, and use the customer data that is created and collected in all parts of the organization.

Big database companies like Oracle and NCR can help build large "data warehouses" to collect, store, and help manage customer data. Companies like Micro Strategy or E.piphany offer solutions that help pull together various pieces of customer data into more useful forms so managers can put it to good use. These "data marts" help marketing managers create management reports, design marketing campaigns, and measure results better. Specialists in "customer analytics" like SAS and Quadstone help direct marketers mine customer data to test brilliant marketing ideas, better understand how they behave when they shop, and target the ones that are most profitable.

Collaborative CRM: These are tools that help make conversations with customers go more smoothly. These technologies help customers conduct these conversations through many different points of interaction—Web sites, telephone, kiosks, or cash registers—with marketers. These solutions help organizations collaborate more with customers through many different media and they even keep track of the dialogue as it moves from one media to another.

This includes hundreds of new CRM technologies that allow customers to track orders though customized Web sites, "click and connect" to tele-web center agents, or share an online "whiteboard" with a remote sales engineer. ("Shared whiteboards" were recently highlighted in Ameritrade television ads where a remote telephone agent has accessed the personal computer of a prospective investor through the Internet, and together they are coming up with the right portfolio to meet his needs.) Marketers can expect many new names and tools because there is a lot of room for technical innovation.

Together, these three categories of applications comprise the CRM "ecosystem." It is safe to expect that many new flavors will come and go. Some software manufacturers will try to do it all. The large players in this industry—like Siebel, E.piphany, Oracle, and SAP—are working to pull all the parts into one box into comprehensive suites. This may not work very well because there are still too many new tools, ideas, and approaches coming out with alternative approaches for one "box" of CRM to have all the parts you need.

Creating a Blueprint for CRM: Nine Customer Exit Barriers

Unfortunately, today there is no proven blueprint for the best way to build a new and solid wall. It is the job of sales and marketing leaders to define with greater clarity what "customer exit barriers" should look like and how they will work within their own industries. Without this direction, organizations risk wasting expensive CRM investments or even going out of business.

To get ideas for their blueprint, smart executives will look for insights from businesses where traditional switching costs have already been eliminated. These are highly competitive segments and include long distance, travel, and consumer financial services. Modern Web portals and online retailers also have low switching costs.

These industries have been struggling for years with very high "customer churn" rates and have wrestled longer with the problem of recreating exit barriers. A few have started to come up with solutions. They include Consumer banks such as Wachovia and Keycorp, Web portals such as Yahoo and AOL, online merchandisers BMG Direct and Amazon.com, travel industry players American Airlines and Priceline.com, catalogers like Lands' End, and credit card companies such as Visa.

Not surprisingly, they are some of the biggest spenders on CRM technology. Consumer banking companies spent far and away the most money on customer analytics and analytical CRM. Telecommunications firms, who have call centers dialing around the clock asking customers to switch their long-distance and local telephone accounts, were the second biggest spenders.

To help "architect" the wall, nine different exit barriers that are likely to work in the future have been identified. These draw upon the strategies these leading companies have used to successfully attract and retain customers. Most depend on customer information and technology to deliver value (in the form of content, community, and convenience) to customers. These should serve as useful "design points" for assembling walls with CRM technologies.

Nine customer exit barriers for the future

1. Customer Learning Curve: Being Easier to Do Business with Than the Next Guy
2. Process Integration: Becoming a Part of the Way Your Customers' Work
3. Personalization: Using Information to Match Offerings to Customers' Tastes
4. Mass Customization: Expanding Choice So Customers Won't Look Elsewhere
5. Risk Reduction and Trust: Making Yourself the "Safer" Choice
6. Loyalty Programs: Giving Economic Incentives for Customers to Stick Around

7. Brand Affinity: Giving Emotional Incentives for Customers to Stick Around
8. Collaboration: Talking and Listening to Customers More
9. Standards: Finding Ways to Become the Only Choice

These are more fully described in the Special Section at the end of this chapter. Marketing leaders should expect to develop more than one new exit barrier just to compete. Think of each as a building block to create a new "wall" around your most profitable customers. The more building blocks you can put in your wall, the more difficult it will be for your customers to look over and leap to the other side.

BMG Direct: Building Walls Using Personalization

BMG Direct, the world's largest music club, has become a leader in the competitive world of online music by investing heavily in personalization. Selling CDs over the Internet is extremely competitive. The product is a relatively simple commodity sold by a large number of competing e-commerce sites. New comparison shopping sites such as RUsure.com, Dash.com, and MySimon enable consumers to compare CD prices across many Web sites with the click of a button, encouraging fickle customer buying behavior. Plus, online music retailers like BMG face formidable competition from the leader in e-commerce, Amazon.com, who has cleverly built an array of exit barriers into its customer relationships.

For example, Amazon offers selections, both across and within product categories (e.g., books, CDs, and toys); promotes customer collaboration and interaction (e.g., through book and music reviews, and through online auctions); and utilizes customer information in sophisticated ways (e.g., suggests books or music to customers based on what other buyers in their demographic are purchasing). For the purposes of the latter, Amazon has over 10 million registered customers and a huge (2 terabyte) customer database (BMG Direct, by contrast, has 2 million registered customers). Amazon also benefits from widespread customer familiarity and positive brand identification.

To meet the challenge, BMG embraced personalization as the key exit barrier for its customer base. BMG built an entire department dedicated to personalization and cross-sell programs. The company works to personalize its products and services and generate customer loyalty by making its customers members of a club and developing a deep database of their musical tastes, buying habits, and service preferences.

While many competing sites employ "personalization engines" to make product and service recommendations, BMG has also built an online infrastructure that helps it cluster and evaluate customer segments. Such clustering is based on more than 240 behavioral characteristics, including the promotion through which members joined, the length of membership and favorite types of music and, of course, the total of CD purchases.

Armed with this data, BMG conducts regular permission e-mail campaigns to target only certain of its customers with special offers. The company also experiments extensively with segmentation targeting, message formatting, campaign timing, and other factors to better understand response function dynamics and continually refine its marketing approach. BMG mines its rich customer databases aggressively and combines them with personalization technologies to attract and retain its customers.

Short-Term Strategy: Viewing Products and Markets Through Different Eyeglasses

Organizations risk wasting their large investments in CRM if the programs are not designed to keep their best customers happy. Any CRM project that does not use these customers as a "design point" is likely to fail over the long term.

To be better designers, marketers need to have a clear picture of how a customer wants to be treated and served throughout his or her customer relationship. A typical customer life cycle includes creating awareness of a product offering, generating interest and the desire to obtain additional information, conducting the transaction, and receiving post-sales service and support.

This is the "relationship" factor of customer relationship marketing. Discovering how the customer wants to define his or her own relationship is the path to creating a better relationship—and building more effective exit barriers.

For example, Hewlett Packard knows that 15 percent of its customers prefer self-service on the Web over dealing with traditional business partners. Avon understands that its younger prospects like to reorder cosmetics on the Web without the help of an "Avon Lady" sales rep who initiated the original sale with a hands-on demonstration.

Online retailers often identify customer segments such as "kamikazes" or "one-click" shoppers (customers who dive into a Web site, get what they want, and leave quickly). Examining a range of customer behavior has helped electronic retailers learn to identify profitable segments—and avoid targeting retention effects on the least profitable segments, such as "cherry pickers" who only buy items on sale, or "sling shots" who buy garments, wear them, and then return them using the "free returns" value-add.

Specifically, there are three steps to identifying your most important customer buying patterns:

1. **Get more and different information about customers;**
2. **Resegment customers and products;**
3. **Creatively cluster customers based on revenue, profit, and behavior.**

1. Get more and different information about customers

If companies creatively rethink market and product segmentation, they can make better decisions and come up with better design criteria for their CRM systems. Traditional market segmentation leads to traditional thinking. General Motors, for one, still splits its marketing budgets, product management, and channel resources along product lines of Chevrolets, Cadillacs, and Buicks. On the other hand, Microsoft recently shook things up, breaking up its products (for example Windows, Explorer, NT) into customer groups—consumers, small business, large business, and the community of software developers—to better tune their marketing approach to the needs of this market.

2. Resegment customers and products

Instead of segmenting markets by traditional methods (size, geography, industry) marketers should try rethinking customer segmentation based on buying behavior. This forces them to evaluate the critical experiences throughout the customer life cycle, such as:

> What level of product understanding do customers have?
>
> What campaigns and medium are they likely to respond to?
>
> What selling channels and points of interaction do they prefer to communicate?
>
> How do they like to receive delivery and pay bills?
>
> What level of personalization do they expect during interactions?
>
> Do they prefer self-service or handholding?

For instance, for many clients, going out for a meal is no longer a strong relationship builder. A study by Arthur Anderson shows that business buyers increasingly prefer a fast response from a tele-rep in ten minutes to lunch with a salesperson next week. And marketers looking to build relationships with Generation Y teenagers may have better success reaching them using viral marketing and permission e-mail campaigns rather than traditional media like TV. These teenagers (born from 1979 to 1994) routinely dismiss the Pepsi ads on TV that make baby boomers drink 8 gallons of the stuff a year. Instead, these teenagers have built Mountain Dew into one of Pepsi's stronger brands using "word of mouth" in Internet chat groups to spread that word that this noncola had a big caffeinated punch.

Likewise, product segmentation must factor in different attributes of the product and service. For example, there are many aspects of a product that impact customer buying patterns beyond price and size. These can include:

> How complicated is the product to buy?
>
> How many varieties are available?

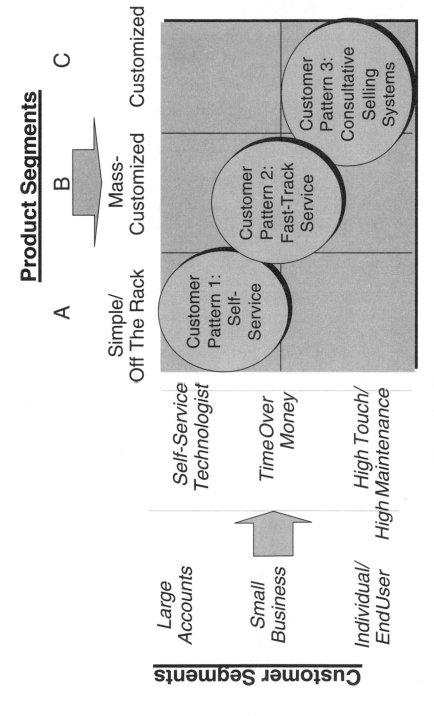

Figure 11.2.   Identifying customer patterns.

How customized or standard is it?

How is the product distributed?

How well are its attributes conveyed through electronic channels?

Product complexity in particular can be an important segmentation criteria when deciding which tasks can be completed electronically and where software can help simplify things for buyers. For example, General Electric's utility customers have expressed interest in getting certain (but not all) types of technical support online for things as complex as computer hardware and stream turbines. Given the cost of providing technical-support knowledge bases through extranets (secure client Web sites), knowing exactly which service tasks the customers prefer to do online with regard to turbines can make all the difference. The design criteria outlined in Chapter 1 offer useful ideas for creatively re-segmenting products in ways that will help marketers better design for CRM systems.

3. Cluster revenues around buying patterns

The above framework can help marketers creatively search for clusters or patterns of customers demonstrating certain behavior. Marketers can then "pull out" those groups that are the most attractive from a revenue, profitability, or cross-sell potential perspective. With persistence, the most valuable customers can be identified.

These patterns will then suggest priorities for CRM investment. If a significant volume of revenue comes from sophisticated customers who buy "off-the-rack" products, it will probably pay to invest in CRM solutions that will automate more functions for buyer self-service.

Dell and Cisco have had great success with Web site configurators, electronic transactions, and online technical support for savvy IT professionals seeking to purchase simple PCs and less complicated servers. Likewise, a busy executive who values time over money would respond to a "fast track" CRM solution that offers speedy and convenient purchase for a few select models.

Alternatively, high-maintenance customers who need handholding might require a high-touch approach from a tele-web agent that can supply live voice support as both agent and buyer view the same Web site screens. Each of these patterns fulfills unique customer needs, has varying levels of revenue potential, and can serve as design points for prioritizing investment in CRM solutions.

Long-Term Imperative: Picking the Right CRM Building Blocks for the Wall

Once you have identified the customer clusters you want to take advantage of, the long-term challenge is picking the right CRM "building blocks" to build a wall that will actually keep these customers from leaving. Because each organization is different, marketers will need a unique portfolio of "blocks" to build a wall that works for them. For example, a capital equipment provider will invest in selling technologies that help salespeople customize factory equipment because they know that every factory they sell to is different and their salespeople burn most of their time "engineering" proposals. A window manufacturer will invest in technologies that allow them to assure customers that they actually have the windows in stock and they will arrive on the same day they will be installed. They know that being on time is the number-one issue with the building contractors they sell to.

An IMT Strategies study of 50 CRM programs showed that consumer financial services organizations spend far more heavily on customer analysis. They are struggling to get inside the heads of small investors and figure out how to keep their millions of existing customers, navigating the subtle differences that tell them why they pick one credit card or mutual fund versus another. The same study showed that high-technology firms throw most of their CRM dollars at "operational" solutions that help their sales forces run faster because these companies are in a desperate race to "acquire" market share and need to help their sales force grab as many new clients as possible.

Finding the best building blocks to erect exit barriers is an ongoing cycle of trial and error. Marketers who experiment will get smarter over time. Leading marketers will get smarter faster if they attempt to translate customer behavior patterns into CRM program priorities.

How can this translate quickly into added value? Take the example of the "fast track" customer pattern identified earlier. A "fast track" customer would probably value timely notification of an opportunity or discount, the ability to buy fast with no hassles, immediate delivery, and streamlined customer service. These needs point to certain CRM solutions—for example, a permission e-mail alert service to notify the customer of an offer at the right time. If busy customers are interested, they will prefer "one-click" buying on the Web that links to a customer profile so they don't have to enter any data or waste time repeating themselves. They will expect express 24-hour delivery and a personal shopper service if they call with questions or returns.

General Electric's Electronic Distribution and Controls business used this approach to target their "fast-track" clients, which helped them to reduce inventories and improve product margins. The Electronic Distribution and Controls division makes thousands of different types of buttons and switches that control electrical industrial equipment. Most clients liked custom buttons and switches that matched their machines, so over time GE found itself making and storing too many spare parts that could not be easily sold to other customers. As a result, inventories were high, factories were clogged with custom orders, and delivery times were slow.

When GE's management looked closely, they realized the 80/20 rule applied. They could serve most of the market demand with very few "mass-customized" buttons. The key would be finding customers who were willing to trade off a little customization to get faster delivery. For a select few "fast-track" products, GE streamlined production to reduce costs, created a special distribution process for rapid fulfillment, and at the same time raised prices. Given the choice between a custom button in 10 weeks and a "mass-customized" but more expensive button much sooner, these "time-over-money" clients chose the higher price and speed. The customers were happy and GE made more money through higher margins.

Bottom Line

Marketers will have to use the customer as a "design point" to assemble the right mix of CRM technologies to create a wall that holds customers in.

Special Section: Nine Customer Exit Barriers for the Future

1. Customer learning curve: being easier to do business with than the next guy

Familiarity breeds customer retention. Finding ways of making your customers familiar with you enhances their "ease of use." This can be accomplished by providing customers with a more accessible base of knowledge about your company's products, processes, and range of endeavor. For example, eBay uses extensive online help menus that made millions of people see themselves as "experts" in the art of the auction.

In the business-to-business arena, the traditional methods of "educating the customer" can be adapted to lower-cost electronic channels. Sponsored industry seminars, for example, can be presented as live Web video and audio presentations. E-mail newsletters that combine high information value with an incentive (special sales, legislative alerts, couponing) are a very popular method of presenting company information, either to select groups of industry clients or broadly to the buyers of consumer products.

2. Process integration: becoming a part of the way your customers work

It is hard to change the spark plugs on a car when the engine is still running. Becoming tightly integrated with a customer's business can make it expensive, inefficient, or painful for that customer to sever the relationship.

Organizations can build this exit barrier through shared equipment and durable purchases or contractual commitments like volume purchase agreements. For example, the Sealed Air Corporation does not sell its famous bubble-wrap packaging products to its biggest clients. Instead it provides them with a "bubble wrap" machine that applies customized packaging right at the end of the assembly line while they are getting the product ready for shipping. Switching to a cheaper brand of packaging (like polystyrene peanuts) is a relatively easy decision. Stopping and changing the assembly line to pull out the custom equipment is far more disruptive.

IBM and Federal Express have translated this same concept into customer "extranets" that offer customized pricing, less paperwork, and package tracking. IBM's corporate extranets to its largest clients have custom pricing, order status, and help in administering "distributed buying" (which means hundreds of employees can do all the work to buy their own PCs, but the purchasing manager is still in control of the big things like price, service contracts, and negotiations).

3. Personalization: using information to match offerings to customers' tastes

Using information about the customer can enhance the buying experience and overall relationship. Personalization has become highly competitive, with most online retailers attempting it to some degree. As discussed in Chapters 3 and 4, consumers respond well to personalized marketing and now expect it as part of the shopping experience. Personalization is impossible without CRM. Companies need to collect and analyze customer information like click streams, buying behavior, and stated preferences. Technologies that can help build this exit barrier include:

Basic customer databases

Programs that track customer behavior

Online customer preference surveys

Dynamic personalization throughout the selling process

Personalization engines

Targeted marketing (e.g., permission e-mail) and response function analysis

Personalization is evolving far, far beyond "Hello [insert name]!" In 2001, an IMT Strategies survey of marketers found that over 50 percent of firms were actively capturing, storing, and using more of this type of information in their marketing campaigns. Specifically, over 50 percent of respondents indicated their marketing departments were targeting marketing campaigns with information about customers' stated preferences, geographic location, scheduled events like anniversaries, and account histories, account status, as well as customer-defined privacy and permission guidelines. BMG Direct collects 240 categories of information on customers and uses these to customize in cross-sell and e-mail campaigns (see case study, this chapter).

4. Mass customization: expanding choice so customers won't look elsewhere

Relationships, no matter how strong, get stale. Marketers can prevent customers from looking elsewhere by offering a broad selection along with the ability to customize services to meet unique needs. Offering variety, mass customization, or rapid product evolution can minimize a simple desire for change.

For years, car dealers knew that "new car smell" was a subtle but powerful psychological force to help hesitant consumers trade in their dirty old car full of old coffee cups, cigarette butts, and loose change, and drive off in a clean sedan. In many situations, the competition has one primary asset— they are shiny, new, and different. They will use this to pry customers loose. Steal your customers back with this same tactic. Mass customization is one way to simulate new car smell by offering new solutions, new configurations, and new service bundles. Expanded product selection also helps keep the relationship fresh.

Personalization and configuration tools also make it possible to offer products not available anyplace else, while catering to a mass audience. Levi Strauss, for example, has undertaken several mass-customization initiatives: "Personal Pair" in 1994, and more recently, "Original Spin." Customers could design their own jeans by choosing from three basic models, five colors, and two zipper types, which yielded thousands of potential customer combinations. Neither experiment has continued, but each provided many gigabytes of customer preference data that the manufacturer could mine.

Using Web-based partnerships to expand selection is really a case of "fighting fire with fire." Content aggregators on the Web, such as price aggregator MySimon and the portal Yahoo, offer comprehensive selection in one place, giving customers no reason to look elsewhere first. One solution is to bring in Web partners that expand the selection and complement in-house products to create the impression of a more comprehensive product line.

5. Risk reduction and trust: making yourself the "safer" choice

Safe is better than good. Marketers can build loyalty by reducing the risk of using a company's products or services and generating trust through accumulated service history and support. Companies that adopt this exit barrier use psychological strategies to make switching appear too risky, even in the face of more attractive solutions. IBM has long benefited from the perception within IT organizations that "nobody ever got fired for buying IBM." DLJ Direct invokes customer trust in its online brokerage by stating that it "puts its reputation online."

How can CRM turbocharge this useful strategy? Organizations can build this exit barrier by implementing programs that track customer history or provide a high level of security for transactions. Warranties and guarantees can be linked to automated customer care programs that send e-mail reminders about scheduled maintenance or warn that a part should be replaced.

Proven performance and technical leadership burnish trust. Amazon's success can be attributed to the reliability of its patented "one-click shopping" process. Customers also trust that the product will be delivered on time. Amazon built this trust through a combination of customer experience, innovative technology, and delivery performance. After Toys "R" Us botched Christmas delivery schedules in their first online retail foray, they turned to Amazon in an alliance deal to woo back risk-adverse online customers.

6. Loyalty programs: giving economic incentives for customers to stick around

Delivering incentives or benefits for frequency of usage ("loyalty") or increased levels of usage are tangible ways of motivating customers to come back to you. Loyalty programs like Green Stamps and frequent flier miles have been a mainstay of marketers for years. Technology just makes them better and easier to weave into the sales and marketing process. Technology permits incentives for more specific consumer activities like reading an ad or filling out an online survey. This response gives marketers the flexibility to fine-tune the customer experience and motivate critical behavior.

Long staple of bricks-and-mortar retention programs, examples of innovative loyalty strategies include American Airlines, which pioneered the frequent flyer program (subsequently embraced by all the major airlines), and Lycos, which has offered frequency rewards from NetIncentives for use of the Lycos portal. An early adopter of the "points" system now in use throughout e-commerce, its success helped launch literally thousands of incentive-based loyalty campaigns.

"Point" and frequency programs, volume discounts for business buyers, referral awards for the clients of service companies, and similar strategies have all been renewed with CRM technologies, which make it easier to test, adjust, and retest their usefulness across a variety of customer segments.

7. Brand affinity: giving emotional incentives for customers to stick around

Marketers can build loyalty by establishing a brand's "psychic" value through positive affinity or affiliation with a community. For example, cKOne, the Calvin Klein fragrance, targets Gen Y consumers through a worldwide cyber soap opera carried out via e-mail (see Case Study, Chapter 3.) The idea is to draw consumers of a particular demographic into a story and set of characters that they can identify with, and define the image/lifestyle of the cKOne customer community. Linking your e-commerce site to "Destination" sites (e.g., ivillage.com, webmd.com) creates brand affinity through aggregating products and editorial content specific to a particular interest or lifestyle.

Individual organizations can build this exit barrier, using their own Web sites, by encouraging "virtual communities" with forums and chats. Kotex has done this successfully for years with its "girlspace" pages on kotex.com. Another tactic that works is making a company Web site into a "destination" Web site—the first stop for seekers to find related Web sites, or a clearinghouse for information on a specific business issue. This worked for CNET, widely considered the "CNN" of the Internet, because it consistently provided a wide range of reliable news and generous links to sources. This didn't work for Disney's original Web site, and its later

Go.To.com portal. Both ventures failed because they too rigidly controlled outbound links and never created a community beyond a focus on Disney products.

8. Customer collaboration: talking and listening to customers more

Keep the customer's attention by maintaining an ongoing, value-added dialogue. This applies to customer interactions with the company itself, supply chain partners, and/or other customers. AOL and Priceline are effectively using collaboration to hang onto customers even though their core services are no longer leading edge because collaboration and switching costs are very low.

AOL builds customer loyalty through chat communities and buddy lists. Parents who buy AOL could easily save a few dollars and improve service by switching to a less-expensive Internet service provider. They don't because they fear the wrath of their sons and daughters. Leaving AOL would cut these teenagers off from the proprietary "instant messaging" network where they spend endless hours collaborating with their classmates or in exclusive chat groups.

Organizations can build this exit barrier through:

Extranets

Groupware

Web-phone integration

Customer Interaction Centers

E-Care (Interactive Customer Service)

Customer portals

Web conferencing

Shared white boards

Trading partner networks

Priceline.com stood out among a new breed of online price aggregators and auction sites in the competitive travel industry because it leveraged customer collaboration to build repeat business and customer loyalty. Priceline.com's innovation was that it enabled customers to name their price and participate in an auction. They reintroduced haggling, which appealed to a "fringe element" of customers for whom securing bargains was a religion. In other words, Priceline.com found a way to bring its customers into the process of airfare purchase. The innovative "name your price" hook helped make Priceline.com one of the first Internet "megabrands"—one of seven Internet brands recognized by over 50 million customers.

Priceline.com further managed retention through varied programs. One of the first was a dynamic e-mail management system that pursued customers after the first buy, with e-mail alerts and special offers that might be targeted around which airline the customer used most, or which category of destination. Unresponsive customers were dropped from the e-mail alert list at a speed that might alarm traditional direct-mail managers. Responsive customers and "frequent buyers" were rewarded with an upward cycle of special offers, incentives, and even more personalized product pitches.

Buyers liked the satisfaction of negotiating and "naming their own price," which makes this collaboration a good exit barrier even though Priceline's business model was not perfect. The "reverse auction" pricing model actually gives most of the advantage to the seller, because only the airlines know the true cost and true availability of seats. Most travelers can make more informed decisions and in many cases get better deals on sites like travelocity.com where they can better see what fares and routes are available. But Priceline.com was effective because it made the customer feel like they were even more involved in the process. Bargain frequent flyers, it seems, would rather get their price than the best price.

9. Becoming a standard: finding ways to become the only choice

Being the only choice is still a good way to keep customers. This involves dictating industry standards, either proprietary standards (in a closed environment) or industry standards (in an open environment). The classic example is Microsoft, which has been using this strategy in operating systems (Windows), then browsers (Internet Explorer), and to some extent portals (MSN). So successful were its efforts that it attracted attention by the Justice Department. In the open credit-card environment, Visa is trying to become the standard by pushing the ubiquity of Visa acceptance among all merchants to combat the prestige of American Express. Beverage manufacturers also vie for exclusivity in delis and supermarkets across the world. No one can buy a Pepsi at a soda fountain when the only cola available is Coca Cola.

Restraint-of-trade issues aside, organizations can build this exit barrier through electronic channels by supplying "Freeware"—free software applications that only work with your own products.

The Internet environment provides more examples of *de facto* standards created through first-mover *selling channel innovations* than it does for market standards created whole out of first-mover *brand awareness*. The lesson here is that finding better ways to sell mousetraps is just as important to customer share as simply making better mousetraps.

Buying Outside Services:

Managing a New Universe of Technology Services, Agencies, and Solution Providers

Technology is forever changing the relationships marketing managers have with their traditional services and agencies. This is because the e-business and CRM programs that marketers must run to compete in today's markets are very different from the advertising and promotional programs they executed in the past. These technology-enabled marketing programs have more "moving parts." Many of those parts—like software, networks, and programming skills—involve technologies and services that are foreign to most marketers. Also, these parts do not come with instructions for easy assembly.

As a result, sales and marketing organizations will have to get help in new and different places. This means outsourcing relationships will become more like marriage than dating. The best marketers will strive to make sourcing outside services a core competency and become adept at forming new types of partnerships with agencies and suppliers. This chapter not only describes what marketers must know to understand what they are buying, it also offers strategy and outlines four keys to picking the right partners and making sure these relationships get results. Sales and marketing executives must have a better understanding of what they buy, and get good at buying it—because buying technology is not getting any easier.

Beyond IBM: Buying Technology Is No Longer Easy

Buying technology was once far simpler than it is today. In fact, up to the late 1980s, over two-thirds of all computer-related business technology was purchased from one company: IBM. At that time, there were perhaps 20 technology companies of any great scale, or even listed in the Fortune 500, and only a few hundred firms were publicly traded on the NASDAQ or other stock exchanges.

Fast forward to the year 2000: IBM at this time represented less than 10 percent of all technology sold. Over 25 "large-cap" technology firms (technology stocks with large market capitalizations like Microsoft, Cisco, and Nortel Networks) supplied combinations of hardware, software, and networking solutions that could be used to create complete stand-alone systems for CRM or sales automation. Over 1500 firms were traded on the NASDAQ alone; counting privately held companies and start-ups, over 10,000 vendors existed to provide technology. Factoring in the agencies that supplied human beings to make these tools work, the universe of third parties to partner with was larger still.

Finding good partners among them is not easy, as technology firms come and go out of business regularly. The estimated "churn" for technology vendors has ranged between 10 and 15 percent (depending on the year and the economy). This means that over the next 10 years, 1000 new vendors will appear, and 1000 will disappear every year. In other words, managers who buy and use technology must keep track of over 10,000 different technology providers, learn about 1000 new companies every year, and keep an eye on another 1000 that will either go out of business or be merged or acquired by a different company. The indigestion associated with this "technology churn" is what keeps technology buyers up at night worrying and technology analysts like the Gartner Group, Forrester, and META Group in business.

Managers looking for simple solutions have not been finding them. Twenty years ago, the executive in charge of technology—the Chief Technology Officer or CTO—went to sleep at night knowing that if things went wrong he had IBM to take the blame. ("You never got fired for hiring Big Blue.") This is no longer true, as the elements that make up sales technology may be spread widely about. For example, a typical Customer Relationship Management (CRM) project for a Global 2000 company can cost over $20 million and involve 50 different types of software. Tried and true vendors like IBM may sell some of these parts, but the rest must be chosen, and assembled, from hundreds of alternative technology providers.

Marketers Must Understand How to Buy Technology

Sales and marketing organizations have always needed outside help reaching their markets. A food producer like Green Giant has to distribute millions of coupons to get customers to buy their creamed corn. Credit card companies like Citigroup need help sending letters to get new card members.

Traditionally, marketers have relied on outside advertising and marketing agencies to help them do these things. These "trusted partners" did the heavy lifting of creating and executing marketing programs like ad campaigns, coupon drops, mail campaigns, and special events.

Adding technology to the sales and marketing formula changes the relationships between marketing managers and outside agencies. Sales and marketing organizations are relying more heavily on service providers—not just to build and run technology-enabled selling programs, but also to counsel them on what technologies to buy in the first place.

For example, when the IMT Strategies study asked 50 e-business heads how and where they were using technology in their sales and marketing operations, a third of these reported they outsourced over half of their budgets to third parties. Some 83 percent of the e-business managers said outsourcing e-services was critical or important to their business. A good 6 percent said they could not live without it. And half said they would outsource more.

Sales and marketing professionals will increasingly be responsible for selecting technology and managing technology-enabled marketing programs. A recent CMP Media survey indicated that 50 percent of senior sales and marketing executives were involved in specifying products to buy and participating in the selection of service providers. The same survey indicated 7 out of 10 technology providers said they were planning to focus on selling to business people. Sales and marketing executives can expect to field more sales calls from these folks and sit in on more meetings deciding which software to buy. To keep ahead of the competition, there will still be a need to review the parade of new capabilities and marketing tools that can give your organization an edge.

As the list and variety of service providers continues to proliferate and get confusing, single-source relationships will be history. A recent Cutter Consortium Outsourcing survey of 154 companies, for example, showed that 83 percent were currently engaged in multiple vendor relationships.

Entering many new types of service relationships can be complicated. In the Cutter survey, 41 percent of respondents involved in outsourcing with multiple partners said they didn't pick the right vendor for the job. These respondents also reported that 17 percent of their outsourced IT agreements had to be renegotiated within six months.

This is not unusual. Many organizations remain somewhat unsophisticated about outsourcing services, for a very good reason. Historically, contracted services have not made up a significant component of overall selling costs. As a consequence it receives little senior management attention, and procurement of services has been (until recently) a backwater for talent.

The death of one-stop shopping

Outsourcing sales and marketing used to be simple. The Chief Marketing Officer generally had one agency relationship to manage things. Organizations that care a lot about marketing, like Coca Cola, Microsoft, American Express, Sprint, LL Bean, and

GM will generally have a strong relationship with some type of service provider for a bulk of their sales and marketing and promotional programs.

Even at smaller organizations, finding good help or changing suppliers was not much of an issue. If the agency creative got stale, or the execution was not satisfactory, throwing them out was an easy answer. Calling for an agency review would bring a parade of shiny new people putting their best foot forward to win your business. In this regard, outsourcing to agencies was more like dating than marriage—no long-lasting commitment was necessary, and you could always change partners if it didn't work out.

Today, no single firm can possibly collect the hundreds of capabilities needed to execute a complicated e-business project. Ad agencies are excellent at developing creative ads, executing campaigns, and even putting up Web sites, but they do not have the technology and strategy horsepower to provide all the support needed to have a successful e-business program. For a while the Venture Capital community and marketers themselves wanted very badly to believe that all the elements needed to set up an e-business program could be provided by one organization. A wave of so called "e-services" firms (firms that claim to be "one-stop shops" for setting up all aspects of e-business programs like iXL, MarchFirst, U.S. Interactive, and Razorfish) emerged to fulfill that promise. Now the myth of "one-stop-shopping" has begun to unravel, with the well-documented downsizing or outright failure of many of these firms reinforcing that point. Both MarchFirst and U.S. Interactive have filed for bankruptcy protection.

The reality is that no agency has the money or management discipline to pull all the parts into one place. Not surprisingly, many sales and marketing executives are looking for not just a different kind of partner, but a different kind of relationship as well.

How things will change for marketers

Moving from a reliance on a single vendor to orchestrating the combined efforts of many vendors will create changes in the way sales and marketing departments operate inside and outside their organization. Marketers should be mindful of several trends that will impact their jobs:

More Internal Coordination: Marketing will have to increasingly rely on and coordinate with others in their own organizations (IT, shared services organizations, cross-functional teams) to get things done. Sending a unified message to third parties is critical.

Hiring for Outsourcing Skills: Marketers will need to make outsourcing a competency by developing or acquiring people with the skills to handle procurement and outsourcing tasks. Costs for this may involve new training for existing staff, paying a premium to acquire people with these skills, (6–11 percent premium) or creating contracts (typically with 4–15 percent commissions) to obtain freelance outsourcing specialists.

More Accountability: Higher levels of accountability will be written into third-party contracts (service-level agreements). This is a direct result of the failure of many "dot-com" advertising campaigns and the growing importance of performance testing throughout the advertising industry. The ad industry has had very low levels of accountability for a long time, dating back to the days when it took months to clearly see the effect of a branding campaign or a direct-marketing test. Agency payment models will become more performance-based. Hybrid performance measurements based on the selling process and business objectives will have to be assembled.

Deeper Partnerships: You can't just fire your core e-business partner. The scale and scope of integration and resources forces more complicated levels of business partnership and joins you like a marriage bond to your service provider.

All of this creates risks and opportunities for sales and marketing managers. A primary risk to marketing executives is reduced independence and control over budgets, supplier selection, and oversight. Marketers can also plan on having less flexibility and leverage with suppliers. This means it will be more difficult to call an "agency review" to stir things up. Deeper partnerships with high degrees of process integration mean you cannot switch suppliers as easily or lean on them. Locking in deeper partnerships can also hinder creativity, risk taking, and the competitive edge that ad agencies traditionally had from the pressure to compete for business.

Also, there will be a cost of acquiring and developing new skills to manage these relationships. For example, sourcing skills will go for a premium. Employees who understand "horizontal leverage" and have joint venture or contracting skills can cost up to 10 percent more. Outside consultants who help write and oversee service provider contracts as sourcing experts can charge commissions worth 5 to 10 percent of the contracts, depending on the project type.

The opportunities will arise because learning how to outsource technology faster and more efficiently than your competitors is a valuable skill that gives you and your company a significant strategic edge. Speed was the number one reason for outsourcing in the *Information Week* survey. A well-managed outsourcing relationship provides the flexibility to quickly adjust the mix of selling resources and change selling costs quickly. Specifically, this means companies can scale up or down more easily to react to changes in demand or market conditions. If something happens to work, third parties can allow a program to grow faster than hiring internally would allow. Alternatively, if a program is a bust, it goes away quickly and quietly, rather than laying off employees or having idle capital equipment around. For example, if an advertiser got frustrated with low response rates, and wanted to shift its entire interactive marketing budget from banner ads to permission e-mail programs (which perform 20 times better) a service provider could make that happen.

In addition, outsourcing with the right service lets marketing executives take advantage of technologies they do not understand well. Outsourcing in many cases lets marketers circumvent overburdened internal technical staff that cannot put capabilities in place fast enough to keep pace with customer needs. Lastly, as the parts needed to execute marketing programs expand, having fewer and deeper partnerships reduces the span of control, allowing marketing managers to focus on a few key relationships.

Short-Term Strategy: Know What You Are Buying

A wide variety of skills and services will be needed to build and run sophisticated technology-enabled sales and marketing programs in the future. Executives should plan on outsourcing a significant portion of their sales and marketing budgets to a new generation of business partners, including marketing agencies, e-commerce utilities, and e-channel partners to obtain specialized talent, technical expertise, faster deployment, and cost-efficiencies.

Sales and marketing executives better know what they are buying and get good at buying it if they plan on being successful. As a starting point, marketing executives need to understand the four primary ingredients needed to run technology-enabled sales and marketing programs. These are the basic building blocks common to any e-commerce, CRM, and interactive marketing program. These competencies fall into four traditional buckets:

Strategy: This includes business process analysis and the core strategy behind the e-business plan. It is important because without a "blueprint" for how an organization's strategy, structure, and processes must change, technology will make little difference in business results.

Agency: This includes creative media placement and the execution of marketing programs and campaigns. It is important because revenue-generating marketing programs need excellent creativity and execution to succeed.

Systems Integration: This includes custom programming and application integration and customization. It is important because many parts need to be assembled, glued together, and customized so they actually work in an actual business setting.

Technology Solutions and Infrastructure: This includes the software, hardware, and infrastructure behind e-business. It is important because these solutions provide the bandwidth, processing power and databases that create selling leverage and new opportunities to innovate the selling process.

Since there is no single recipe for success, marketers need to assemble the right mix of help. Skepticism about these new flavors is in order in heavy doses. Service providers that combine many capabilities sound great but may not actually deliver the goods.

Separating the wheat from the chaff (what's easy, what's hard, what's new?)

When selecting a third-party service provider, it is important to know what is difficult to do and what is window dressing. Marketers who can sort the "wheat from the chaff" will be able to value and more easily select the right partners. The easy stuff should be priced accordingly or taken in-house. The hard stuff is where management needs to pay attention and where marketing service providers will need to prove their mettle. The new stuff needs to be sniffed out to see if there is a diamond in the rough that can give marketers a real leg up.

What's easy?

Building a Web site, for example. In the early days of electronic selling, organizations either turned to their existing advertising agency (which had quickly sprouted or acquired an Internet division) or hired one of many trendy boutique "cyberagencies" that specialized in Web work. In many cases, the funding for building a Web site would come out of a "special projects" budget. Like the Web site itself, the outsourcing was of little concern to senior management because the project was experimental.

As Web selling channels have matured, they are becoming more integrated into the selling and marketing mix. Skills for this "easy stuff" have since become marginalized to small niche service firms, taken in-house, folded into off-the-shelf hardware/software packages, or available through a larger service provider (such as an ad agency). For example, Internet ad serving, which basically distributes Web banner advertisements, seemed difficult and unique in the late 1990s. Now it is deemed a commodity service, and the innovators that pioneered the service (former e-marketing luminaries like 24/7, Engage, and Doubleclick) are on life support.

In the long run, certain skills and competencies will be regarded as easy and become commoditized. Currently, the list will include:

Hosting a Web presence

Hosting software applications

Third-party marketing campaign execution

Ad serving and affiliate networking

Hosting and managing customer databases

Business requirements definition and business case development

Web site development

What's hard?

On the other hand, putting together a $20-million-dollar, unified CRM program is still hard. Technology solutions that require different parts of an organization to share data, require significant capital investment, or create major changes in corporate strategy require a higher level of involvement in partner selection. Outsourcing the management of IT functions, as is required for enterprise marketing programs or the building of databases visible to business partners or customers, makes more sense to organizations who do not want to hire legions of engineers and data entry operators. Sales and Marketing staff need to participate in buying these skills and selecting partners, as they will play a large role in managing the partner relationship day-to-day.

In the IMT study of 50 companies, executives identified five areas where they expected to continue to need outside help. They are:

1. *Marketing and customer analysis to understand customers better and design more targeted programs.*
2. *Data warehouses to store and manage customer information collected from all over the organization.*
3. *Electronic commerce to build online sales channels and link up demand chain partners.*
4. *Sales force automation to make sales forces more effective and help them coordinate with other parts of the organization.*
5. *Content management to make sure product information gets into online catalogs, supports Web personalization, and makes self-service Web sites work better.*

Certain skills and competencies will remain difficult. These include:

Creative and content development

Custom application development

Competitive best practices and analysis

Software and hardware installation and configuration

Web site architecture

Web site user experience design

Database integration

Online/offline convergence initiatives

Project management

Channel integration

Sales process analysis

Business modeling/supply chain analysis

What's new?

Keeping track of the new stuff remains important. The most important thing to remember is (a) There will always be new things on the horizon, and (b) new, flashy capabilities will require new skills that can command a premium price, but only for a short period of time. Ultimately, new technologies and skills will mature and smart competitors or users will figure them out (i.e., HTML). Over time new capabilities may be folded into broader services firms, or marginalized to niche specialists.

For example, in the early 1990s telephone switches were new and hot. Most people who ran large call centers bought them and they worked pretty well. Most call-center managers got their money's worth in the form of tele-agent productivity and happier customers. This success helped pave the way for a wave of "add ons" that take advantage of the intelligence built into our phone systems and support Web-phone collaboration, voice recognition, and sophisticated cross-sell and upsell marketing programs.

In 1994 marketing Web sites were new. Now most organizations have them, they work pretty well, and the folks who made their living exclusively by building them are either out of work or selling you newer stuff (like marketing analytics, rich media, or wireless technology).

More recently, wireless communications and "ASPs" (Application Service Providers, companies that let you rent software instead of buying it) are new and hot. The ads and the sales pitches are just as urgent as they were before: buy this or die. Technology firms like IBM paint images in television ads of Wall Street analysts pummeling executives because cell phones were not central to their strategy. The Gartner Group sends images of millions of headset-clad Europeans spurning America's "PC based" e-commerce as "antiquated."

The different recipes for success (and failure)

Just like a cook can combine ordinary ingredients into a variety of recipes, businesses will struggle to combine these four basic ingredients into offerings that make them appear unique, relevant, and in some cases valuable. The right recipe for success has eluded most firms.

Given the capacity for the high-tech industry to create new acronyms and catch phrases, this could get quite confusing to everyone involved in contracting and using these services. Beyond the "one-stop-shops" mentioned earlier, many new flavors and combinations will likely emerge in several areas.

In the area of outsourced infrastructure and software, we can already see different variations on a theme: Two of the popular types are Internet Service Providers (ISPs) and Application Service Providers (ASPs). ISPs help large and small organizations network with each other and their customers, mainly through the Web. ASPs are a little different. These are services that host software applications for you, effectively "renting" you the software on their own servers so you don't have to buy and support it. These mostly benefit small companies who are not technically sophisticated by allowing them to easily set up for Web commerce and access many new technologies that they could otherwise not afford or understand. On top of that expect to see service providers who will take just about any marketing task off your hands, such as telephone support, Web site hosting, and the distribution of Web advertisements.

Specialty services will emerge. Some will perform difficult and important tasks, like data cleansing services that clean up and add information to marketing lists so they perform better. In addition, entirely new types of businesses will come along, trying to fill gaps where services are needed or significant value can be created. For example, "build-to-order" integrators will help assemble parts from many different providers. This will likely be useful in the long term because customers have demonstrated they would rather buy complete solutions than individual parts and get exactly what they want instead of what is available. Rapid response logistics—the companies that ship stuff fast—are valuable additions to the distribution network. They are probably going to be pretty important as electronic commerce firms increasingly compete on delivery cycle times. Further, many customer segments have demonstrated the willingness to pay a premium for rapid delivery. Variable-cost field forces allow organizations to shed costly full-time staff and only use field sales where and when they are needed. These are also valuable for a virtual organization.

Long-Term Imperative: Four New Keys to Developing Strategic Partnerships

All organizations will need help managing many different service provider relationships. As things get more complicated, sales and marketing organizations will struggle with different approaches to working with many outside service providers. Organizations will need help in order to keep track of the many parts. Current efforts to assemble and manage many different capabilities fall into these general categories.

> One-stop shopping: Getting all the services you need in one place

> Do-it-yourself: Handling everything in-house

> Partnership networks: A trusted partner who acts as a general contractor to assemble the right capabilities

Most executives who are managing large e-business initiatives surveyed by IMT Strategies wished there was a one-stop-shop that would take care of all of their third-party services needs. Most knew that one-stop-shopping for e-business support was an unattainable fantasy, but given the complexity of managing so many contacts, they saw value in having one relationship to deal with. They also wished they had the time and skills to manage these relationships in-house because they felt they were too strategic to let go outside the company. The desire for control tended to lead them to overestimate their ability to handle all of these decisions. On a practical level, neither option is feasible for most organizations.

This leaves partnership networks. Most felt that a partnership network, administered by one primary service provider, was the most viable plan in the long term. Much like a homeowner will use an architect and general contractor to build a house, selling organizations are learning to entrust the assembly and management of third-party service providers to select strategic partners. When building a house, a general contractor may divide the work into subcontractors (electrical contractor, plumbing contractor). This provides the advantage of specialty teams; the general contractor doesn't have to know about plumbing codes and electricity grid requirements; the subcontractors are entrusted to know their specialty, be able to expertly purchase the needed materials, and bring their own tools and employees to help.

Organizations will be forced to pick one or two strategic "e-business partners" because they don't have the management bandwidth to manage many services relationships. Much like the homeowner will use an architect and general contractor to build a house, organizations entrust the assembly and management of third-party service providers to these select strategic partners. These "trusted partnerships" will become far more heavily integrated into selling processes compared to the "episodic" projects or retainers that they are typically engaged in today.

Disney, for example, got fed up with its e-services firms and consultants (Razorfish, among others) who were building their struggling online portal, GoTo.com, and turned to their trusted advertising agency to find out who might help them build a better strategy. While Disney recognized that this agency did not have specific skills in e-business, it also recognized that a long-term relationship made the agency fit for the task. Specifically, (1) the agency knew Disney's business and was already familiar with its corporate philosophies regarding other sales channels, and (2) the agency had a good track record for performance as well as Disney's trust.

Disney decided that many of the relationships it would have with Web-related service vendors would be transitory, and could be subordinate to the primary trusted partner. Apparently these things will become important again. All other relationships will be "transitory" or subordinate to the primary "core" partner (e.g., they better get aligned with them or not be there for very long). As one executive put it, "consulting is dating . . . outsourcing is more like marriage . . . for better or for worse."

Making a Good "Marriage"

Picking a partner is a lot like marrying into a family in many ways. You must choose well, because you will likely be together for a long time, through good times and bad. The rules will be very different from dating. Separating can be painful and always has significant consequences.

An analogy like this is actually valuable if it helps you to focus on the most necessary aspects of developing a rewarding relationship with technology partners. There are four keys to doing a better job buying the services needed to support e-business, and they are all about relationships:

1. **Get good introductions and references to marry into a good family (align with a trusted partnership);**
2. **Find a house to live in together (define new organizational approaches to services procurement);**
3. **Get help from a spiritual advisor (expert advice to support decision making);**
4. **Have a good prenuptial agreement (get great at contracting).**

1. Get good introductions and references and marry into a good family (align with a trusted partner)

When it comes to managing third-party relationships, it pays to remember that such a marriage may include a large extended family of countless brothers, sisters, in-laws, and cousins. In the case of getting help for technology-driven sales and marketing programs, the things you look for in your primary partner include good references and a good reputation. They must have:

1. A trust relationship with you and a broad set of relevant service and solutions providers
2. An excellent understanding of how to use technology
3. Industry- or process-specific expertise
4. Skills in portfolio management and assembly

This partner must be able to help you identify and assemble the right ingredients to support your technology-driven sales and marketing program. A recent *Information Week* survey of executives buying e-services reinforces the fact that breadth of partnerships, knowing how to use technology, and trust are going to be the basis of future service provider relationships. Half (52 percent) of the respondents ranked the range of applications available as the number-one selection criteria for an e-services vendor. The second most important was that the agency provides partnerships and adds value. A deep understanding of e-business strategy and legacy systems were also identified as key selection criteria by 49 percent of those responding. Trust counted, too. Brand names and trusted relationships were also identified as top selection criteria for picking an e-services provider. For example, JP Morgan created an outsourcing structure called the Pinnacle Alliance; it is headed by JP Morgan's VP of sourcing management. CSC Index—a systems integrator—is the lead partner, along with three other partners (Andersen Consulting, Bell Atlantic, and AT Solutions), and this team accounts for one-third of JP Morgan's technology budget.

Given these criteria, the core partnership will likely be with a major systems integrator. Firms like KPMG, IBM Global Services, and PWC have the best shot because they have the most experience in the role and a lot (but not all) of the parts in place. Specifically, they understand technology, have broad partnerships with a wide variety of technology partnerships, and can assemble and integrate technologies.

More than likely, the advertising agency will take a back seat to the integrator. In consumer-driven businesses, like retail or consumer electronics, where branding, awareness, and traffic generation are paramount, ad agencies have a shot at being the core partner. For this to happen, one of the surviving e-services agencies (for example, Sapient) or a major ad agency conglomerate like InterPublic or WPP Group PLC might scale up and develop the breadth of skills to win a seat at the head of the table. Perhaps one or two of these players will have the scale, assets, and funds to acquire the skills and capabilities to do this. Other possible contenders for the "core" partnership relationship could include:

A dominant (trusted brand) hardware supplier like Hewlett-Packard, Cisco Systems, or IBM (who can credibly do this via its Global Services consulting arm). This probably makes sense where the buyer manages a significant amount of technology assets and trust. Risk management and sustainability are paramount. For example, IBM Global Services is the primary partner behind Goodyear's partner extranet, a Web channel designed to support their 4000 dealers with online services. Goodyear management happily pays a price premium because one partner makes life much easier.

A dominant (trusted) industry player who makes the e-business market in that industry. For example, Enron in energy markets and Wal-Mart in retail. Covisint, the online marketplace for the automotive industry, could hold this position for the thousands of suppliers to that industry if it were spun off and became an independent agent for the industry. (For more about Covisint, see Chapter 2.) This probably makes sense in homogeneous industries where processes, suppliers, and buying practices have a lot in common. Industries like packaged goods, automotive, and retail speak a very different language than other businesses.

This is not to say that agencies, and their cousins (strategy consulting, technology solutions, infrastructure providers, specialists) will not have a major role. They will probably not get to sit at the head of the table, and like all siblings, they will have to figure out how to coexist with other parts of the family while elbowing each other for a bigger piece of meatloaf or pie. Their input is still important: programmers who excel in coding complex software must defer to advertising agency partners when a question addresses brand strategy issues.

2. Find a house to live in together (define new organizational approaches to services procurement)

Companies will need new organizational forms to facilitate these relationships with so many outside service providers. Organizations that are reasonably good at applying professional purchasing practices to the factory generally don't yet apply that discipline to outsourcing and services. Both IT and purchasing organizations are much better at sourcing and integrating many parts than marketing and sales.

Smart managers will translate traditional procurement disciplines to services and agency relationships. These will become what have been called a "shared services organization." Of the e-business executives interviewed by IMT Strategies, 82 percent wanted some form of centralized or "federated" (where business units have some controls but report to a higher authority) governance of e-services outsourcing.

Several organizations have done this by setting up a single administrative umbrella staffed with a full-time professional. For example, a Chief Resource Officer position may be created. However, unlike traditional purchasing operations, these organizations cannot be cost centers. They will need to become profit-and-loss centers (pay for performance, revenue and risk-sharing types of relationships) to attract talented managers, effectively measure performance, and capture value from revenue generating. Companies already deploying shared services include the banking giant Chase Manhattan and Delta Airlines. Delta has a "business partners unit" that oversees 250 vendors and 2600 contracts.

One important benefit of these umbrella offices is they will facilitate cross-functional outsourcing. This means getting sales, marketing, information technology, and purchasing people to put their brains together to make better sourcing decisions. Instead of loosely assembled project teams, they will create more formal processes where many organizations can contribute to defining clear business requirements for selecting partners and active oversight of the ongoing relationships.

On the downside, this will shift decision-making authority from business units (read the sales and marketing function) to companywide resources (read an enterprise sourcing Czar). Getting things done will involve tasks such as "tin cupping" for funding from many different groups, negotiation skills across organizations, and power shifts from marketing to procurement. Internal selling and deal-making skills will be more important than ever to sales and marketing management.

3. Get a spiritual advisor (get expert advice to support decision making)

Marketers should get help finding, selecting, and managing third-party service providers. There are plenty of places to get advice on simple purchases like a DVD player or a PC. Complex outsourced relationships are another story. However, help is needed. The Cutter Consortium survey revealed that 17 percent of IT outsourced agreements are renegotiated within six months. Complicated outsourcing contracts can be up to a foot thick when the details are sorted out. The average marketing organization does not have the resources to negotiate these.

To fill this void, a new variety of consultants and online services are emerging that specialize in helping marketers with the selection and assessment of external service providers or new technologies. Marketers can hire sourcing advisors with experience, specializing in negotiating contracts from IT to marketing services. These consultants act just like a "general contractor," assembling the best subcontractors into a team and riding herd over them.

Several online marketplaces have emerged that provide online resources for finding services and managing them simply. For example, one pioneer—Ajunto—has a buying service that automates the buying of complicated technology services. In the service, a buyer can get references, reviews, and tools for developing and evaluating different alternatives or developing documents that lay out exactly what is expected from a third-party partner. When a buyer gets in trouble, they have access to expert analysis from industry experts like the META Group. Another resource is IQ4Hire.com; they are advisors who help develop requests for proposal documents (RFPs), identify potential service providers, and actually help facilitate selection. They take 4 percent commission for doing this. Depending on the importance of the service relationship, this can be viewed as "cheap insurance."

Most organizations lack procurement experience when it comes to outsourcing. According to the Cutter study, half do not ask for help (50 percent) in structuring contracts. This is probably because most do not view contracting third-party agencies as strategic. Seventy-five percent of those participating in the survey treated their outsourcing engagements as special projects rather than strategic relationships.

4. Have a good prenuptial agreement (get great at contracting)

Like marriages, closer partnerships require higher levels of accountability. As relationships with external services providers progress from dating to marriage, then the service contracts (or service-level agreements) will need to be viewed more as "prenuptial" agreements.

The old agency model allowed the ad industry to survive very low levels of accountability for a long time. This poor level of measurement will not hold up in an era where marketing services providers are tightly integrated into marketing operations. Agency payment models will have to change from pass-through (agencies take a cut of ad dollars spent by the client) to performance-based (agencies get paid based on a documented number of sales, or leads generated, or a number of impressions made). Agency performance measurements will need to better reflect how they support business objectives.

More mature outsourcing relationships are governed by sophisticated Service-Level Agreements (SLA). These are typically used with call centers to define clear expectations of customer service, such as response times and first pickup.

Marketing services contracts are evolving further, from performance benchmarks and remedies (negative/nonperformance incentives) towards more sophisticated partnerships, risk sharing, and even equity relationships. In addition, people will pay a premium for speed. Execution, in the form of time to market (or time to value) is more important than getting money back or penalties.

For example, eGM—GM's online channel organization—manages a variety of third-party service providers to support its e-business initiative. EGM is staffed with 150 professionals and has one of the largest online marketing budgets in corporate America. However, most of the operations and tactics are outsourced to a variety of partners, including a strategy consulting firm

(A.T. Kearney), an agency (Modem Media), and a technology provider (IBM and EDS) who provide hosting, data centers,and application development. Projects are measured on speed. A typical project is measured in a 90-day cycle time.

Bottom Line

Technology will forever change the relationships marketing managers have with their traditional marketing services agencies; relationships will become more like marriage than dating.

Special Section: The Outsource Universe

Executing all e-business, CRM, and Web marketing programs will require a combination of many different capabilities. Fundamentally, these competencies fall into four traditional service "buckets":

1. Strategy: Strategy and business case development
2. Agency: Marketing agency and services
3. Systems Integration: Integration and customization
4. Technology Solutions and Infrastructure: Application selection and installation, other services, infrastructure, and support

Strategy

Good corporate strategy is necessary to successfully incorporating technology into the sales and marketing process. Unfortunately, strategy is hard to define and its value is highly subjective. This does not stop organizations from spending heavily on this area. Management consulting is a $58 billion industry, according to Kennedy Information Group. The industry is filled with hundreds of specialty bou-

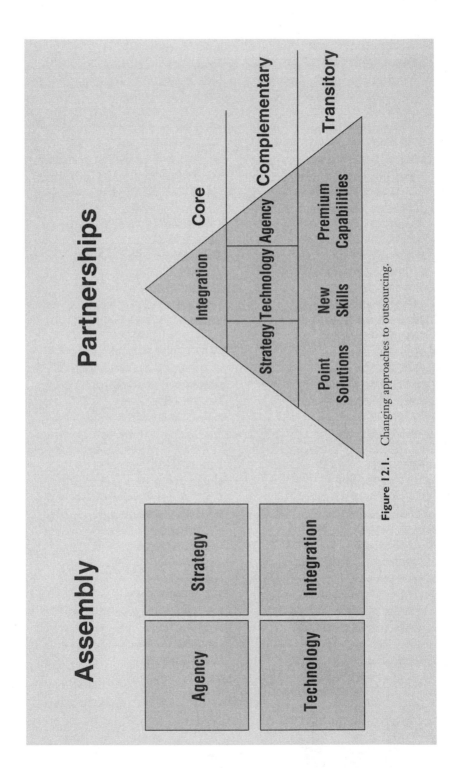

Figure 12.1. Changing approaches to outsourcing.

tiques. Most of the major players are exclusive private firms like Bain & Associates, Boston Consulting Group, McKinsey & Co., and A.T. Kearney. Specialists in marketing or channel strategy include Mercer Management Consulting, and Peppers and Rogers Group.

According to a survey of e-business managers in 2000, the top things e-business heads were looking for from strategy providers were:

Competitive analysis

Process Analysis (business modeling)

Market segmentation and customer targeting based on behavior

All manner of firms will include strategy as part of their offering. However, few are equipped to do it well. In the long run, ad agencies and software solutions providers have neither the intellectual horsepower, credibility, objectivity, or business models to do this right. For example, the failure of e-services firms to gain credibility with executive-level management and materially change their business processes has hurt them with their Global 2000 clients. This is because real corporate strategy involves the painful process of redefining markets, processes, compensations, and organizations. It also involves getting executive-level management to think and act differently. These are not trivial tasks.

Agencies

Agencies have helped marketers design, develop, and execute marketing programs for years. They generally help with the biggest chunks of the marketing-investment mix—media advertising, promotions, direct mail, and telemarketing. The most familiar agency is the ad agency because it involves the most money and has the most visibility. The fruits of ad agencies' labor is pervasive across media—television, print, newspaper, outdoor, radio, cable, and now the Web. And it most cases, it is still one of the biggest areas where marketers spend. In 2000 U.S. marketing organizations will spend $157 billion on advertising through this mix of media.

According to a survey of e-business managers in 2000, the top things e-business heads were looking for from their agencies were:

Creative and content development

Media placement

Campaign execution

Web site and user experience design

Campaign development

Agencies have fragmented and specialized in the last 20 years as marketing programs have become more sophisticated. Direct marketing, for example, has become an important weapon in the marketing arsenal. Organizations will spend $43 billion on direct-marketing programs in 2000. Specialists like Wunderman Cato Johnston and Blau Direct emerged to fill this need.

As organizations shifted more and more sales to low-cost, high-value tele-channels, agencies that deliver call-center outsourcing also emerged. U.S. marketing organizations spent over $100 billion on telemarketing in 2000, and about $99 billion was given to call-center agencies specializing in these fields.

Interactive marketing is the newest kind of specialty agency. It will make up only 2.6 percent of total marketing spending in 2000, but that percentage is expected to climb to 5 or even 7 percent by 2003. Interactive marketing has spawned thousands of specialty agencies to help execute targeted Web advertisement, permission e-mail, e-promotions, and online personalized promotions. (For more on this, see Chapter 4, "Interactive Direct Marketing.")

Systems Integration

Systems Integrators are professional services organizations. They used to be called the big six, which became the big five, Pricewaterhouse Coopers, KPMG, Ernst & Young, Deloitte and Touche, Accenture, and will ultimately be restructured and renamed. These are the folks that help incorporate technology into businesses. They select, install, and integrate software. They do many elements of putting together strategy and process analysis. They are a selling channel for all major software. The industry is dominated by several very large professional services firms and many small specialty shops. Recently, e-services emerged as a specialty category.

According to a survey of e-business managers in 2000, the top things e-business heads were looking for from systems integrators were:

Custom application development

Software and hardware installation and configuration

Web site architecture

The old rule in the consulting game is that every dollar of strategic consulting generated $10 in purchases for systems integration. As a consequence, all systems integrators have tried to get into the corporate strategy business, and major technology hardware firms are building, buying, or investing in services organizations. IBM has over 120,000 consultants in its systems integration division. This division is driving growth, makes up a big 36 percent today, and will make up 46 percent of the company by 2005, growing 13 percent per year. Along the same lines, Cisco Systems invested $1 billion in KPMG. Other major hardware suppliers Compaq, Sun, and Hewlett Packard are under pressure to do the same.

Technology Solutions and Infrastructure

All told, today there are about 30–50 large firms who provide the lion's share of technology infrastructure to corporate America, depending on who is counting. They provide the hardware, network, and software that make up the foundation for e-business by building out services for organizations. These are the firms that make up a good chunk of the equity in the NASDAQ and have become household names to day traders. In stock, traders call them "large cap" technology companies. They include hardware manufacturers like Hewlett Packard, IBM, Cisco, Sun, Dell. Firms like Oracle, Siebel Systems, and Computer Associates make the software to run on those machines. The networks and telecommunications technologies that link everything together are made by the likes of Lucent, ATT, Sprint, MCI/Worldcom, and others.

According to a survey of e-business managers in 2000, the top things e-business heads were looking for from technology providers were:

Custom application development

Software and hardware installation and configuration

Things get pretty specialized and complicated from there. For example, the outsourcing of technology infrastructure has become a major industry. This is because firms have decided that buying, installing, and managing technology is expensive, complicated, and requires special skills and solutions. Outsourcers let companies like these use technology to help them sell, but help relieve the burden of IT ownership and management.

Ross Perot figured this out and funded his presidential aspirations this way. He gave up selling mainframe computers with IBM to build EDS by outsourcing mainframe computing in the 1960s. The outsourcing market for IT exceeded $85 billion in 2000, according to the META Group.

Outsourcing IT is becoming more strategic as organizations move from outsourcing production processes (like data centers, factories, etc.) to sales and marketing processes (managing partner-networked and Web sites). There are close to 10,000 service providers who will outsource your networks, software, and hardware. These have fancy names and permutations. Two of the primary types are Internet Service Providers (ISPs) and Application Service Providers (ASPs). ISPs help large and small organizations network with each other and their customers, mainly through the Web. ASPs mostly benefit small companies who are not technically sophisticated by allowing them to easily set up for Web commerce and access many new technologies they would not otherwise afford or understand.

In general it is very hard to mix the four key ingredients—(strategy, agency, technology, and systems integration) because it is too expensive to bring all of those capabilities under one roof, and the four lines of business are very different from an economic perspective. Simply put, they make money in very different ways. That makes managing a company that does all four key ingredients a lot like "herding cats."

For instance, marketing agencies make money by taking a cut on the ads their clients place but bill their people out at very low dollars per hour. The relationship part is just a means to an end. On the other hand, strategy consulting firms bill their people out at a very high rate to make a profit. Fees per professional are very important to them. Software companies basically sell products, and any consulting is really just a way to get licensing fees. Systems integrators sell programmers by the hour and like software only because it is an excuse to sell as much custom programming and wiring as possible.

Index

About the Author

STEPHEN DIORIO IS FOUNDER AND PRESIDENT OF IMT STRATEGIES, A LEADING SALES AND MARKETING STRATEGY FIRM. A former marketing executive with Citicorp and GE, Diorio is a popular speaker and established authority on sales and marketing strategy.